AIRCRAFT CARRIERS

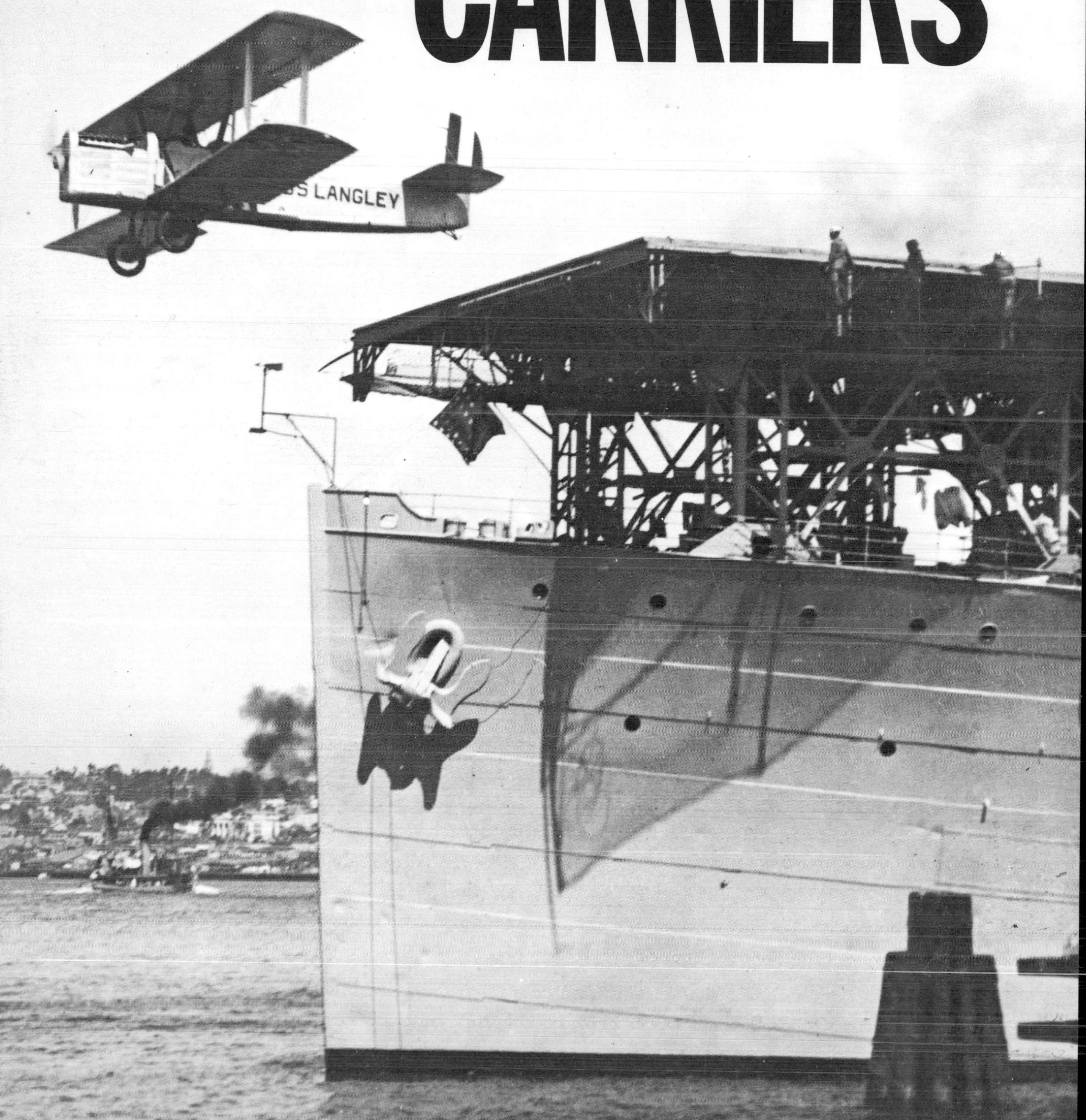

AIRCRAFT CARRIERS

THE ILLUSTRATED HISTORY

Richard Humble

MICHAEL JOSEPH
LONDON

First published in Great Britain by
Michael Joseph Ltd.,
44 Bedford Square,
London, WC1B 3DU.
1982.

ISBN 0 7181 21503

Produced by Winchmore Publishing Services Ltd.
48 Lancaster Avenue,
Hadley Wood,
Herts, England.

Edited by Sue Butterworth
Designed by Bob Burroughs
Picture Research by Jonathan Moore
Maps by Richard Natkiel
Line Drawings by Pierre Tilley

Printed in Hong Kong by Lee Fung Asco Ltd.

First published 1982
Reprinted 1983

CONTENTS

1. THE FIRST CARRIERS, 1903-1920

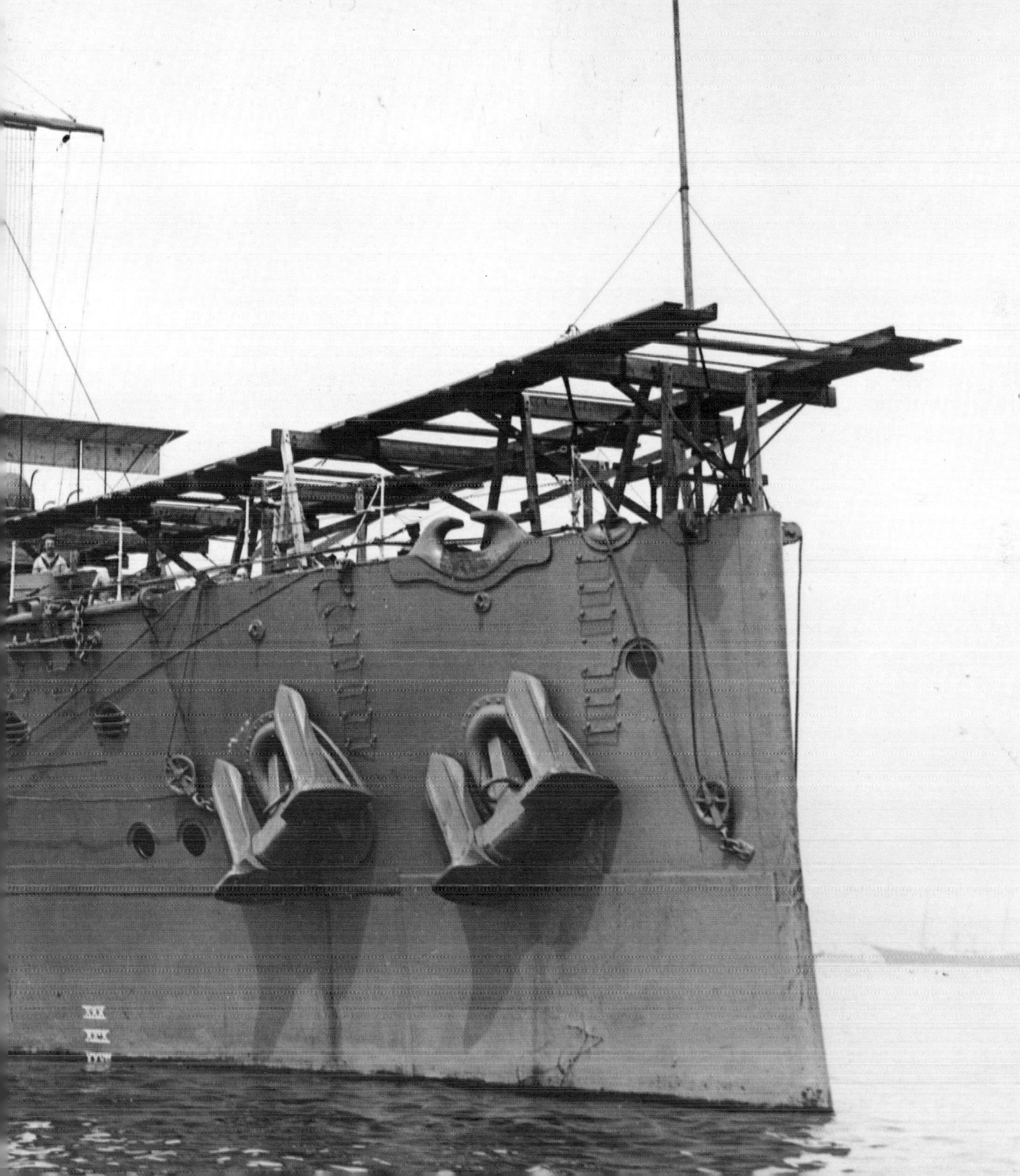

Previous pages: The first cautious step in marrying aviation to sea power – flying-off platform mounted on HMS *Hibernia* 1912

IN THE UNEASY ERA of strategic nuclear deterrence there is a natural temptation to regard all conventional weapons as puny or obsolete, but this is a misleading urge. The military history of the post-1945 'atomic age' is replete with confrontations and wars which have repeatedly proved that conventional weapons remain vital 'front-line' tools of defence. This applies to warships as it does to aircraft and land weapons – and to no type of warship more than the aircraft-carrier, the most majestic and versatile instrument of modern sea power developed this century.

As with many descriptive names, that of the aircraft-carrier is only partially accurate. An aircraft-carrier does not merely carry *aircraft* for launch and recovery at sea. She also carries the essential ground crew and hardware for storing, servicing, fuelling, arming and repairing her aircraft, because without such facilities the carrier could never venture beyond flying-range of a friendly shore base.

An aircraft-carrier is therefore far more than a ship from which aircraft can take off and return. She is an ocean-going, self-propelled – and, for as long as can be contrived, *self-sufficient* airstrip and service base. Designed to serve with conventional surface warships – cruisers, frigates, destroyers – the aircraft-carrier makes it possible for a fleet to survive and win naval battles without either side's ships ever sighting the other. The carrier's aircraft make her an invaluable weapon of anti-submarine warfare; no other type of warship can cover so much ocean. The carrier can strike at shore and inland targets and provide air cover for amphibious landings; her helicopters can land and recover specialised troops, such as marines or commandos. For operational range, versatility and hitting-power, the aircraft-carrier has never been surpassed by any other warship type.

It is helpful to list all these attributes of the modern aircraft-carrier, because the process reveals another area in which the type is unique. Nearly all the abilities mentioned above were developed in the carrier's middle and latter years, in and after the Second World War: an evolving multiplicity of roles not to be found in any other warship type. Thus the battleship and, to a lesser extent, the cruiser, remained a platform for heavy-calibre fire-power. The destroyer remained the fleet's skirmisher, its prime duty being to intercept and repel surface and submarine torpedo attack. The frigate, with its name exhumed from the age of sail but its ancient role assumed by the cruiser, remained a specialised submarine-hunter. But the aircraft-carrier went from strength to strength until, in only 25 years from its first appearance, it had replaced the battleship as the undisputed arbiter of naval warfare. And few if any of its acquired roles were dreamed of when the first cautious experiments were made with naval aviation and carrier design.

Shape of things to come, as imagined in the days when manned flight was still science fiction and looked like remaining so. This 'shilling shocker' sketch of a futuristic air combat, from 1900, shows 'aerial cars' bombing each other

The first suggestions that aircraft might be of any use at sea were made in the balloon era, when lighter-than-air contrivances looked like remaining the only safe way of flying. Certainly, for nearly ten years after the Wright brothers' immortal experiments at Kitty Hawk in 1903, there seemed little prospect that heavier-than-air machines would ever be made safe enough to operate over land, let alone over water. Crashes were so prevalent that national newspapers ran articles agitating for legislation to stop the slaughter. Flying over water was still considered the height of folly, and the English Channel still seemed an impassable gulf, when an unsuccessful French would-be aviator penned the first startlingly accurate blueprint of the aircraft-carrier. His name was Clement Ader and he had given up attempts to devise a heavier-than-air flying machine after hair-raising crashes in 1890 and 1891. Undeterred, his faith in the future of aviation unshaken, Ader turned from experimentation to theorising and wrote *l'Aviation*

Militaire. He not only insisted that air reconnaissance would transform the practice of land warfare: he argued that this boon would also be an invaluable asset to battle fleets, which must necessarily take their aircraft with them in specially-designed ships.

Ader was the first to use the term *aircraft-carrier* (*'porte-avions'*) in the modern familiar sense. Such ships, he stated with uncanny prescience, would look like no other ship that had ever put to sea. They would have unimpeded flight-decks, a high turn of speed, and elevators to strike down the aircraft (their wings having been folded back) for repairs and maintenance on a hangar deck below.

None of Ader's soberly-argued ideas seemed any less fanciful than H.G. Wells' *The War in The Air*, written in 1907. This apocalyptic fantasy forecast inter-continental bombing raids by fleets of airships, cutting the nightmare of war free from the manageable confines of traditional battlefields and bringing about the speedy collapse of world civilisation. Like Ader, Wells took it for granted that practicable heavier-than-air flying machines would be developed sooner rather than later, but treated them as secondary to gas-filled dirigibles. Space forbids a detailed commentary here, but one of the most interesting details was Wells' inclusion of aircraft not only in a fighter defence role against the airships, but as dive-bombers against conventional warships. In the fifth chapter of *The War In The Air*, 'The Battle of the North Atlantic', the German air fleet on its way to knock out the United States intervenes in the death-grapple between the German and American battle fleets below. At the moment when the American battleships seem to have the upper hand, heavier-than-air *Drachenflieger* slip their tows, swooping down from their parent airships and bombing the American fleet to ruin.

It was in the five amazing years after Wells published *The War In The Air* – 1908-12 – that heavier-than-air flight became an unquestionable, practicable, passenger-carrying and joy-riding reality. Nothing like it was to be seen until the similar period 50 years later, from the first artificial satellite launches to the first manned flights in Earth orbit between 1957 and 1961. But there was a profound difference between the birth of aerodynamic flight and that of space flight only 50 years later. The birth of space flight was urgently induced by the superpower rivalry between the Soviet Union and United States, with vast resources and prodigal sums of state funds expended in pursuit of predominantly military goals. Not so with the aviation pioneers of 1908-12: dedicated amateurs all, whose achievements were viewed with massive scepticism by the military and naval 'establishments' of the day. Aeroplanes would frighten the cavalry's horses, while it was equally plain that no weapon which an aeroplane could carry had any chance of inflicting serious damage on Dreadnought battleships.

The great breakthrough began with Wilbur Wright's visit to France in 1908. At Le Mans between June and December that year, Wilbur's series of demonstration flights put the powered hops made by European pioneers in 1906-8 (Santos-Dumont and Henri Farman) to shame. Wilbur shattered his own records as fast as he made them, ending the year with an endurance flight of 123 kilometres in 2 hours 20 minutes (31 December 1908). The most important outcome of Wilbur Wright's *tour de force* was a spate of big-money prize offers prompting further achievement. Foremost among these prizes was Lord Northcliffe's offer of £1,000 for the first cross-Channel flight, which Louis Blériot claimed in July 1909. Blériot's Channel triumph was followed within a month by the Reims Aviation Week of August 1909, which at one stage produced the unprecedented spectacle of no less than six aircraft in the air at the same

August 1908 – Wilbur Wright in action at Le Mans. His superb series of demonstration flights acted as the vital catalyst to European aviation, leading to a succession of record-breaking flights – and accelerating the development of the aircraft as nothing else could have done

July 1909: Blériot's monoplane rests on its collapsed undercarriage under the walls of Dover Castle after the first triumphant Channel crossing – which even the British could not ignore

Below: The Hon. 'Charlie' Rolls heads out from Dover in his Wright aircraft on the first two-way Channel crossing

moment. At Reims Hubert Latham set up a new altitude record (508 feet), Farman established a new endurance record (179.2 kilometres in 3 hours 4 minutes) and the American Glenn Curtiss won the Gordon Bennett speed trophy (46½ mph).

Apart from these feats, the Reims meeting of August 1909 marked the beginning of serious British military and naval interest in heavier-than-air flight. The Royal Navy sent Captain Scott (of Antarctic fame), the Army Generals Henderson, Grierson and French as observers. But what really mattered was the insatiable Press and public interest in flying, all the keener because the events of 1908-9 proved that of all the world powers Britain was the biggest outsider in the flying stakes, and the least air-minded nation. Britain 'hosted' the next big aviation contest, the cross-country London-to-Manchester race of April 1910. This was narrowly won by the Frenchman Louis Paulhan against a strong British challenge by Claude Graham-White, flying a Farman machine. The French lead was further reduced in June 1910, when the Hon. Charles Rolls achieved the first two-way Channel crossing (Dover to Calais and back). But within a month Rolls was dead, killed in a crash at Bournemouth – the second fatal crash in a week, adding to the ammunition of the sceptics who still dismissed flying as a suicidal stunt rather than a revolutionary new form of transport.

But the 'firsts' kept coming. In August 1910 the American John B. Moisant made the first flight from Paris to London, carrying a passenger for additional distinction – a cross-country struggle against repeated mishaps lasting from 16 August-6 September. Five days later Robert Loraine made the first flight across the Irish Sea. In the same month George Chavez piloted the first aeroplane across the Alps via the Simplon Pass, only to die of injuries incurred when crashing on touch-down at Dondossola. In October Graham-White won the second Gordon Bennett contest, held in the USA at Belmont Park on Long Island. And in November 1910 a light cruiser of the US Navy became the first warship in the world to fly-off an aeroplane from a deck platform.

The motive for this stunt was not an excited rediscovery of Clement Ader's prophecies, nor any sober re-reading of Wells' *The War In The*

November 1910 – Eugene Ely's Curtiss Hudson takes off from USS *Birmingham* in Hampton Roads. In these early days it was not realised that the art of shipboard take-off required steaming into wind at top speed – but though Ely's aircraft hit the surface he managed to keep aloft and land safely ashore

Air. Indeed, the only real military motive was the possibility of ship-launched foreign aircraft penetrating American waters, possibly on spy flights, without American ship-launched aircraft being able to perform likewise. The German Hamburg-Amerika line had proposed flying-off mail-carrying aircraft from liners to speed the transatlantic mail. The first successful launch would be a natural publicity stunt and Captain Washington I. Chambers, of the Navy Department's *matériel* branch, was determined that the publicity would come the Navy's way. Wilbur Wright refused to try but Eugene B. Ely, one of Glenn Curtiss' exhibition pilots, readily volunteered. Nothing in these years yielded so many 'firsts' as the fear of being beaten by a rival, and this was no exception; another Curtiss pilot, J. McCurdy, had been sponsored by *The World* to make the first shipborne take-off from a liner. McCurdy's first attempt on 12 November was foiled by propeller damage, and the Navy seized its chance. Frantic work on the 13th completed a wooden platform 83 ft long and 24 ft wide, sloping gently down from the bridge to the forecastle of the light cruiser *Birmingham*. Ely's aircraft was hoisted aboard early on the 14th and the trial was made in Chesapeake Bay that afternoon, with *Birmingham* steaming at 10 knots. It was a near-disaster, but despite hitting the water and splintering the tips of the propeller-blades Ely managed to claw his aircraft off the surface and land safely ashore.

The question now was whether or not an aeroplane could be *landed on* a ship – a very different proposition, in view of the potentially lethal obstacle of any ship's superstructure. Ely nevertheless volunteered for the new trial, held at San Francisco on 18 January 1911. Over the quarterdeck of the cruiser *Pennsylvania* was built a 102 ft-long platform. Ely's aircraft was fitted with undercarriage hooks to engage one or more of 22 transverse wires stretched across the platform and anchored with sandbags. In these days of painful ignorance before the need to take-off and land into wind was accepted as imperative, *Pennsylvania* was moored stern-on to a 10-knot wind. This gave Ely a touchdown speed of 40 mph and he was still airborne well up the deck, but his hooks caught the twelfth wire and brought him to a perfect halt. He then showed his considerable nerve by having his aircraft turned round and making the second shipborne take-off, again landing safely ashore.

Much had been established as practicable in these three flights – the ability of a ship to launch and recover aircraft, using a flight-deck and arrester-wires, and all within eight years of the Wright brothers' first flight. But Ely's feats in 1910-11 were more of a curiosity than a revelation. Today the work of the test pilot is a recognised and respected facet of aviation, but in the years before 1914 every pilot was, willy-nilly, a performer. The newspapers, city corporations and champagne firms who put up the cash for the first flying prizes naturally expected a show for their money, which made the first pilots stuntmen and stars combined. In practical terms Ely's operations achieved little more in the short run other than persuading the US Navy to start

September 1912 – the new marvel. Commander Schwann taxying one of the early A. V. Roe 'aero-hydro-planes' – in the days before Winston Churchill insisted that 'seaplane' was a much better word for such aircraft

Opposite: May 1912. A seaplane perches on its flying-off platform aboard HMS *Hibernia* during King George V's inspection of his Fleet

training its own pilots instead of having to rely on stuntmen like Ely. All he got from the Navy was a letter of thanks and the award of the Distinguished Flying Cross – the latter 25 years after his death in a crash, which occurred later in 1911.

Apart from the fact that this was one more stunt in an age of stunts, shipborne flying in 1911 offered little to any navy. Once a warship had been fitted with bow and stern platforms it would clearly become useless as a warship, because the platforms had to be built over the guns. But further deck-landing experiments after January 1911 were almost immediately rendered unnecessary by the new 'star performer' of aviation in 1911-13: the seaplane. Here was a new aircraft type which did not require flying-platforms to go to sea. Provided that wind and water conditions were right, the seaplane could be lowered straight into the sea from a parent ship; then, on return, hoisted aboard, folded up and stowed away – all without detriment to the ship's fire-power.

But seaplanes were no more than an exciting novelty at air displays at the inevitable moment when aeroplanes were used for the first time in war: the Italo-Turkish conflict of 1911 which ended with Italy ousting the Turks from Libya. *Capitano* Piazza flew the first air reconnaissance mission over hostile troops on 23 October 1911; *Tenente* Cavotti dropped the first bombs (four 2-kilo grenades) on 1 November 1911.

The last two years of peace down to August 1914 saw the powers of the *Entente* – Britain, France and Japan – developing modest land and naval air forces, and experimenting with ship conversions for the conveying and launching of seaplanes at sea. In Britain Lieutenant Charles Samson, first commander of the Royal Naval Air Service (established 1912), eagerly copied Eugene Ely with flights from the battleships *Africa*, *Hibernia*, and *London* in 1912. The French Navy was first in

the field with an operational seaplane carrier: *Foudre* (1912), converted from a former torpedo depot-ship and able to embark up to eight seaplanes. In 1912-13 the British, experimenting with the old cruiser *Hermes*, borrowed the American bow-launching platform and added a development of their own: launching seaplanes from platforms, with detachable trollies fitted to the floats. These experiments led to the decision to buy the uncompleted hull of a collier and fit her out as the Royal Navy's first 'aircraft carrier', but she had not been finished by the outbreak of war. And in these same months the Imperial Japanese Navy made a modest start, converting the merchantman *Wakamiya* to carry a brace of seaplanes.

The name of the new British 'carrier' – *Ark Royal* – had not been used in the English fleet since the days of the Spanish Armada. In August 1914 the 'German armada' giving most worries to the British Admiralty was the Imperial German Navy's fleet of Zeppelin airships, not the warships of the High Seas Fleet. For most of the war the Zeppelins enjoyed range, lifting-power and climbing speed far beyond the reach of the skimpy Anglo-French air forces. Luckily for the Allies, and the British Grand Fleet in particular, the Zeppelins were never used to full advantage; but the British Admiralty at the outset of the war nevertheless feared that the German battle fleet would be better served in the air than the British.

In an attempt to trim the balance, the Royal Navy commandeered fast-steaming passenger ferries and pressed them into wartime service as seaplane carriers. Speed was required to enable the carriers to keep up with the fleet; this was the first recognition of one of Clement Ader's most striking prophecies in *l'Aviation Militaire*. The first three, *Empress, Engadine,* and *Riviera,* were cross-Channel steamers. They needed the minimum of conversion-work to instal hangar space and cranes on their promenade and boat decks. None of the three could launch her seaplanes while under way. For all that, these three 'cheap and available' converted Channel packets carried out the first deliberate attack of naval aviation.

This attack took place on Christmas Day 1914 and was the third attempt to reduce the Zeppelin menace by bombing the airships in their sheds. The first two had been carried out by land-based Royal Naval aircraft, first from Antwerp (October 1914) against Cologne and Düsseldorff, then from Belfort (November) against Friedrichshafen on Lake Constance. Despite the puny weaponry of the attacking aircraft, these early raids met with consider-

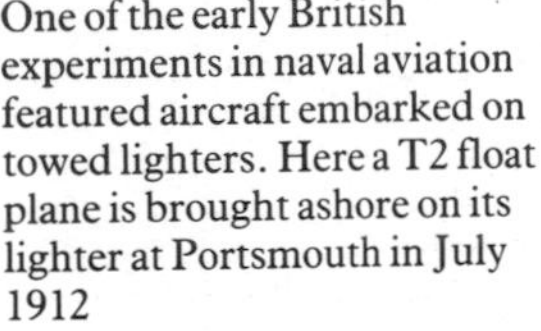

One of the early British experiments in naval aviation featured aircraft embarked on towed lighters. Here a T2 float plane is brought ashore on its lighter at Portsmouth in July 1912

Britain's first 'aircraft-carrier' – the converted collier HMS *Ark Royal*, destined for sterling service to the Royal Navy in two world wars. Her début in active service was at the Dardanelles in May 1915

able success: at Düsseldorff a Zeppelin was blown up in its shed. But even without the fall of Antwerp on 10 October, Allied land-based aircraft of 1914 lacked the range to carry out attacks on the sea and air bases of the High Seas Fleet in North Germany. The raid of Christmas 1914 gave the shipborne seaplanes of the RNAS their chance, and the target was the Zeppelin and naval base at Cuxhaven.

Seven seaplanes were hoisted out by the three carriers, after an audacious approach to a point barely 12 miles north of Heligoland. Three of the seven turned back early, foiled by low cloud screening the Zeppelin sheds from view; they returned safely to the ships and were hoisted in, only to find that two Zeppelins had not only spotted the force but had tried to bomb it. The force duly withdrew before the High Seas Fleet could pounce on it, leaving submarines to recover the four crews still in the air. The latter were also foiled by bad visibility at Cuxhaven but made a useful survey of the German fleet base and anchorages, dropping their bombs on the dockyard area before returning to the rendezvous. Three were neatly retrieved by the waiting submarine *E.11*; the fourth had the bad luck to be picked up by a Dutch trawler, and was subsequently interned.

This remarkably early demonstration of the versatility of naval aviation encouraged the continuing British development of seaplane carriers. The next batch of ferry vessels to be converted was *Ben-my-Chree, Manxman* and *Vindex,* all larger than the first three. They joined the fleet early in 1915, as did *Ark Royal,* and were sent to the Mediterranean to support the Gallipoli landings. But the confident pre-war belief that the seaplane would prove a deadly anti-submarine weapon was not justified at Gallipoli; indeed when U-boats reached the eastern Mediterranean in May 1915 there was little doubt that seaplane-carriers were infinitely more vulnerable to submarines than vice versa. At 7,020 tons displacement, *Ark Royal* was the biggest carrier in the world; she could carry the Short S.184 seaplane capable of dropping a 14-inch torpedo (a feat first achieved by Squadron Commander A. Longmore on 28 July 1914). But *Ark Royal* could only make 10 knots and it would have been suicidal to keep her forward during a submarine scare. She was withdrawn from the Gallipoli forward area in the best of company, including the brand-new 'super-Dreadnought' battleship *Queen Elizabeth*; and the onus of seaplane work was passed to the 24-knot *Ben-my-Chree*.

Opposite: The vital option – torpedo-carrying naval aircraft meant that enemy ships were now vulnerable to air as well as surface torpedo attack. This is a Short 184, dropping a 14-inch torpedo in 1915 – the combination which accounted for the first ships to be sunk by airborne torpedo attack, in August 1915
Inset: Curtiss 'F' flying-boat in early catapult-launching tests at Pensacola, Florida, in 1915. The US Navy led the world in developing not only catapult launching but arrester-gear for safely halting aircraft in deck landings

It was an S.184 seaplane from *Ben-my-Chree* which claimed the first air-launched torpedo 'kill', a Turkish supply-ship, on 12 August 1915. This claim was indignantly disputed by a British submarine in the area; but five days later two S.184s caught another supply-ship and tug, and sank them both. Such was the combat début of the carrier torpedo-bomber – decidedly before its time. No current seaplane could lift the standard 18-inch torpedo carried by surface warships (let alone the newer 21-inch); and the 14-inch torpedo was inadequate for the massive armoured belts and defensive 'blisters' protecting capital ships. The British did develop a torpedo-bomber later during the war – the Sopwith Cuckoo – but this most promising type arrived too late to see action.

By the end of 1915, therefore, carrier-based seaplanes had already established themselves in the role of *reconnaissance*; they had acted as *bombers against land targets*; they had *supported an amphibious landing* and shown themselves capable of *sinking enemy shipping*. British seaplanes added a further distinction to this list before the war ended: *participation in a fleet action*. This was the famous prelude to the Battle of Jutland (31 May 1916) when one of *Engadine*'s Shorts got off three sighting reports of the oncoming German fleet, before being forced down by a broken fuel pipe. But one vital task always remained beyond the reach of the seaplane with its low operational ceiling: *high-altitude interception* of the Zeppelins, whose surveillance made it impossible for the British fleet to operate undetected in the North Sea. After the supreme frustration of the German fleet's escape at Jutland, the British buckled down to the problem of finding a shipborne aircraft-carrying system which could shoot down Zeppelins and make another surface fleet action easier to bring about.

By the second half of 1916 it was crystal clear that only the lightweight fighting scouts, evolving in the increasingly vicious air war over the trenches of the Western front, had a chance of engaging Zeppelins – and thus the nettle was cautiously grasped at last. A carrier ship would have to be devised on which these wheeled-undercarriage scouts could land – with some form of long flight-deck unencumbered by superstructure amidships. The only alternative was to fly-off the scouts from bow platforms and require the pilots to ditch in the sea when their fuel ran out; and by late 1916 the rising tide of casualties in the land/air war was already sufficiently appalling to discourage further additions at sea. The through-deck carrier was obviously the best solution.

Yet, that is the easy sequence of events as viewed by hindsight. The actual birth of the

through-deck carrier between 1916 and 1919 was far less straightforward. No Admiralty planner cried 'Eureka!' and drew the basic outline of the first through-deck carrier. In fact the new design stemmed from two repetitions of a familiar theme: the conversion of large hulls to carrier duties.

The last big conversion job had been the ex-Cunard liner *Campania*, whose fore-funnel had been divided in two to extend her bow flying-off deck further aft. In 1916 another liner was purchased for conversion, this time uncompleted so that all possible wartime experience could be built in to her. This was the *Conte Rosso,* construction halted on the outbreak of war until her purchase by the Admiralty in August 1916 and subsequently completed as HMS *Argus*. The second of the new conversions began as an experimental warship, so patently unsuited to any other form of service with the fleet that conversion to an aircraft-carrier seemed the only chance for her. HMS *Furious*, launched the same month as the purchase of *Conte Rosso*, was the third of three 'light battle-cruisers' ordered before the brutal lessons of Jutland. They were the awkward offspring of Admiral Lord Fisher's fallacious belief that 'Speed is Armour'. *Glorious* and *Courageous* had four 15-inch guns apiece; *Furious* was designed for a single 18-inch gun fore and aft. None of them had any armoured protection worthy of the name; monstrous though their main armament was, they lacked enough heavy guns to range accurately at high speed. In early 1917 it was decided not to instal *Furious*' fore 18-inch gun but build hangar space and a flying-off deck on her foredeck, and add her to the carrier fleet. By April 1917 the job was done. With her flight-deck forward and massive lone gun-mounting aft, *Furious* was the world's biggest naval oddity since the Russian attempt to introduce circular battleships 40 years before.

Squadron-Commander E. H. Dunning and the pilots of her air group were nevertheless determined to exploit *Furious*' high speed and make regular landing-on possible. They had the luck to be flying one of the most docile aircraft produced in the war – the Sopwith Pup – and noticed that when *Furious* steamed flat-out into a stiff breeze and a Pup flew alongside at just above landing-speed, there was very little in it. With a gentle sideslip, the Pup could be eased over the flight-deck even when *Furious* was anchored head-to-wind. As the ship had no arrester-wires and the Pup was not fitted with brakes, the problem was staying down once down. Dunning fitted his Pup with rope toggles, briefed a handling-party to grab hold and hang on once he was down – and on 2 August 1917 carried out the first deck landing on a carrier steaming into wind. On a repeat attempt two days later, Dunning was drowned when a burst tyre sent his aircraft cartwheeling into the sea before the handling-party could intervene, and all similar attempts were forbidden.

Dunning's place in naval aviation is secure – because, rather than despite, of his tragic

Opposite: A frantic scramble for the rope toggles as Commander Dunning's Pup makes the first successful deck-landing aboard *Furious* (2 August 1917)
Below: Tragedy – Dunning's Pup cartwheels into the sea, carrying him to his death only two days after his triumphant first landing

Above: *Argus*, the world's first flush-deck carrier. The zebra-like splendour of 'dazzle' painting was designed to break up the ship's silhouette and confound attacking U-boats
Opposite: Sopwith Camels aboard *Furious*, above the bow flying-off deck. The palings enclosing the deck area were intended to stop aircraft from being blown over the side in high winds

death. Having shown that deck landings under way were possible, he showed that his method was mortally unsuitable. The immediate aftermath was a committee of enquiry recommending an unimpeded flight-deck the full width of the ship. This was adopted for *Argus* (launched in December 1917); but as her original design had been for bow flying-off, central superstructure/funnel, stern landing-on, the radical change to an unimpeded flush deck kept *Argus* away from the fleet for another ten months. As for *Furious*, she was sent back to the builders to have a landing-on deck built aft. This was not an attempt to deny the inevitable, but to make her as useful as possible for fleet operations in 1918. When *Furious* returned to the fleet in March 1918 it was soon found that wind eddies round the superstructure at speed made landing-on the stern deck impossibly dangerous for aircraft. For the rest of the war, *Furious* launched only – yet her career was far from over.

In July 1917 the Admiralty had moved two steps further by taking over the battleship *Almirante Cochrane*, which had been building for Chile, and ordering her redesign and completion as the carrier *Eagle*. At the same time *Hermes* was laid down, the first British ship to be built as a carrier from the keelplate up. The big question was which form of through-deck was going to be chosen for the latest carriers ordered. The simple flush-deck, as chosen for *Argus*, created as many problems of command and control as it solved for the airmen. All the bridge facilities and platforms for conning the ship had to be tucked under the edges of the flight-deck; the ban on standing masts gravely impeded radio communication. Then there were the obvious problems associated with abolishing vertical funnels and leading the engine fumes horizontally to vent through the sides or stern.

As all these problems emerged during the completion of *Argus*, the alternative design which was to become the aircraft-carrier's trademark seemed increasingly attractive. This was the 'island' flight-deck devised by Flight-Commander (afterwards Group-Captain) H.A. Williamson, originally submitted to the Admiralty in the summer of 1915. The 'island' grouped bridge, mast, and conventional vertical funnel into a single streamlined unit on the starboard side of the flight-deck – ideal for conning the ship without impeding flying operations. Operating experience during the last months of the war led to the 'island' deck being selected for both *Hermes* and *Eagle* when their construction was resumed after the Armistice. After *Argus* joined the fleet in October 1918 perhaps her most invaluable service was testing the new design. A temporary 'island' structure was built on *Argus*, pilots reporting that it gave them no trouble at all.

But after all the design changes and delays, *Argus* had arrived too late to make possible Admiral Beatty's plan for a mass torpedo attack on the German fleet in its harbours, using torpedo-carrying strike aircraft launched from carriers. If the tools for the job could have been prepared in time, the lessons of Taranto

Below: A Camel comes in to land on *Argus* in 1918. At the right of the picture, raised by the low 'fiddle' extending across the flight-deck, can be seen the fore-and-aft arrester-wires for slowing landing aircraft by the drag of hooks fitted to the undercarriage. The transverse arrester-wires perfected by the Americans in the 1920s were to prove infinitely superior
Opposite: The world's first homogeneous carrier, but too late for service in the First World War – HMS *Hermes* displays her elegant cruiser lines

and Pearl Harbor could well have been thrust upon the world 20 years early. As it was, the last major effort by carrier aircraft in 1918 was a painful throwback to the pinprick raids of 1914. On 19 July 1918, six Sopwith Camels launched from *Furious* attacked the Zeppelin sheds at Tondern in Schleswig. Though two Zeppelins and a captive balloon were destroyed in their sheds, only two of the attackers made it back to the carrier force to ditch beside a friendly destroyer; one was lost without trace, and the other three were briefly interned in Denmark. Judged purely on the combat record, carrier-based naval aviation had taken four years to come full circle, and a pretty small circle at that.

It was a haphazard, fumbling development which cried out for co-ordination and firm direction; certainly there was regrettable waste and duplication of effort. Even so, it is by no means certain that this wasted effort was detrimental to other aspects of naval aviation. Even if, as Group-Captain Williamson has asserted, the British could easily have had a through-deck carrier in service in 1916, this would merely have discouraged the invaluable experiments conducted in the Grand Fleet between 1916-18. These established the value of single aircraft which could be launched from a turret platform mounted in a battleship or cruiser. Though every launch necessarily ended in a sea landing when the mission was done, a Pup launched from the cruiser *Yarmouth* finally achieved the interception and destruction of a Zeppelin (*L.22*). This took place on 21 August 1917 – only 17 days after Dunning's fatal attempt to deck-land on *Furious*. When catapults and float planes were adopted for this purpose between the wars, every ship big enough to

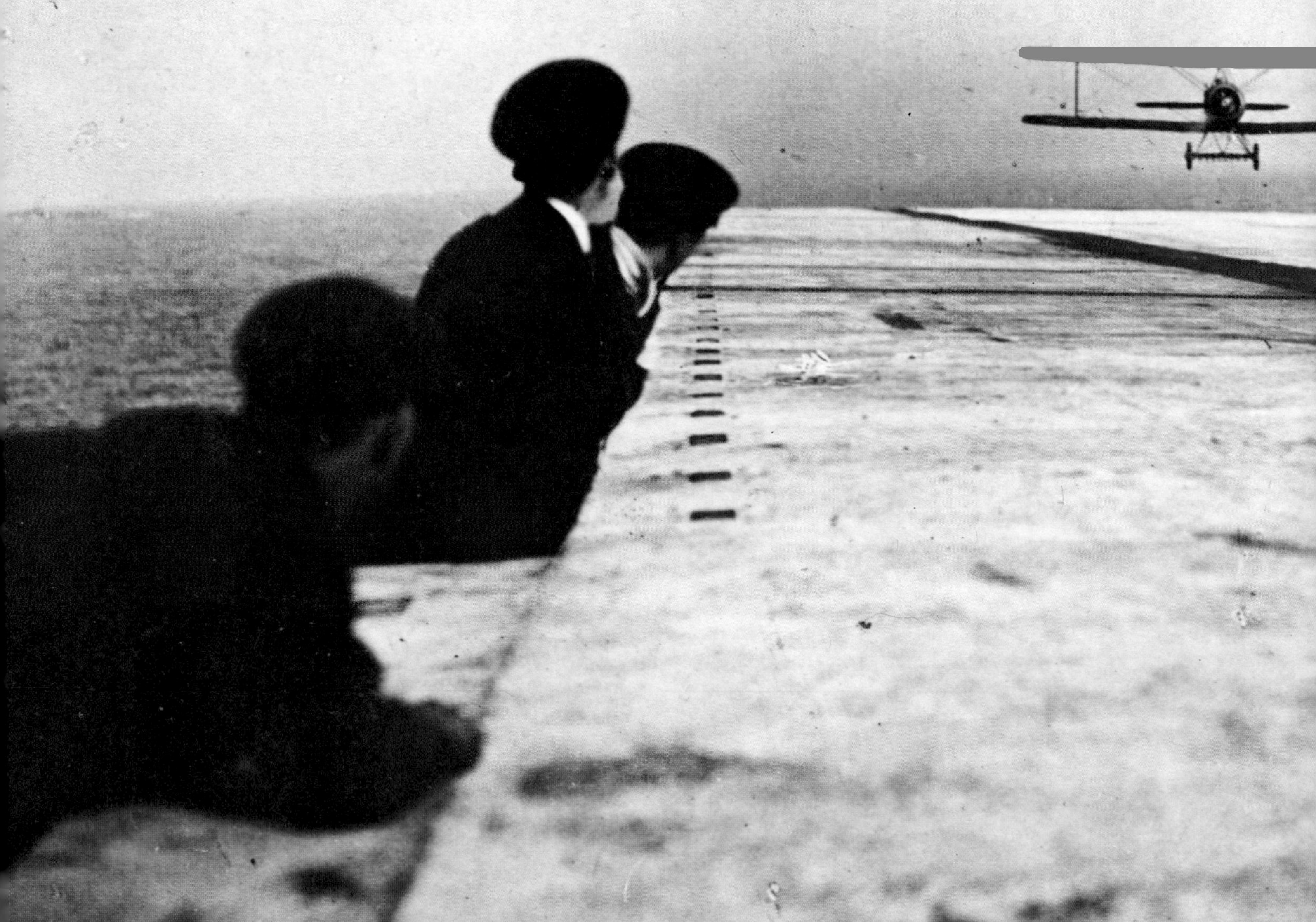

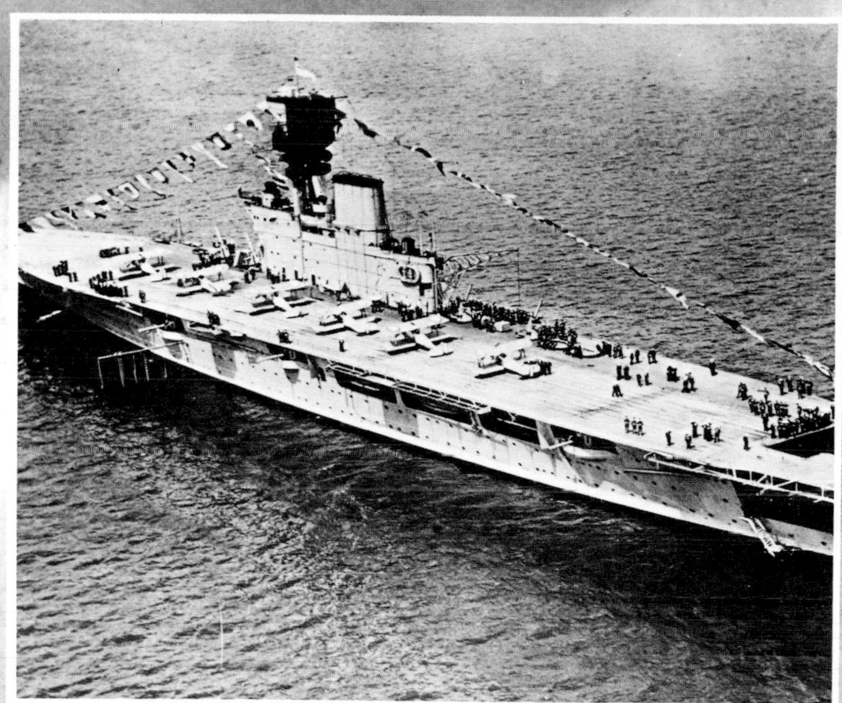

embark catapult and seaplane hangar could fly its own air reconnaissance. But the art was developed in the British Grand Fleet during the impatient wait for the first aircraft-carriers, at the close of the First World War. By the time of the Armistice, when the British fleet put to sea it took over 100 aircraft with it – not one embarked on a carrier.

And yet by July 1919 – only the tenth anniversary of Blériot's first Channel flight, when Britain had been the least air-minded nation in Europe – the British had made themselves first in the world with aircraft-carrier design and development. As the 1920s began, with one 'custom-built' carrier already in service, two more completing and no other nation within reach of the British lead, there was not the slightest indication of how far the British lead would be cancelled out over the coming 20 years.

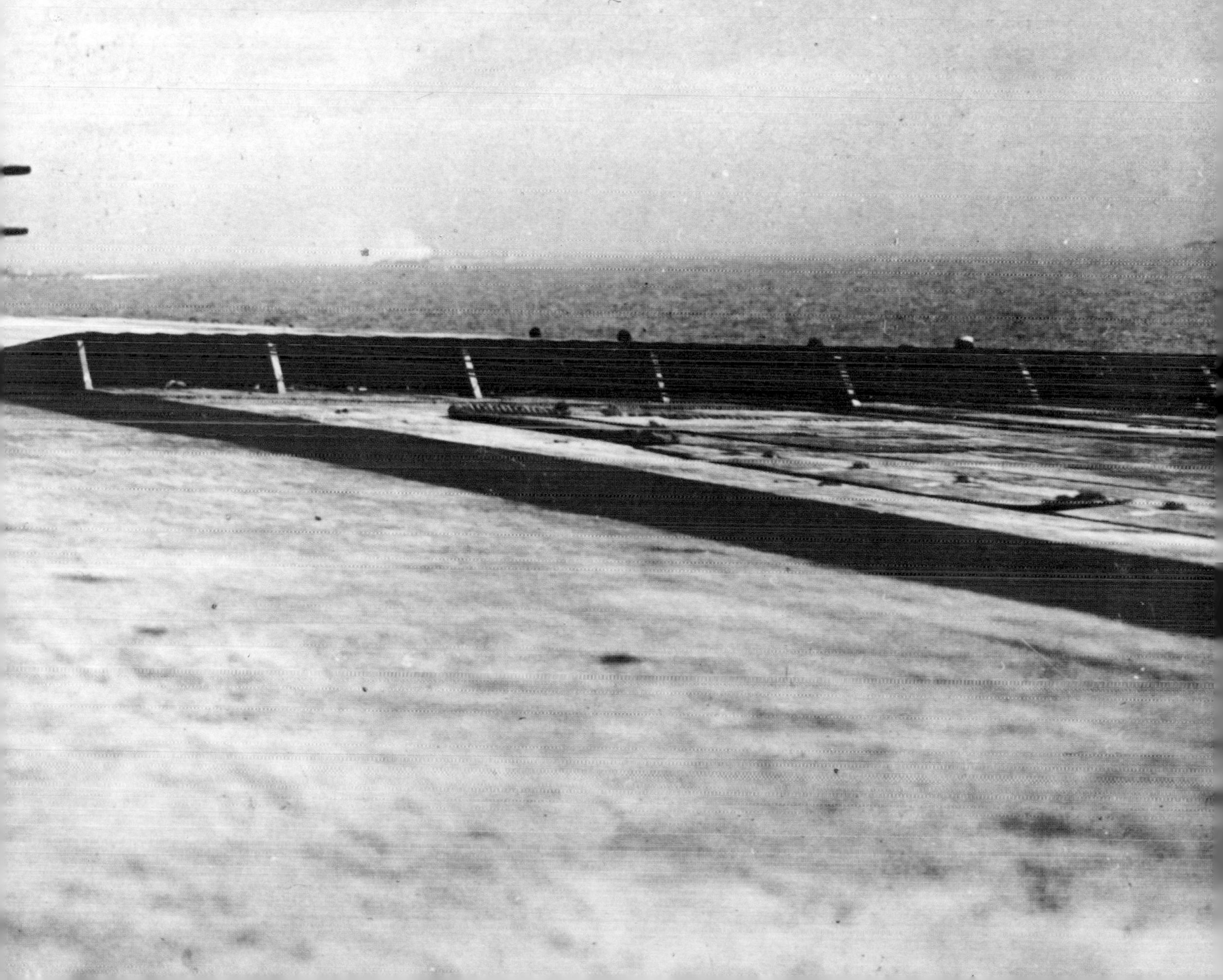

2. THE CARRIER NAVIES, 1920–1939

Previous pages: Britain's HMS *Glorious* takes it 'green over the bows' in a moderate sea – another convincing reason for abandoning the bow flying-off deck, quite apart from the problems posed by faster, heavier aircraft

THE INTERNATIONAL PROLIFERATION and continued development of the aircraft-carrier after the First World War was in every sense as uncertain as the type's beginnings. The carrier concept was taken up gingerly, first by Japan, then by the United States, and cautiously sniffed at in the sharp air of post-war economy. Certainly there was no post-war rush to build carriers, which had a long way to go before they were accepted as anything more than an 'optional extra' to the conventional battle fleet. The battleship was still regarded as the most prestigious of all, and with battleship main armaments moving onwards and upwards from 15-inch to 16-inch and even 18-inch there was every prospect of a peacetime battleship building race. But then something extraordinary happened: the diplomats took a hand and achieved the most successful arms limitation treaty of the twentieth century.

The Washington Naval Treaty of 1922 was a highly successful attempt to redefine international sea power on more reasonable lines. Though it dealt most comprehensively with other warship types, the Treaty's 'public enemy number one' was the big battleship. Given the eventual breakdown of international peace keeping in the 1930s, the effectiveness of the Washington Naval Treaty was in putting the conventional battle fleet permanently out of business. The signatory powers agreed to ration themselves to strict quotas and tonnage limits on future heavy warship construction. Though few of the Washington signatories remained loyal to the spirit of the Treaty, and battleship construction began again and continued throughout the 1930s, enough had been achieved to provide that there would be no re-enactments of Jutland in the Second World War, in which the battle *fleet* had been replaced by the battle *group*.

But the price for this most effective scotching of battleship development was the energetic stimulation of carrier development. One of the most important clauses in the Washington Treaty enabled signatories to convert unfinished battleship and battle-cruiser hulls – 'frozen' by the building moratorium – for completion as aircraft-carriers. This option was taken up by Japan and the United States; Britain, with *Argus* in service, *Eagle* and *Hermes* completing and *Furious* undergoing conversion to a flush-deck, decided to complete her available battleship hulls *as* battleships. The result was that ungainly duo *Nelson* and *Rodney*, their design radically changed to conform with Treaty restrictions and looking as though their stern quarters had been amputated with a blunt bread-knife. Well-armoured and armed with nine 16-inch guns, they nevertheless had a miserable top speed of only 23 knots. The huge American and Japanese 30-knot carriers launched in the same year as *Nelson* and *Rodney* (1925) proved an infinitely better bargain.

The intervention of the Washington Treaty therefore had a most profound effect on the post-1920 evolution of aircraft-carrier design. Before this sudden return to capital ship hulls as bases for conversion to carriers, the optimum displacement for carriers had been anyone's guess but was far lower than those of the first, wartime carrier conversions. Setting aside all speculation over a tactical or combat role, the basic function of any aircraft-carrier was accepted as reconnaissance: serving as the 'eyes of the fleet'. This was the traditional job of the cruiser, and it seemed only reasonable that the first homogeneous carriers ('built from the keel up') should be cruiser-sized – around 10,000 tons or even less, provided that the engines could deliver bursts of maximum speed on demand to make flying operations possible. The fact that *Furious*, *Argus* and *Eagle* had considerably higher displacements was irrelevant: they had, after all, started their respective lives as a light battle-cruiser, a luxury liner and a battleship. Thus the first homogeneous British carrier, *Hermes*, was really an elegant flat-topped cruiser of 10,850 tons displacement. *Hermes* was therefore 3,600 tons lighter than *Argus*, but was 5 knots faster and had a flight-deck 33 feet longer; *Hermes* could also carry the same number of aircraft (20) as *Argus*. Though launched in September 1919, 26 months before her only rival the Japanese *Hosho*, post-Armistice lack

Below: 'CV.1' – America's first carrier, the converted collier USS *Langley*
Opposite: Wings of the future over the truncated past – a Swordfish float plane and the battleship HMS *Nelson*, her stern cut short by the Washington Naval Treaty

K
8502

of urgency meant that *Hermes* was not first into service. By the time she finally joined the fleet in 1923, *Hosho* had already been serving with the Japanese Navy for nine months.

But *Hosho* was not merely the first of the new breed to enter service: she deserves remembrance as one of the most remarkable warships of the twentieth century. For a start she was easily the *smallest* aircraft-carrier ever built; and yet, for all her meagre 7,470 tons, she could operate more aircraft (up to 26) for her size than any other carrier. Apart from being a miracle of economical design, *Hosho* was prophetically equipped with an experimental light-and-mirror system for assisting deck landings. (Here was a classic example of a scientific improvement coming too soon for the technology of its day. Throughout the piston-engined era, carrier aircraft approach speeds would remain low enough for the pilot to be given the information he needed by a deck officer, facing the incoming aircraft and mimicking its flight attitude with a pair of 'bats'.) With all these distinctions it was most fitting that *Hosho* should be fated to be the only one of the ten aircraft-carriers, with which Japan went to war in December 1941, still in service at the end of the war – all the other nine having been sunk.

Though *Hosho* was completed with an experimental island this was removed after first trials, in 1923. So was the down-sloping bow section of the flight-deck – an obvious clue to the extensive early Japanese reliance on the British experience. With her island abolished and her flight-deck levelled, *Hosho* served on as a flush-decked carrier, plain and simple – prototype for all subsequent units of the Imperial Japanese carrier fleet. From the outset, Japanese carrier designers shrank from combining a vertical smoke-stack with the roomy bridge structures favoured by the British and Americans; and wherever island bridges had to be included, as in the case of the bigger Japanese fleet carriers, such islands were kept as small as possible. Of the 28 Japanese aircraft-carriers after *Hosho* to until the end of the Second World War, only four were built with vertical funnel venting combined with an orthodox island bridge. The Japanese soon came to favour the 'bent-over' funnel: flattened and streamlined as with the carrier funnels of other navies, but projecting its smoke downward and away from the hull. In the early days in *Hosho*, however, they experimented with six hinged smokepipes, three to a side: vertical for normal cruising, swung down to the horizontal when flying was in

Stern view of *Hermes*, showing the downward-curving 'round-down' at the after end of the flight-deck.

Opposite: First carrier to enter service – Japan's *Hosho*, showing the experimental island subsequently abandoned

A fine 'portrait-shot' of HMS *Eagle*, showing her distinctive battleship lines and elongated island structure

progress. It was not a success, nor was it repeated – in the Japanese Navy, at least.

As if to demonstrate the almost infinite variety of choices in carrier design in the early 1920s, Britain's *Eagle* had the longest connected island superstructure (in proportion to overall length) of any early carrier. Controversy about the size of *Eagle*'s island was rife even before she was delivered uncompleted for experimental flying tests in late April 1920. *Eagle*'s first Captain hated the thing and regarded it as the worst point of his ship's design. But even pilots who were bothered by that looming mass above their starboard wing found that the island was a useful point of reference, assisting them to get the height right when approaching to land. The evidence of wind-tunnel tests helped produce the more compact island form first used in *Hermes*. But the British showed themselves willing to keep an open mind about the pros and cons of carrier islands. This was shown by the decision on the huge reconstruction that would evidently be needed to convert *Furious* into a proper aircraft-carrier. Broadly agreed in April 1921, 14 months before the reconstruction began, this decision had profound effects on not only British but also Japanese carrier design for the next 15 years.

The most obvious answer to the question – flush-deck or island – was largely dictated by post-war economy. It was clearly easier and cheaper to give *Furious* a flush-deck, like *Argus* – maybe safer too, in the long run, with the debate over *Eagle*'s island still raging. Unlike that of *Argus*, however, the new flight-deck planned for *Furious* was not to extend the full length of the ship. There was also to be a

HMS EAGLE (Britain)
(ex-battleship *Almirante Cochrane*; launched 8.6.18)
DISPLACEMENT 22,600 tons. DIMENSIONS 667 ft (*overall*) x 923/4 ft x 24 ft. MACHINERY 4-shaft geared turbines: 50,000 SHP. SPEED 24 knots. PROTECTION Main belt 4-7 inches; deck 1-4 inches; shields 1 inch. ARMAMENT 9 x 6-inch, 4 x 4-inch AA, 8 x 2 pdr AA. AIRCRAFT 21. COMPLEMENT (*excluding aircrew*) 748

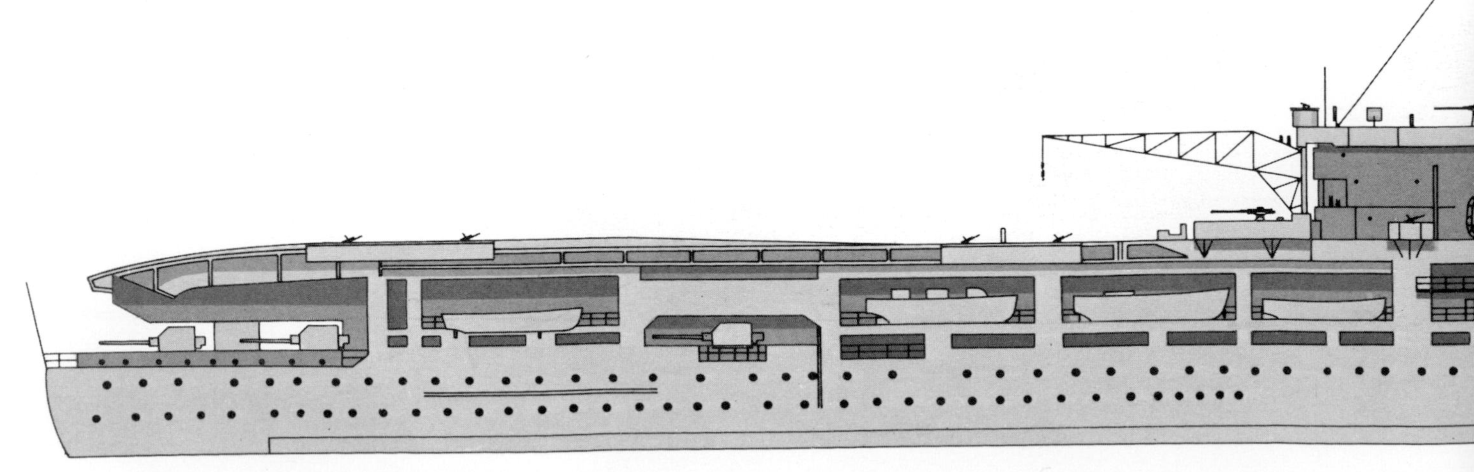

Fairey IIIF reconnaissance aircraft over *Furious* after her final conversion to a full flush-deck. Like the US Navy's *Langley*, her nickname was 'The Covered Wagon'

bow flying-off deck of true wartime stamp, 'next level down' from the main landing-on deck. When flying-off, aircraft were to be wheeled straight from the hangar on to the launch spot at the head of the flying-off deck. The British stuck to this configuration for the reconstruction not only of *Furious* but of her sister-ships *Glorious* and *Courageous*; and it was faithfully copied by the Japanese in their next two carriers – *Kaga* and *Akagi*.

This was mistaken on two main counts. First, and to a lesser extent, there was too much obsession with the experience of the war years, when bow flight-decks or ramps had been the *only* way of launching aircraft. But second – and far more crucial – was the failure to allow for the development of naval aircraft. Of course it would have been impossible, in the twentieth year of the aeroplane era, to have made even a broad estimate of aviation trends

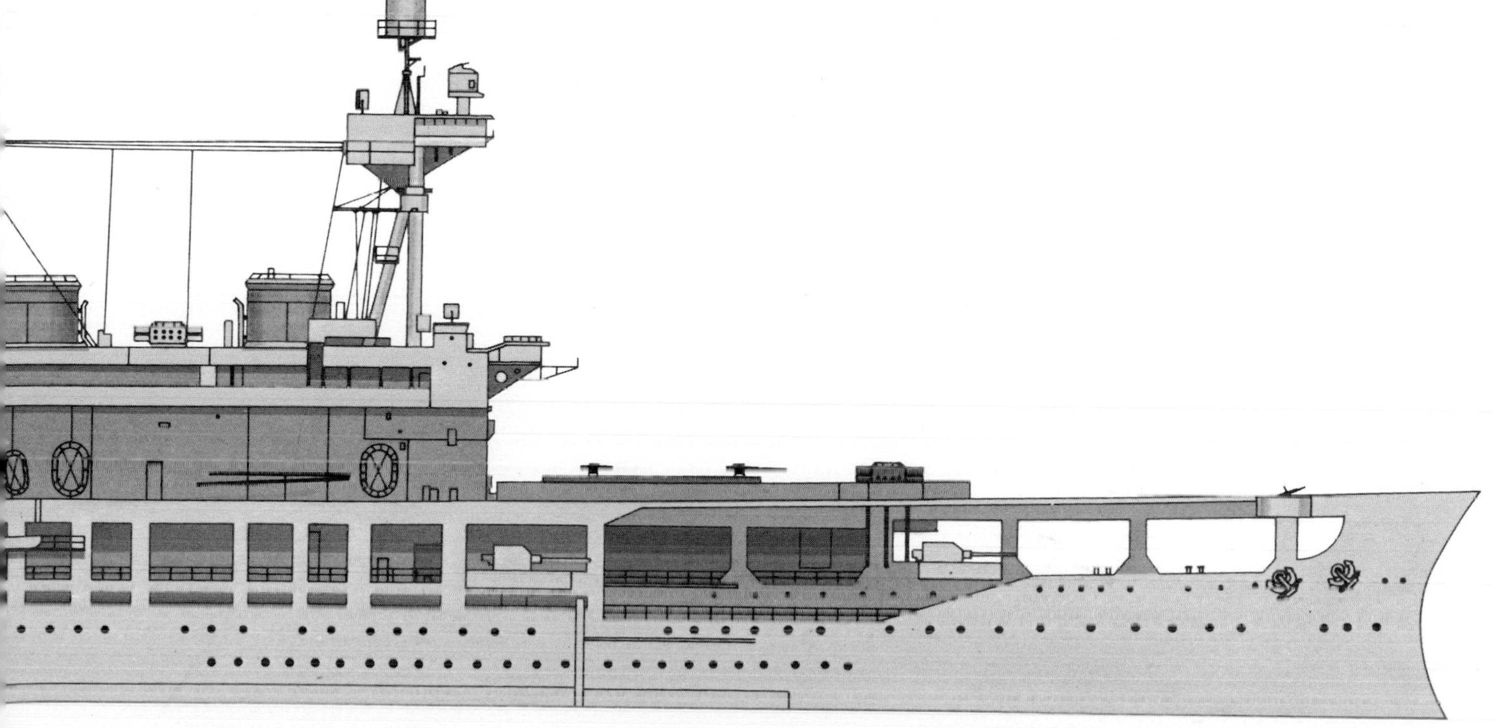

HMS *Glorious* in apple-pie order for the Coronation Naval Review of May 1937. The angular radio masts visible aft were lowered during flying operations

for the coming 20 years; but there were pointers. Aircraft were becoming bigger, heavier, and faster – not, admittedly, in steady or direct proportion, but unmistakeably so. The new Fairey Flycatcher carrier fighter of 1923 had a wingspan only 1 ft greater than that of the Sopwith Camel six years before – but its fuselage was over 4 ft longer than the Camel to accommodate an engine with nearly three times the Camel's horsepower, and the Flycatcher's loaded weight was 2,845 lb – 1,315 lb heavier than that of the Camel. When the Hawker Nimrod began to replace the Flycatcher eight years later, the Nimrod's wingspan was 4½ ft wider than the Flycatcher's; the Nimrod was 4 ft longer than the Flycatcher and its loaded weight 1,022 lb. greater than that of the Flycatcher. (The Nimrod was also 77 mph faster.)

Such impressive increases in aircraft size and performance did not, alas, mean that carriers could handle more aircraft. Much could be done by building more hangar space and by improving the arts of stowage (folding wings and interlocking parking); but faster, heavier aircraft would still need more and more flight-deck in which to take off and land, not to mention all the artificial slipstream the carrier's engines could deliver. The time was fast coming when no modern aircraft would be light enough, small enough or slow enough to take off from a bow flying-off deck.

Given this ever-mounting problem with the aircraft, it was clear that the best-off navies would be the ones which had managed to build the biggest carriers in the first place, for the biggest carriers would need the fewest modifications. In other words, aircraft development would 'grow into' the bigger carriers instead of being cramped and restricted by insufficient space.

In the big new carriers which grew from the Washington Treaty, it became apparent that the British – who had pioneered naval aviation throughout the war years – suddenly had the most to learn. In less time than it had taken to establish the British lead in aircraft-carrier development, that lead had been lost to the Americans and Japanese.

At the end of the First World War, the United States Navy had seemed no likelier than the Japanese to cut back the British lead in aircraft-carriers. Moreover, the US Department of the Navy was under just as much pressure from the Government to implement stringent economies as was the British Admiralty: they wanted to build an experimental American carrier, but funds were withheld. As a second-best, the American planners decided to take a leaf out of the British book by converting a fast collier: the 15-knot *Jupiter*, sent for conversion in March 1920. Two years later she emerged as the US Navy's first carrier (CV.1) – USS *Langley*.

A clean sweep had been made with her upperworks: she was to be a flush-decked carrier whose deep holds (not hangars) could store the biggest shipborne air group ever

Left: A Hawker Nimrod, superbly photographed in the act of taking-off from the main flight-deck of *Furious*

embarked – up to 55 aircraft – by any carrier then built or building. *Langley*'s flight-deck was another novelty. It did not taper, like *Hosho*'s, or gracefully follow the converging curve of the bows, like those of *Hermes* and *Eagle*. *Langley*'s flight-deck was an uncompromising rectangle, aimed at saving the last possible square inch of space for ranging aircraft on deck. Every possible disadvantage was turned to advantage – most notably *Langley*'s low speed, which made the development of a workable arrester-gear absolutely essential. It was aboard *Langley*, the old 'Covered Wagon' as she was affectionately known, that the system of linked transverse arrester-wires was perfected which has been used ever since.

This, then, was the world balance in aircraft-carriers when the Washington Conference was called in 1921. Britain had two carriers completed: *Argus* and (nominally at least) *Eagle*; *Furious* was scheduled for reconstruction, *Hermes* still completing. Japan and the United States had one carrier apiece still in process of completing – *Hosho* and *Langley*.

Reduced to its essentials, the ensuing Naval Treaty laid down the first definition of an aircraft-carrier's vital statistics: a warship of between 10-27,000 tons displacement primarily designed for operating aircraft, carrying no gun heavier than 8-inch and a maximum of ten. The United States and Japan, however, were to be allowed to complete two carriers apiece of 33,000 tons' maximum. This was agreed to facilitate conversion of the big battle-cruiser hulls, anxiety over which had provided the most urgent motive for the summoning of the Conference in the first place.

The result was a fascinating competition. Which pair of converted battle-cruisers would contain the most novelties – Japan's *Amagi* and *Akagi*, or the USA's *Lexington* and *Saratoga*? Circumstances beyond their control obliged the Japanese to revise their 'entry', for *Amagi* was damaged beyond repair in the Tokyo earthquake of September 1923. Nothing daunted, the Japanese merely broke up *Amagi* on the stocks and reprieved the hull of *Kaga* in *Amagi*'s place. *Kaga* was one of a pair of battleships, both launched in 1921, which would have displaced 38,500 tons and been armed with ten 16-inch guns; both were condemned by the Washington Treaty. After *Amagi*'s mishap only *Kaga*'s sister-ship *Tosa* went to her doom as a target ship. *Kaga*'s original battleship design had an inevitable effect on her performance as an aircraft-carrier; battle-cruisers were longer in the keel than battleships, leaner in the beam, built for speed without the battleship's armoured bulk. This meant that although *Kaga* and *Akagi* always operated as a 2-ship carrier division, *Kaga* was 43 ft shorter and some 3 knots slower than her consort.

Hitching a Douglas DT-2 to the catapult of *Langley*. Despite the invaluable experience gained from American catapult tests, unassisted aircraft 'lift-off' was to remain the basic launch practice throughout the piston-engined era

Akagi after her final conversion, displaying her distinctive port side island and 'humped' flight-deck. The latter was intended to make life easier for aircraft taking-off and landing-on – 'downhill' when taking-off, 'uphill' when landing-on

By contrast *Lexington* and *Saratoga* were a perfectly-matched pair of graceful giants. Apart from their sheer size – 888 ft long overall, 36,000-ton displacement, speed of 34 knots, capacity for up to 90 aircraft, complements of 3,300 officers and men (*Kaga* and *Akagi* had 2,019 and 2,000 respectively) they were the best-looking carriers of their day. This in itself was an important turning-point in the history of the aircraft-carrier. 'Lady Lex' and 'Sara' brought *majesty* to the carrier. Here was an unmistakeable emblem of sea power incarnate, no less impressive, in its own way, than the traditional aura of the battleship – and certainly far more impressive than that of the flag-showing cruiser. Apart from their size and their grace, an equally startling aspect of *Lexington* and *Saratoga* was – indeed, still is – the confidence and speed with which they took shape. Without undue effort or wasteful false starts and redesigns, they calmly reaped the benefit of all the key lessons learned in naval aviation over the past ten years. Debates and experiments over such design trivia as bow flying-off decks or hinged funnels – all the stumbling-blocks which had imparted an unmistakable mongrel look to every other carrier in existence – left no apparent scars on *Lexington* and *Saratoga*. In 1927 they joined the fleet, splendid and complete; neither was to require any major reconstruction before the outbreak of the Pacific War in December 1941.

Yet there were many who mocked the two when they appeared. For the first time there was heard the plaint so often repeated over the past 55 years: that the big fleet carrier is a vulnerable waste – too many eggs in too flimsy

KAGA (Japan)
(launched 1928)
DISPLACEMENT 38,200 tons. DIMENSIONS 812½ ft (*overall*) x 106¾ ft x 30 ft. MACHINERY 4-shaft geared turbines: 127,400 HP. SPEED 28⅓ knots. PROTECTION Main belt 9-11-inch. ARMAMENT 10 x 8-inch, 16 x 5-inch, 22 x 25 mm AA. AIRCRAFT 90. COMPLEMENT 2,019

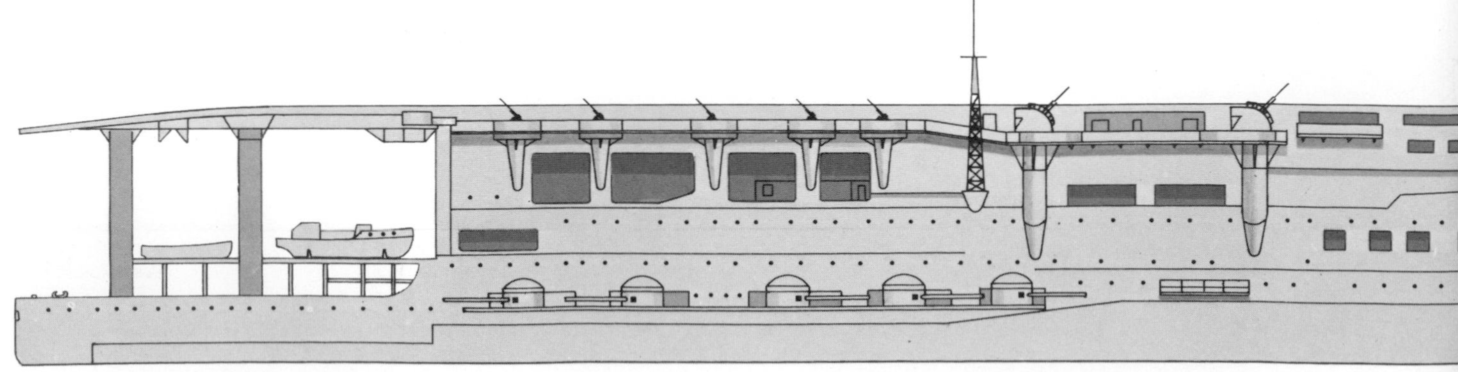

Lexington landing-on aircraft in 1929, displaying the enormous reach of her flight-deck. In the piston-engined era this was the unanswerable argument in favour of the big carrier – note the stack of aircraft ranged forward, safely 'out of range' of landing aircraft

a basket. Also not for the last time, it was asserted that more and smaller carriers was the proper policy, not fewer and bigger. There was much more reason for other criticisms. The gun question was a particularly good one – what was the point in adding a heavy cruiser's full armament of eight 8-inch guns? In *Lexington* and *Saratoga* these were mounted cruiser-fashion, in twin turrets fore and aft of the island with its monstrous, 79-ft smoke-stack. But if they should ever have to fire at an enemy inconsiderate enough to attack from the port beam, the damage those guns would cause from blast alone – particularly if there were aircraft fuelling or arming on the flight-deck – was not pleasant to contemplate.

Apart from this sobering consideration, there was the space taken up below decks by the hoist mechanism, lobbies, handing-rooms and magazines required to serve the guns. All this equipment, which could well be useless in action, encroached greedily on storage and hangar space. And indeed in *Saratoga*'s 1942 refit, which concentrated on improved anti-aircraft fire-power and flying capacity, the old 8-inch gun battery was the first to go. (The 8-inch guns were replaced with 5-inch dual-purpose guns, which at least could be swung vertically to shoot at aircraft.)

The guns of *Lexington* and *Saratoga* reflected the fact that despite all the theorising, nobody could tell what the combat role of the big carrier would turn out to be. There was not a shred of evidence to show that carriers, operating alone or in concert, could liquidate conventional warships with their aircraft alone. It took the Second World War to prove that when massed carriers operated with the

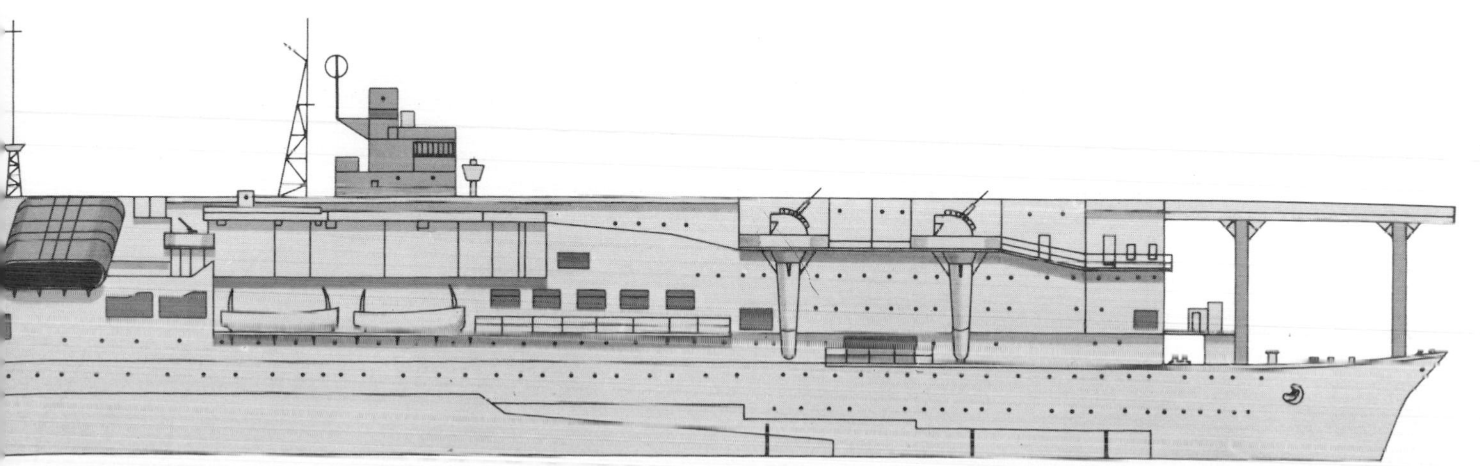

Saratoga, with a particularly fine view of her monstrous 8-inch gun armament – expressive of the inter-war doubts as to the carrier's true role. Should the type poach on the cruiser's traditional preserves – or should her aircraft give her an entirely separate role? The 'cruiser-sized' 8-inch turrets were removed at the earliest opportunity as soon as the Pacific War broke out

battle fleet in support, carriers could not only win battles: they could win wars. When *Lexington* and *Saratoga* entered service in the late 1920s the proper combat role of carriers was believed to be operating in support of the battle fleet, cruiser-fashion. (As already mentioned, precisely the same assumption in the British Admiralty had produced the cruiser-carrier *Hermes*.) Hence the instinctive 'issue' of standard heavy-cruiser gun armament to *Lexington* and *Saratoga*. It represented not so much a 'belt-and-braces' caution, as a reluctance to admit that the cruiser and the aircraft-carrier were separate species with separate functions.

In September 1925 Britain's *Furious* returned to service after her reconstruction as a full carrier. After all the vicissitudes of her early years, *Furious* now embarked on 19 splendid years as probably the most popular and certainly the most successful of the Royal Navy's 'first generation' carriers. As the last flush-decked British carrier, *Furious* blazed the trail for her sister-ships *Courageous* (conversion completed 1928) and *Glorious* (conversion completed 1930). Though the recommissioning of *Furious* took place in the same year that *Saratoga* and *Lexington* were launched, it was virtually impossible to find a single obvious feature that *Furious* shared in common with the American giants (other than flight-deck lifts). One of the most significant differences was the notable British freedom from uneasy nostalgia over gun mountings. The flight-deck of *Furious* was neither imperilled nor cluttered by cruiser-style gun turrets; her twelve 4-inch AA guns were deployed sensibly in 2-gun mountings, leaving the flight-deck completely clear.

A comparison of *Akagi* and *Kaga* with *Lexington* and *Saratoga*, as completed, shows first the extent to which Japanese designers were still following British patterns; and second the tremendous lead established by the Americans. Nobody could be blamed for guessing, on looks alone, that *Akagi* had been launched six years before *Lexington*, not a mere six months. Here were the two biggest flush-deck carriers ever completed, with not one extra flying-off deck forward, but two! It was a most eye-catching salute to the British influence on Japanese carrier design, but one rendered all the more bizarre when the next two British carriers were completed with island flight-decks. In the arrangmeent of Japanese gun mountings the British influence was again very discernible. The Japanese kept the 8-inch gun (ten for *Kaga*, six for *Akagi*),

A fine bow shot of *Courageous* at sea in the spring of 1932, preparing to fly-off aircraft (note lowered radio masts) from her main flight-deck. The faster, heavier biplanes of the 1930s made the shorter bow flying-off increasingly dangerous and the practice had been abandoned long before 1939

but in single mounts. Apart from the fact that it used the heavier 4.7-inch gun, the main AA batteries in *Kaga* and *Akagi* were direct copies of the one used in *Furious:* six twin mounts, pinned to the ships' sides atop distinctive structures resembling hanging buttresses.

But there could be no atoning for the drastic reduction in the number of aircraft made inevitable by the inclusion of forward flight-decks. Whereas *Lexington* and *Saratoga* could operate 80-90 aircraft, *Kaga* and *Akagi* could only operate 60-70 aircraft. Given the maximum dimensions available in the Japanese ships this was a depressing total. It was a crucial deficiency not put right until 1935-38, when drastic reconstructions of *Kaga* and *Akagi* extended the main flight-decks right up to the bows and raised the aircraft total to 90.

After *Lexington* and *Saratoga* all American fleet carriers were of homogeneous build (with the exception of the nine-ship 'Independence' class, converted from 'Cleveland' class light cruisers under the 1942 war emergency building programme). The same applied to the best of the later Japanese fleet carriers: *Soryu* and *Hiryu* (1935, 1937), *Shokaku* and *Zuikaku* (1939), and *Taiho* (1944). By December 1941 both the American and Japanese navies contained more carriers of homogeneous design than converted ships: five out of seven in the US Navy, six out of ten in the Japanese Combined Fleet.

With the full mobilisation of the vast American shipbuilding industry on the outbreak of war, Japan's absolute reliance on hand-to-mouth conversions to keep up the strength of the carrier fleet would be revealed. By the early 1930s, however, the American and Japanese navies each had a balanced pair of fleet carriers, enabling carrier to be pitted against carrier in fleet exercises and war games and hammer out the tactics of attack and defence. But not one of these training studies ever even vaguely suggested that the big battleship's day was done; and the Japanese Navy's remarkable investment in carrier power was set fatally at risk by the exhorbitant super-battleship building programme of the 1930s. The time, effort, manpower and materials consumed by the 'Yamato' class super-battleships between 1934 and 1941 arguably lost Japan the war. If in the high summer of 1942 the Japanese Navy had had six more medium fleet carriers instead of two 18-inch gun, 70,000-ton giant battleships which never saw action for the next two years, it is highly likely that the Japanese would have won the knockout victory they sought.

One of the most important reasons why Britain fell astern of the United States and Japan between the wars is that the American and Japanese navies each had its own air force. Britain had fought the First World War with separate air forces for the Army (Royal Flying Corps) and Navy (Royal Naval Air Service). These were amalgamated into the new Royal Air Force in April 1918, and for the next 20 years the Navy lacked control of its own air forces. Having suffered an immediate and exhaustive transfer of 2,500 aircraft and 55,000 men to the RAF, the Navy was only partly appeased by the formation of the RAF's 'Fleet Air Arm' in 1924. This left the RAF providing the aircraft, maintenance crews and nearly half the pilots, subject to Navy discipline when afloat and RAF discipline when ashore. Between 1924 and 1937 (when the needful independence of the Navy's air arm was finally conceded) the RAF found it hard enough to procure adequate modern aircraft for itself, let alone the Navy. The Hurricane and Spitfire fighters only just entered RAF service in time for the Battle of Britain. The Royal Navy's fighter aircraft in September 1939 were the biplane Gloster Gladiator (maximum speed 253 mph) and the Blackburn Skua (225 mph) – the Skua also 'doubling' as a dive-bomber when required. These were the aircraft pitted against the German Messerschmitt Bf 109E with its top speed of 357 mph, not to mention double the fire-power augmented by twin cannon.

And yet, despite the deplorable obsolescence of its aircraft, the morale and professionalism of the British Fleet Air Arm remained second to none. In a crazy way, the professionalism rose with every deficiency in the cramped confines of the ageing British carriers. After an amateurish series of experiments with fore-and-aft arrester-wires in 1920-26, the Fleet Air Arm had abandoned *any* form of arrester-gear and relied on skill alone until transverse arrester-wires arrived for good in 1933-35. When they did arrive, diehard Fleet Air Arm pilots were heard to grumble that the new luxury would ruin the standard of flying. This absurdity apart, Fleet Air Arm training and exercises, concentrating on torpedo attacks and, from 1935, night flying operations, was in deadly earnest and bore abundant fruit at Taranto (see p. 60).

Marvellously agile but hopelessly outpaced and outgunned by the modern monoplane fighters – the Gloster Gladiator, in its Sea Gladiator variant, was the Fleet Air Arm's fighter mainstay at the outset of the Second World War

The last naval power to be prodded by the Washington Treaty into aircraft-carrier development was France. Not surprisingly for a nation which had been a battlefield throughout the First World War, France's defence priorities in the 1920s were for security on land. But the French Navy did have five 'Normandie' class battleship hulls whose construction had been halted in 1914; and one of them, *Béarn,* was selected for conversion to a carrier in April 1922. (*Béarn* was destined for a special niche in carrier history: the only 'first generation' carrier to survive into the 1960s.) The French designers relied heavily on the British experience with *Eagle,* but added some unique touches of their own. *Béarn* was the only carrier whose flight-deck lift shafts were closed by gigantic hinged doors, and not by the lift-platform resting flush with the deck when fully 'up'. She also introduced a hot air/cold air 'mixer', with hot funnel gases blended with cold air to cut down turbulence over the flight deck. Despite her lumbering 21½ knots (barely faster than Britain's *Argus*) *Béarn* put in enough good work over her first ten years in service for two homogeneous successors, *Joffre* and *Painlevé,* to be ordered in 1938. But only *Joffre* had been laid down by the outbreak of the Second World War.

The growing uneasiness of the 1930s, increasingly frequent resorts to force and the breakdown of world peace – all were reflected in the warships of the day. The 1930s saw the leading navies once more laying down new battleships, of which only the British 'King George V' class paid full obeisance to the Washington Treaty and its successor, the London Treaty of 1930. The latter was the last naval restrictions treaty signed by Japan. She had laid down her second homogeneous carrier in 1929: *Ryujo,* a deliberate attempt to cram maximum aircraft into a small carrier below the lower Treaty limit. This not only proved

impossible – *Ryujo*'s displacement worked out at well over 10,000 tons – but uneconomical and positively dangerous. *Ryujo* could only make 29 knots; she carried 48 aircraft, but was so top-heavy that she needed a major reconstruction. She was the first obvious attempt to solve the riddle of whether several small carriers are a better bet than a few big ones, and for all her faults she yielded invaluable experience to the benefit of her successors.

Soryu, launched in December 1935, was Japan's first island carrier (though without vertical funnels) and at 15,900 tons was the last Japanese carrier designed to comply with Treaty restrictions. A sister-ship, *Hiryu*, launched two years later, was cut to more generous cloth and displaced 1,600 tons more than *Soryu*; both could operate 73 aircraft and led directly to an expanded design, *Shokaku* and *Zuikaku*, launched in 1939. These latest carriers displaced 25,675 tons, could steam 34 knots and carry 84 aircraft. Given the superior quality of Japanese carrier aircraft in the early months of the Pacific war, *Shokaku* and *Zuikaku* were the fastest and toughest fleet carriers in the Pacific before the arrival of the American 'Essex' class in 1943.

The influence of Treaty restrictions, though waning, rested more heavily on American carrier design in the 1930s. The US Navy, like the Japanese, sought to follow up its pair of 1920s giant carriers with an experimental small carrier. The result was *Ranger* (launched February 1933) – the first homogeneous American carrier. She was originally intended to be the first of five 13,800 carriers; she repre-

Above: *Béarn* after her 1935 refit, which extended her flight-deck fully forward. She was the only pre-war carrier destined to do yeoman service clear through to the jet age.
Below: Japan's top-heavy lightweight *Ryujo*, showing her dangerously low forecastle

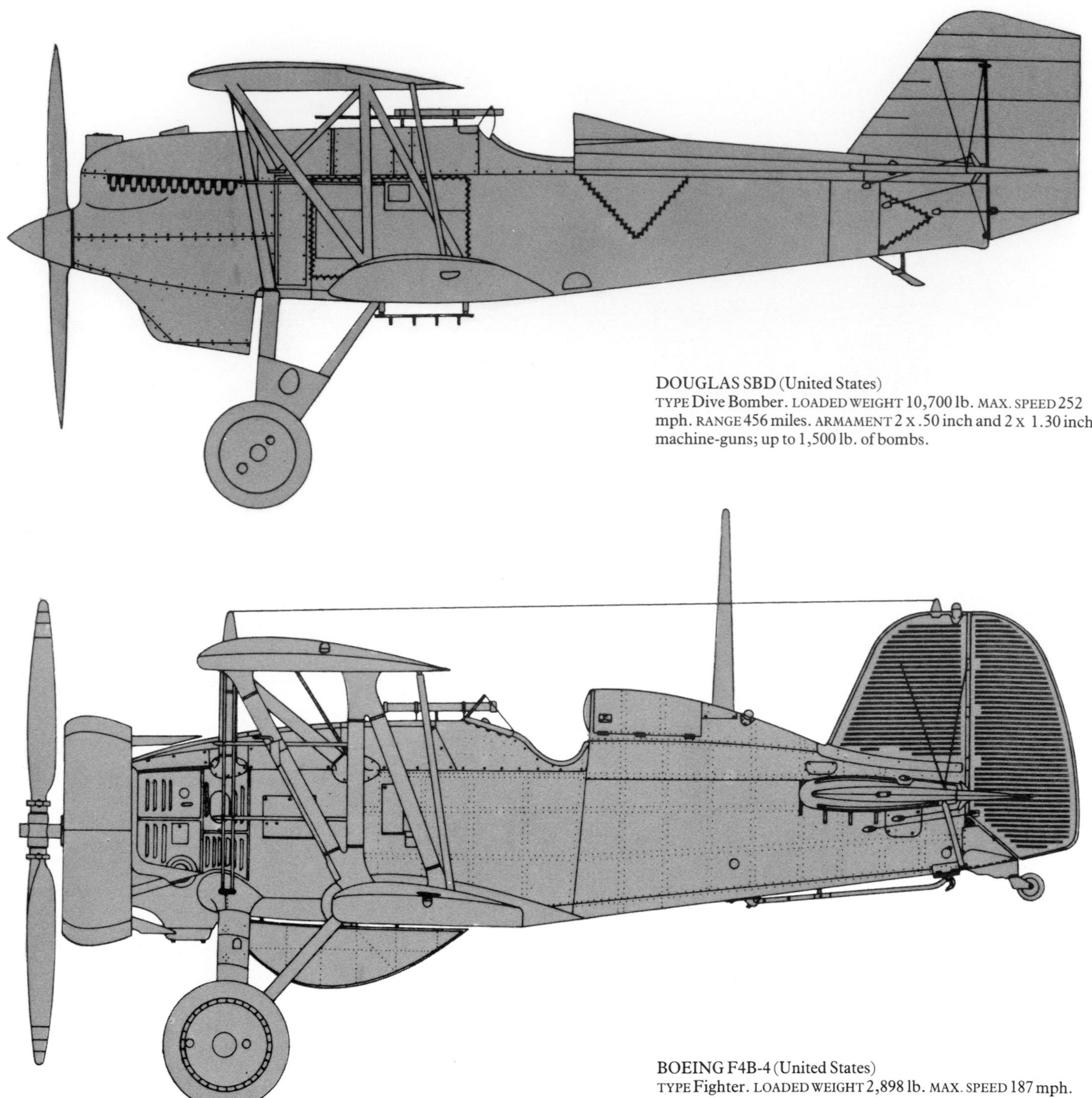

DOUGLAS SBD (United States)
TYPE Dive Bomber. LOADED WEIGHT 10,700 lb. MAX. SPEED 252 mph. RANGE 456 miles. ARMAMENT 2 x .50 inch and 2 x 1.30 inch machine-guns; up to 1,500 lb. of bombs.

BOEING F4B-4 (United States)
TYPE Fighter. LOADED WEIGHT 2,898 lb. MAX. SPEED 187 mph. RANGE 585 miles. ARMAMENT 2 x .30 inch machine-guns.

sented, like *Ryujo,* an attempt to get more ships out of the permitted maximum tonnage. With a maximum speed of only 29½ knots *Ranger* was not a complete success; in an almost ludicrous reaction from the giant superstructures of *Saratoga* and *Lexington,* she carried six hinged smoke-pipes aft, in the style of *Hosho,* and a diminutive island. *Ranger*'s great contribution was her entirely new hull design, extending beam construction above the waterline to unheard-of limits to increase inner capacity. Thus, while *Ranger*'s displacement was 18,500 tons and her overall length 119 ft *less* than those of *Saratoga*, *Ranger*'s extreme beam measurement (at 109½ ft) was 4 ft *more.* This method of lateral hull extension was the great American contribution to aircraft-carrier design, permitting the embarkation of greater striking power without a proportionate increase in overall displacement. It was expanded into the 20,000-ton *Yorktown* and *Enterprise,* launched in 1936 – the first carriers of the '100-plane' category. The Japanese held to their preference for 'long and lean' carrier hulls; it will be noted that the 'Shokakus', though three years later than the 'Yorktowns'

Left & below: Contrast in carrier hull/flight-deck designs of the 1920s and 1930s. Britain's *Hermes* shows the graceful flare of her bows influenced by her cruiser design . . .

. . . while *Enterprise*, in the mid-1930s, carries a full rectangular flight-deck atop a laterally-expanded hull

Japan's *Taiho*, laid down in July 1941 – the exception to the rule with Japanese fleet carriers. First Japanese carrier fitted with an armoured flight-deck, she was not completed until the Japanese naval air arm had suffered crippling and irreplaceable combat losses

and of nearly 6,000 tons greater displacement, carried 16 fewer aircraft than the 'Yorktowns'.

Before the third 'Yorktown' was begun (*Hornet*, launched in December 1940) the US Navy had one last try with the small-carrier format. The USS *Wasp*, launched in April 1939, featured the basic *Ranger* hull design with all its advantages, but with a *Yorktown*-style island and funnel instead of the clumsy smoke-pipes. Yet the power problem was the same: 29½ knots was not good enough for fleet work in a 33-knot age. *Wasp* had a glorious if brief career before her in the Second World War, but the wise decision was made to build *Hornet* as the prelude to the main heavy carrier fleet: the 'Essex' class carriers (27,100 tons, 33 knots, 100 aircraft).

Meanwhile the first of Britain's new carriers, *Ark Royal*, was ready for service. The Royal Navy's decision to build a new generation of fleet carriers was a particularly bold one, on two counts. It was made at a time when there was no prospect of the Admiralty recovering control over its own aircraft; and it was made without any prior experimentation of the kind the Americans had made with *Ranger*. The British had started with small carriers, and had learned their limitations only too well – but this did not imply that they were impatient to build giant carriers. The aircraft problem made it impossible for the Admiralty to think in terms of large air groups; on the other hand, the Fleet Air Arm had developed a remarkable proficiency in its operations amid the modest confines of *Furious*, *Courageous* and *Glorious*. The worst defects of these three popular conversions in 1935 were held to be their speed – at 30½ knots still impressive for ships 20 years old, but slipping behind the speeds of more modern types – and their flight-deck layout. The blend of lower bow deck and 'three-quarters' main flight deck was acceptable as long as aircraft remained small and light; but by the middle 1930s the heavier new biplanes could no longer use the bow deck in safety and it was so much wasted space. A

TAIHO (Japan) Displacement 29,300 tons. Dimensions 854 ft × 91 ft × 31 ft. Machinery 4-shaft geared steam turbines: 180,000 shp. Speed 33 knots. Protection sides 6 inches, deck 3 inches. Armaments 12 × 3.9 inches, 71 × 1 inch AA. Aircraft 15; complement 1751.

Yamato, expressive of the Japanese Navy's fatal reliance on the super-battleship concept. She never fired a gun in anger until the Combined Fleet's carrier arm had been decisively beaten. The manpower and material devoted to these colossal 'white elephants' were one of the invisible long-term assets working to the advantage of the American carrier arm

second conversion programme (which in the case of *Furious* would have been the *fourth*) might create more flight-deck and hangar space but would certainly not yield more speed. A new carrier, prototype of the class which would eventually replace the ageing trio, was far and away the best solution; and the result was *Ark Royal,* the most famous British carrier of the Second World War.

To emphasise the importance attached to the new ship, she was carefully given the same name as the Navy's first 'aircraft-carrier' of 1914. Still performing yeoman service as a catapult and training ship, the old veteran was renamed *Pegasus* to release her name to the new carrier, launched in April 1937 and commissioned in November 1938. As the first of a new class of heavy British warship, no less detailed planning had gone into the new *Ark Royal* than had gone into the first Dreadnought battleship 30 years before. They increased *Ark Royal*'s manoeuvrability by dropping her length-to-beam ratio (10:1 in *Soryu*, 9:1 in *Ranger* and *Yorktown* but only 7.6:1 in *Ark Royal*). They hung a flight-deck 800 ft long on a hull with a perpendicular length of only 685 ft, saving vital tonnage to give extra armoured protection to hangars and fuel tanks. This protection was to become the most distinctive feature of British aircraft-carriers in the Second World War; but it was achieved at the expense of aircraft capacity. *Ark Royal* had been designed for 72 aircraft, but this had to come down to 60. Even so, this was 12 more than *Courageous* and *Glorious* with their 500 extra tons displacement apiece. *Ark Royal* displaced 22,000 tons and was a clear knot faster (31.75 knots) than *Courageous* and *Glorious*.

Ark Royal had not even been launched when the Admiralty ordered the first two of her successors, the improved, better-armoured 'Illustrious' class (1936 Estimates). Despite excellent service in the Second World War and the undoubted need for them, it is equally true that if there was one naval power which should

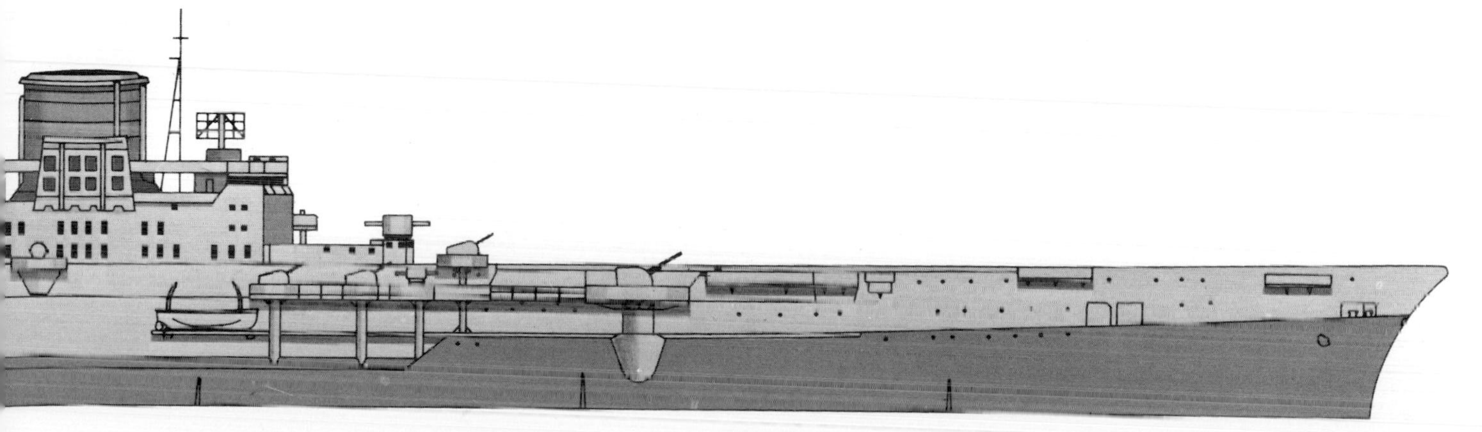

GRAF ZEPPELIN (Germany)
DISPLACEMENT 23,200 tons. DIMENSIONS 820 ft x 88½ ft x 18½ ft. MACHINERY 4-shaft geared turbines: 200,000 SHP. SPEED 33½ knots. PROTECTION Sides 4-inch, deck 2-inches. ARMAMENT 16 x 5.9-inch AA; 12 x 4.1-inch AA; 22 x 37 mm AA; 28 x 20 mm AA. AIRCRAFT 40. COMPLEMENT 1,760.

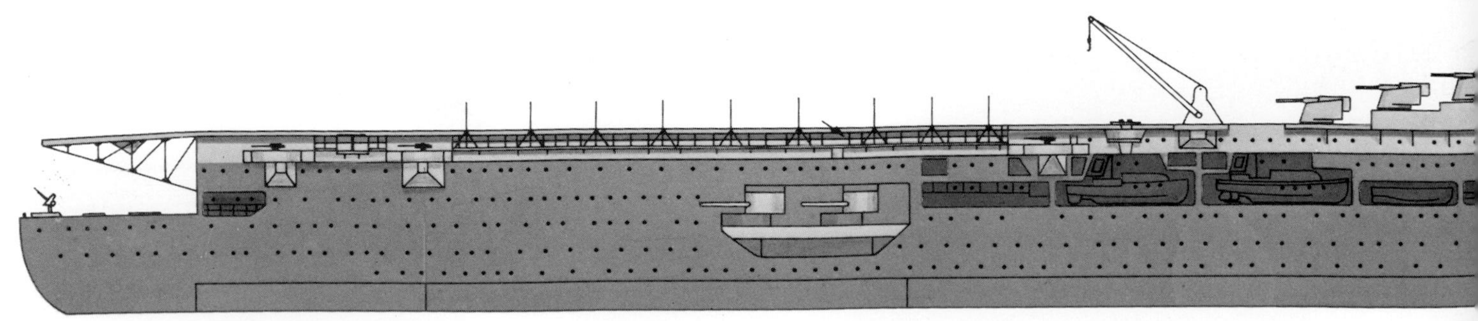

have invested in more smaller carriers – or even fewer carriers and more anti-submarine craft – that power was Britain. The new German U-boat fleet would prove far more deadly than the big new surface warships built for the German Navy between 1933 and 1939. And one of the latter in particular represents perhaps the most fascinating might-have-been of the aircraft-carrier story: the German carrier *Graf Zeppelin*.

She was launched in December 1938, the first of two carriers for a balanced German fleet envisaged, by the intricate 'Z-Plan', as being ready to challenge the Royal Navy in about 1944-45. Grand-Admiral Raeder's idea of a 'balanced fleet' was nothing if not obsolete, harking back to the good old days of the Dreadnought heyday. Two carriers would have had their work cut out in trying to support eight battleships, five battle-cruisers and three pocket-battleships. Only *Graf Zeppelin* was launched, and she was never completed; the main reason for this was the virulent opposition of *Luftwaffe* supreme commander Marshal Göring, who hated the Navy as a service institution outside his control and did his best to keep it starved of aircraft. By the time that Albert Speer replaced Göring in 1942 top priority for new naval construction had passed irrevocably to U-boats.

For all this the British can count themselves extremely lucky, given the wartime Atlantic sorties by *Admiral Scheer, Scharnhorst, Gneisenau*, and *Bismarck*, and what they managed to achieve *without* carrier support. It is easy to pick holes in *Graf Zeppelin*'s design and write her off as a mish-mash of other navies' ideas. But she would certainly have been fast (33 knots), well armoured, and – without Göring's hostility – possessed of what would have been unquestionably the best carrier aircraft outside Japan. These would have been the naval version of the Messerschmitt 109 fighter, the Me Bf 109T – 'T' for *Träger*, or carrier – and Junkers Ju-87C dive-bomber. In view of the Ju-87's deadly prowess off Norway, Greece, and Crete in 1940-41, the prospect of carrier-borne 'Stukas', even in conjecture, is not an attractive one.

As a final comment on *Graf Zeppelin*'s happily unrealised potential, she would have been given an impressive battery: sixteen 5.9-inch guns and an excellent array of 4.1-inch and automatic AA weapons, far better than the AA provision in most pre-war carriers. The interesting point, given the high reliance of the German surface fleet on commerce raiding, is that *Graf Zeppelin* would have made a formidable surface raider in her own right, without a single aircraft aboard. If completed according to the original specifications, she would have been given the highest surface-to-surface armament of any aircraft-carrier before the Soviet Union's *Kiev*, 37 years later.

In September 1939 the only two carrier navies directly opposed to each other, Japan and the United States, still had two years of peace before their supreme trial of strength in the Pacific War of 1941-45. In those two years the task of establishing the combat role of the aircraft-carrier, and proving its unique potential in the Mediterranean, Atlantic and Arctic, fell primarily on the Royal Navy.

Left: *Ark Royal* under the shield of her Swordfish on the eve of the Second World War. At her stern can be seen the enormous overhang of her flight-deck 'round-down', the contrivance by which a full-size flight-deck was hung on a medium-size hull

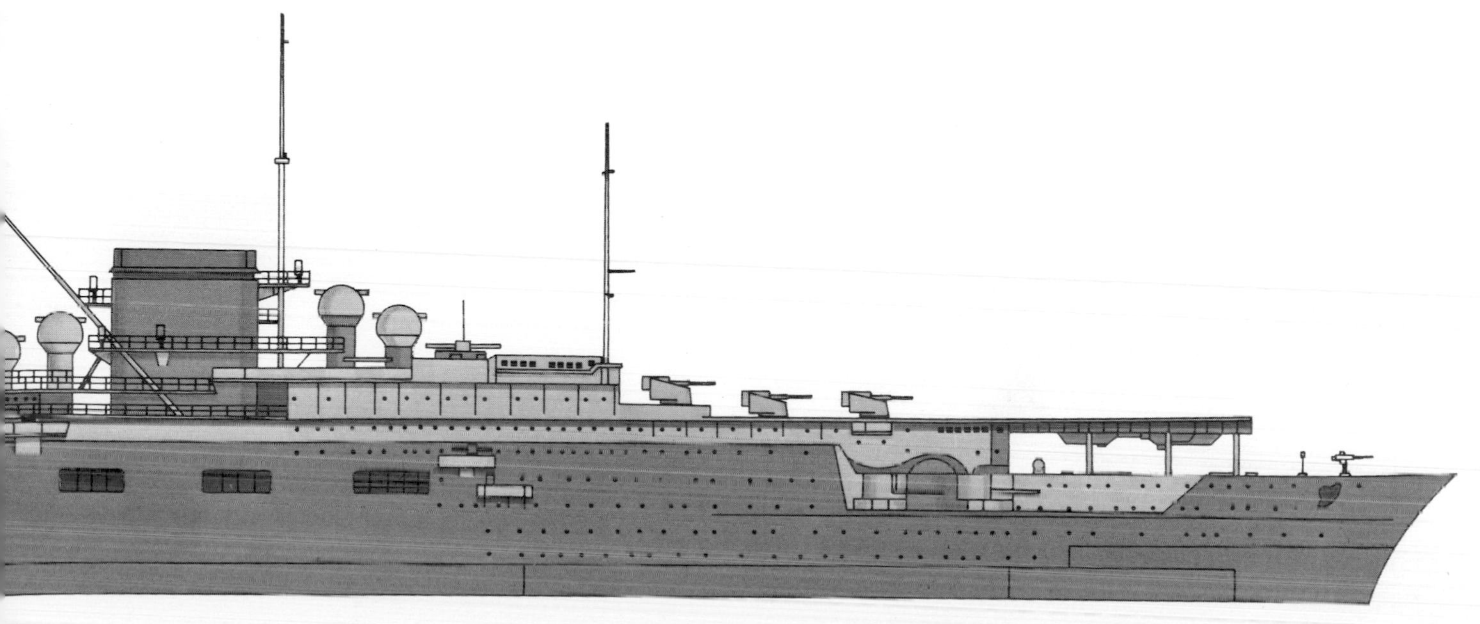

3. ATLANTIC AND MEDITERRANEAN, 1939–1945

Previous pages: Albacore torpedo-bombers aboard HMS *Indomitable* in June 1942, having their wings folded before being struck down to the hangar

THE OUTBREAK OF THE EUROPEAN WAR in September 1939 found most of the British carriers in home waters. *Argus* was no longer regarded as operational, though she still had invaluable work to do in training and ferry duties. *Ark Royal* and *Furious* were with the Home Fleet at Scapa Flow, *Courageous* and *Hermes* with the Channel Force. *Glorious* was with the Mediterranean Fleet and *Eagle* about to be recalled from the China Station. This basically favourable deployment for a war with Germany was all the more improved when, contrary to expectation, Mussolini did not bring Italy into the war as Germany's ally. Though a welcome surprise on many counts it nevertheless disconcerted the Allied strategists, who had looked forward to attacking Italy as the weakest partner of a German-Italian alliance.

The first task to which the British Admiralty set its carriers was operating in small hunting groups – usually a carrier and two or three destroyers – hopefully to clear British home waters of U-boat marauders. This plan was lucky not to end in total disaster. It betrayed a fatal over-confidence in what would nowadays be called 'Western technology', the technology in 1939 consisting of the recently-perfected Asdic apparatus. Asdic (referred to from this instance by its more familiar modern appellation, sonar) enabled surface ships to detect submarines, a breakthrough which in 1937 prompted the British Admiralty to boast that U-boats would never imperil Britain again. But sonar expertise against 'live' submarines could only be painfully learned in wartime conditions; water disturbance interfered with the sonic pulse, or 'ping', which meant that anti-submarine forces using sonar had to proceed at slow speed. The result, in the first weeks of the war, was immensely valuable aircraft-carriers and destroyers nosing about in search of U-boats, having sacrificed the surface ship's biggest advantage over the submarine: speed. In any case the whole strategy was wrong: the First World War had taught that *hunting* for U-boats was a waste of time. The infallible recipe for trapping U-boats was to force the U-boat to attack well-defended convoys – the classic gambit of luring the opponent onto ground of one's own choosing and destroying him there. The clumsy British carrier/destroyer patrols of September 1939 were as dangerously misguided as they could be.

'Asdic' operator in his cabinet. Excessive faith in this device cast the British fleet carrier in the U-boat hunting role in the opening weeks of the war – with near catastrophic results

On the morning of 14 September 1939, *Ark Royal* turned into wind to launch three Skuas; the aircraft were to rendezvous with SS *Fanad Head*, which had just reported a torpedo attack. Barely had the aircraft taken off from *Ark Royal* when she was narrowly missed by two torpedoes: she had headed straight for *U-39*. The *Ark*'s escorting destroyers counter-attacked and by great good fortune blew the U-boat to the surface with the second depth-charge pattern; *U-39*'s crew surrendered, and the submarine foundered. So far so good – but when the *Ark*'s Skuas caught *U-30* still attacking *Fanad Head*, two of them bombed so low that they blew their own tails off and crashed in the sea, their crews promptly being taken prisoner by the undamaged *U-30*. Superbly handled, *U-30* evaded a machine-gunning attack by the surviving Skua and a later attack by six Swordfish torpedo-bombers from *Ark Royal*; she got back to Germany with her prisoners. Such was the combat début of *Ark Royal*, and indeed of the aircraft-carrier. As far as the *Ark* was concerned the events of the 14th added up to a humiliating near-disaster, with two aircraft written off and four men prisoners-of-war for nil return – *U-39* had been the destroyers' kill, not the *Ark*'s. Of course it could be, and was, written up as a masterpiece of teamwork between carrier and destroyers; but *Ark Royal*'s part in *U-39*'s destruction had been more of a horrified decoy than a master of the hunt, while her attacks on *U-30* had been an unmitigated fiasco.

When the inevitable happened three days later it was a miracle that the victim was *Courageous* and not the brand-new *Ark Royal*. At sunset on 17 September *Courageous* was sighted in the St George's Channel by *U-29* (Lt Schuhardt). Though *Courageous* had aircraft aloft they failed to detect *U-29*'s periscope as Schuhardt stealthily approached, keeping right in the blazing eye of the setting

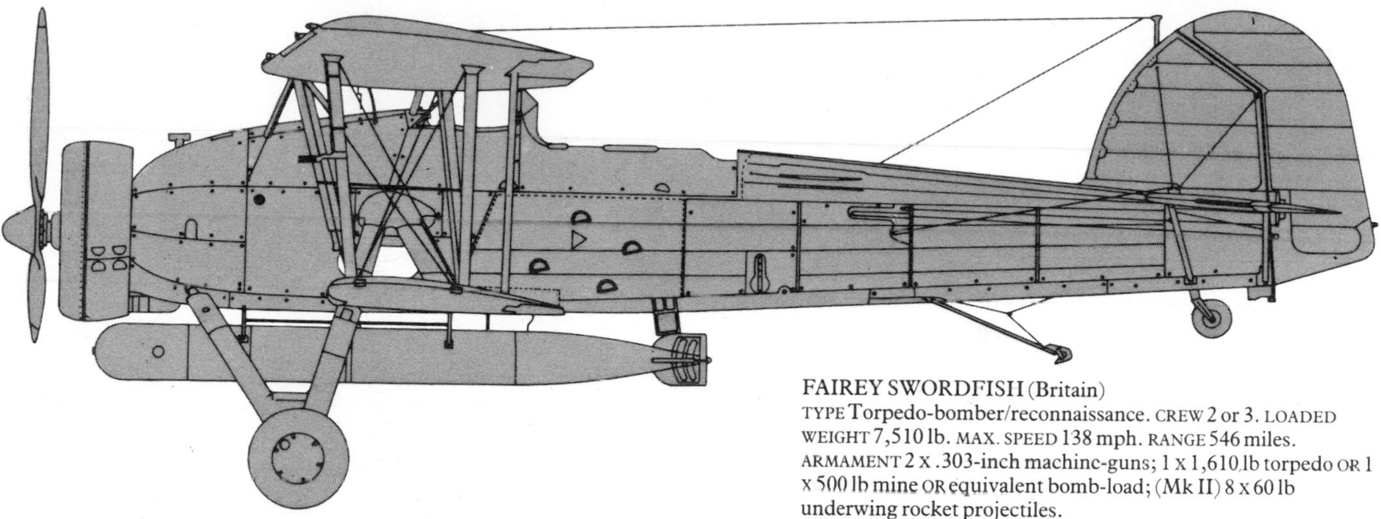

FAIREY SWORDFISH (Britain)
TYPE Torpedo-bomber/reconnaissance. CREW 2 or 3. LOADED WEIGHT 7,510 lb. MAX. SPEED 138 mph. RANGE 546 miles. ARMAMENT 2 x .303-inch machine-guns; 1 x 1,610 lb torpedo OR 1 x 500 lb mine OR equivalent bomb-load; (Mk II) 8 x 60 lb underwing rocket projectiles.

sun and showing the minimum of periscope. Two of *Courageous'* accompanying destroyers had been detached to investigate an alarm raised by a merchant ship in the vicinity; the other two also failed to sight *U-29*'s periscope. Even so, Schuhardt was on the point of giving up after a two-hour stalk when *Courageous* suddenly altered course to fly-on her aircraft. In so doing she placed herself perfectly to receive a model torpedo attack at 3,000 yards. Torn open by two of *U-29*'s three torpedoes, *Courageous* heeled over and sank within 15 minutes, taking with her Captain Makeig-Jones and 518 of her 1,216 officers and men. Instant but indiscriminate depth-charge attacks by the two destroyers were wide of the mark and *U-29* escaped with little difficulty. The first major British warship sunk in the Second World War had been one of the precious aircraft-carriers, which were immediately withdrawn from U-boat hunting. However essential, this admission of defeat amounted to a strategic as well as a tactical setback for the aircraft-carrier.

In less than a fortnight *Ark Royal* was back in the news again, earning immortality in the process. She sortied with heavy units of the Home Fleet – battleships *Nelson* and *Rodney*, and the battle-cruiser *Hood* – to cover the retrieval of the damaged submarine *Spearfish* by a cruiser squadron. Later in the morning of 26 September, the *Ark*'s airborne reconnaissance patrol sighted three shadowing Dornier Do-18 flying-boats 10 miles to the south-east. These were, it must be remembered, the days before shipboard and airborne radar, when first contact was still by 'eyeball'. Later in the war, with radar surveillance afloat and aloft, no reconnaissance plane could hope to get anywhere near as close without being detected. *Ark Royal* promptly launched no less than nine Skuas, one section of three per Dornier, to cope with the interlopers. Even allowing for good German evasive tactics down at wave-top level the escape of two of the Dorniers, given the force sent against them, was nothing to cheer about. But one of them *was* forced down, to be sunk after its crew had been made prisoner – the first German aircraft shot down by the British in the Second World War. (The

Ark Royal with the destroyer *Wren* in 1939. The carrier/destroyer U-boat hunting groups were a gross misuse of the carrier's true potential

Opposite: Bombing-up a Fairey Albacore. Intended as an improved successor to the Swordfish, the Albacore never matched the prowess of the older type, which served with distinction to the end of the war

Germans had shot down their first British aircraft on 4 September.)

But the Dorniers had done their work: 13 German bombers were hastily sent against the Home Fleet as it withdrew. Cloud cover did not help their search but considerably helped in the final approach once the ships had been sighted. Only one attack shook the *Ark Royal*: Corporal Francke's famous Ju-88 attack, which landed two spectacular but harmless near-misses close to the bows. Francke himself honestly claimed no more than a possible hit – only to find himself proclaimed by Goebbels' propaganda machine as Germany's great war hero, the man who sank the *Ark Royal* with a single bomb. *Ark Royal*'s premature 'sinking' was a classic misfire of Nazi propaganda compounded by *Luftwaffe* High Command, which refrained from indignant denials. Listening-in to Berlin to hear the renegade 'Lord Haw-Haw' demand 'People of Britain, ask your Leaders: where is the *Ark Royal*?' became a popular pastime in Britain, and nowhere more so than in the *Ark* herself. Poor Francke, promoted *Leutnant*, decorated, yet driven to the verge of suicide over the affair, had his misery compounded when the officers of *Ark Royal* officially invited him to become a member of their ward-room.

But on a far more serious level it would have been much better for the British Navy if the feeble German bombing attacks of 26 September (*Hood* actually was hit, but only by a dud) had caused genuine, even serious damage. As it was, the negligible results achieved by the *Luftwaffe* only served to encourage the school of thought which considered bombers to be no match for modern warships. It was a fateful error, not to be entirely dispelled until the terrible lessons taught by the Japanese in December 1941.

After these initial opening moves in home waters the British carriers moved south to join the hunt for the German surface raider, the pocket-battleship *Graf Spee*. This was easily the most extensive search for a single warship, if not the most dramatic, before the chase of the *Bismarck* 20 months later. Eight separate hunting groups were set up, patrolling from Florida to Ceylon; the North Atlantic convoy route was given battleship cover and the support of *Furious*. With *Eagle* at Ceylon, *Glorious* transferred to the Indian Ocean via the Suez Canal, *Ark Royal* off Pernambuco, *Béarn* at Dakar and *Hermes* in the West Indies, it was also the most impressive instance of Allied naval co-operation before the final drive on Japan, in the spring and summer of 1945. *Graf Spee*'s three-month cruise was a feat of skilful and humane commerce destruction. Her great

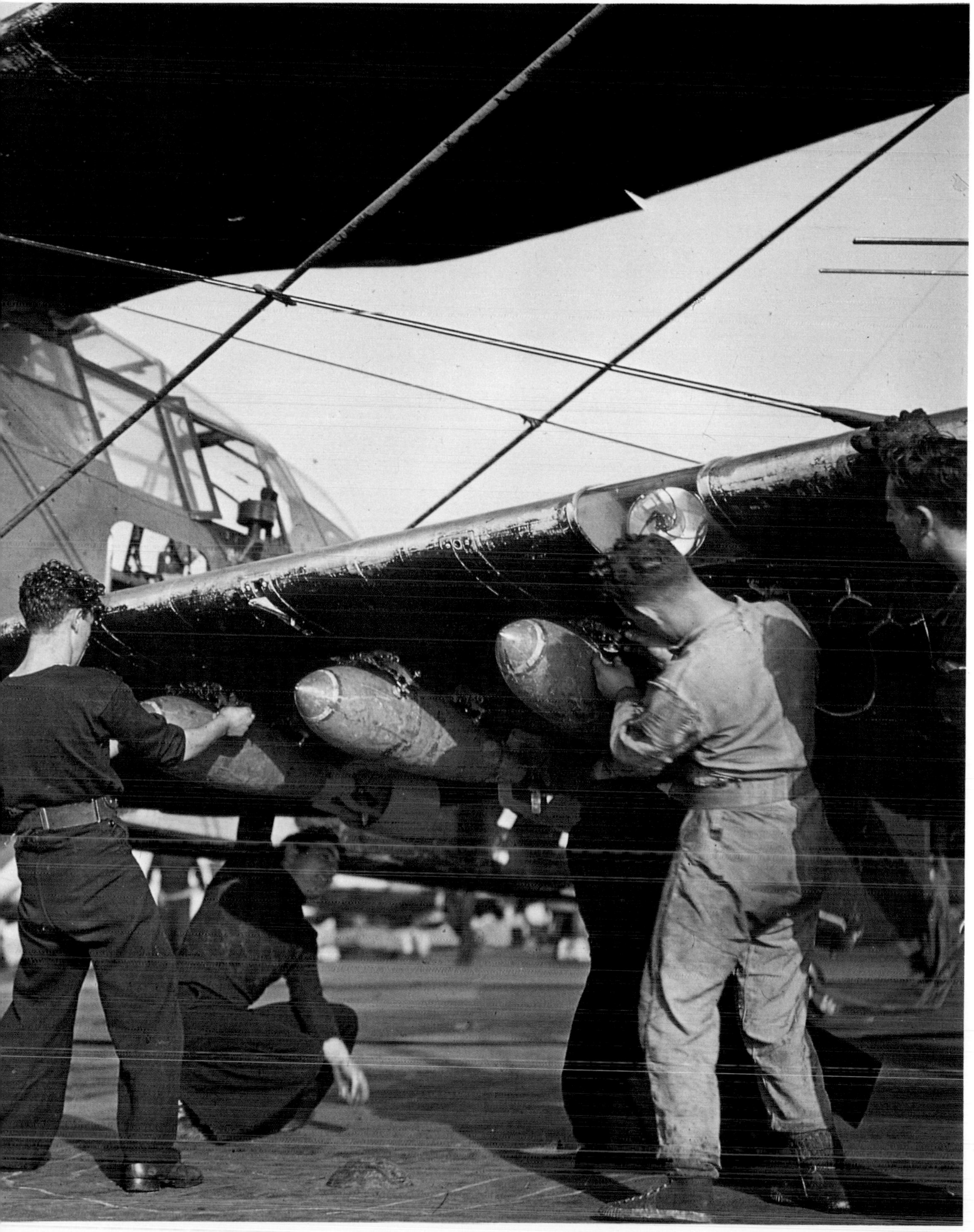

achievement was tying down so much Allied sea power, into which, however, she was bound to run sooner or later. When it happened, on 13 December 1939, *Graf Spee*'s discoverers were the cruisers of Force 'G' off the River Plate.

There were three levels to the Battle of the River Plate: physical, moral and diplomatic. The British lost the physical battle but won the moral one, inducing Langsdorff of the *Graf Spee* to seek shelter in Montevideo. The diplomatic aftermath saw the Uruguayan authorities, prompted by the British, deny Langsdorff the time he wanted to repair his ship: he must sail or face internment. What made Langsdorff decide on scuttling *Graf Spee* was his conviction – also carefully nurtured by the British – that *Ark Royal* and the battle-cruiser *Renown* were waiting for *Graf Spee* outside the 3-mile limit. In fact *Ark Royal*'s hunting group, 'Force K', spent 17 December frantically refuelling at Rio de Janeiro, over 1,000 miles away; and *Ark Royal* had only just sailed for Montevideo when Langsdorff took his ship out on its last brief journey. Langsdorff was probably intimidated just as much by thoughts of the 15-inch guns of *Renown*, battle-cruisers being the only warship type considered fast enough to catch *and* out-gun pocket-battleships. But it is at least possible to claim that even the rumoured presence of an aircraft-carrier helped bring about the destruction of *Graf Spee*. In the hunt for the pocket-battleship, *Ark Royal* had steamed 75,000 miles and her aircraft had flown nearly 5,000,000.

Taken as a whole, however, carrier operations in 1939 were little more than light sparring. The first campaign in which aircraft-carriers were involved to the hilt was the

At the funeral of *Graf Spee*'s dead, Captain Langsdorff gives the correct naval salute – in notable contrast to the attendant priests (note furious glance from the German minister behind him)

Franco-British attempt to eject the Germans from Norway (April-June 1940). This remains a classic modern instance of how superior naval power can be set at naught by a tame yielding of the initiative to a determined enemy. The German invasion of Norway was a seaborne pounce, based on the correct guess that the far stronger French and British navies would never be able to react in time. Having seized all the main ports and airfields and installed the *Luftwaffe* on Norwegian soil, the conquest of the interior could proceed at the Germans' convenience. As the British had no land-based aircraft capable of operating over the Norwegian coast, they would be entirely dependent on carriers for air cover in whatever form of amphibious counter-move could be made.

Unfortunately, when the campaign began on 9 April 1940 with German landings at Oslo, Egersund, Kristiansand, Bergen, Trondheim and Narvik, the only carrier with the British Home Fleet was *Furious*. On her return from the South Atlantic, *Ark Royal* had been given a brief refit before being sent to join *Glorious* in the Mediterranean for joint training. *Ark Royal* and *Glorious* were immediately recalled to home waters but were not available for operations off Norway until 24 April. The German Navy was thus spared from carrier

Graf Spee blazes off Montevideo after her spectacular scuttling on 17 December 1939, brought about by fears that *Ark Royal* was waiting for her at sea. In fact the *Ark* was over 1,000 miles to the north, racing south after a frantic refuelling stop at Rio de Janeiro

attack at its most vulnerable moment: during the actual invasion, when fully extended from the Kattegat to Narvik.

By the time the British Admiralty had grasped the full scale of the operation, all major German warships covering or actually involved in the invasion were on their way home. It had certainly not been a bloodless *coup* for the German Navy: the heavy cruiser *Blücher* had been sunk by Norwegian torpedoes at Oslo, and the light cruiser *Königsberg* rendered unfit for sea by three heavy Norwegian shells at Bergen. After a daring flight from Hatston in the Orkneys, 15 Skuas sank *Königsberg* at anchor on 10 April: the first major warship sunk by dive-bombers. The first attempt to use *Furious* was against the heavy-cruiser *Hipper* and the accompanying destroyers, which had landed the Trondheim invasion force on the 9th. But when the torpedo-carrying Swordfish from *Furious* arrived on the 11th they found the cupboard virtually empty: *Hipper* had sailed for Germany on the previous evening. All three of the remaining destroyers were nevertheless attacked, but all three survived due to the shallowness of the water which intercepted running torpedoes.

A week after the first landings, the German footholds in southern and central Norway were secure; but at Narvik, the iron-ore port in the far north which was the immediate strategic objective of the whole campaign, it was a very different story. Two British surface attacks, with destroyers on the 10th and the battleship *Warspite* on the 13th, had wiped out the German destroyers and supply-ships on which the small German garrison relied. The way was clear for the landing of troops to recover Narvik – but there would be no point in doing this unless the Germans were ejected from Trondheim as well. It was planned to take Trondheim by converging attack from landings at Namsos and Aandalsnes – but supplying and reinforcing these counter-attack forces was impossible under the intense air attacks of the *Luftwaffe*. These were vigorously maintained by X *Fliegerkorps*: 290 bombers, 40 Stuka dive-bombers and 100 fighters, quite apart from 70 reconnaissance float planes and land-based aircraft. To challenge these forces, *Furious* had been rushed to sea without her fighter squadron (in the initial rush to try and catch the German warships); and *Ark Royal* and *Glorious*, when they arrived, only operated 18 Skuas and 12 Sea Gladiators between them. Carrier-launched fighter operations in support of the troops ashore were further hampered by the need for the carriers to stay at maximum range from the coastline (150 miles or more).

Blackburn Skua, the Fleet Air Arm's inadequate dive-bomber-cum fighter, in a bombing dive. In the 1940 Norwegian campaign the Skua's success in sinking the light cruiser *Königsberg* was not repeated in the attempt on *Scharnhorst* on 13 June, when 8 out of 15 Skuas were lost

Though the thing could not be done, the efforts of the Fleet Air Arm pilots against these impossible odds were magnificent: merely to survive in such obsolescent aircraft required nerve and superior flying skill. *Furious* and *Glorious* reverted to a ferry role, shuttling driblets of Gladiators and Hurricanes across to Norway, there to operate as best they could from frozen lakes until the bombers caught them. After the foredoomed evacuations from Namsos and Aandalsnes (completed on 3 May) all efforts were concentrated on the capture of Narvik. With supreme irony, the first gleam of genuine success on the Narvik sector coincided with the collapse of the Allied front in Belgium and the supreme crisis of Dunkirk (10 May-4 June). No sooner had Narvik fallen than it had to be evacuated, in a series of embarkations lasting until 8 June. And this final withdrawal from the Norwegian coast led directly to one of the biggest naval tragedies of the war – surely the saddest and most one-sided action in the history of the aircraft-carrier.

Glorious had embarked the last ten RAF Gladiators on 7 June. None of them had arrester-hooks suitable for carrier deck landings, but their pilots had made a perfect job of their first-ever deck landings. It was different for the eight surviving Hurricanes: no 300-mph monoplane fighter had ever been landed on a British carrier deck before, and orders were given for the last Hurricanes in Norway to be destroyed on the ground. But the RAF Senior Officer in Norway, Group-Captain Moore, found himself besought by his pilots that the attempt should be made. It was a request made from motives of loyalty and practicality combined. Certainly every British fighter would be invaluable in the months ahead, and the stalling-speed of the Hurricane I was only 5 mph more than that of the Flycatcher for which the flight-deck of *Glorious* had been designed; Hurricanes, moreover, had brakes. Given the circumstances, however, the safe arrival of all eight Hurricanes aboard *Glorious* was no mean achievement. But they were the last aircraft ever to be operated by *Glorious*. Detached from the Home Fleet to make her own way home due to fuel shortage, with only the destroyers *Acasta* and *Ardent* in company, *Glorious* was surprised by the 11-inch German battle-cruisers *Scharnhorst* and *Gneisenau* in the afternoon of 8 June. Why *Glorious* had no reconnaissance aircraft aloft, or emergency striking force prepared, will never be known. What is certain is that she was pounded to destruction by 11-inch shells despite the superb courage of the destroyer men in *Ardent* and *Acasta,* both of which were also sunk – but not before *Acasta* put a torpedo into *Scharnhorst*'s bow. Only 46 men survived, out of over 1,500 sailors and airmen in the three ships – more men lost than in the loss of the *Hood* in the following May.

After this tragedy came a crowning humiliation, when *Ark Royal* sought to avenge *Glorious* with a dive-bombing attack on *Scharnhorst* as she lay in Trondheim on her voyage home to Germany. The attack took place on the morning of 13 June, carried out by a force of 15 Skuas eager to avenge *Glorious* and emulate the sinking of *Königsberg* two months before. It was not to be. As the Skuas pressed their attacks they ran into intense flak and fighter opposition, and no less than eight were shot down – the heaviest losses in a single attack ever suffered by *Ark Royal*'s aircrew, As if to add to the sense of failure the one 500-lb bomb which hit *Scharnhorst* failed to explode.

The Norwegian campaign was a definite climacteric: the proof, in battle, of the strategic value of aircraft-carriers. The failures were less important than the potential; it was all too obvious that three carriers were nowhere near enough to have turned the tide, even without their hopeless inadequacy in aircraft. Yet they had certainly shown what could be achieved. In the last week of May, with the German position stronger than it had ever been, the modest helping of fighter cover delivered to the troops by *Furious* and *Glorious* enabled Narvik to be taken. Yet, by the middle of June 1940, after only ten months of war, the British nucleus of four fleet carriers had been reduced by half. *Ark Royal* and *Furious* were left with the puny if valiant aid of *Hermes* and *Eagle* – the latter now brought west from the Indian Ocean to join the Mediterranean Fleet. There could now be no question of trying out, in combat, the carrier group operations which had looked so promising in peacetime exercises. The only ray of comfort was the fact that the first 'Illustrious' class carriers would soon be in service, but it was a pretty thin ray, given the catastrophic run of events since the German Western offensive had broken on 10 May. Apart from the fall of Holland and Belgium, the Norwegian fiasco and the subsequent collapse of France, Italy had entered the war on 10 June. The Mediterranean theatre had come alive.

The British Admiralty had never contemplated naval war in the Mediterranean without the participation of the French Navy in the western basin. With France prostrate there was every prospect of the French battle fleet being parcelled out between Germany and Italy; and it was primarily to contain the French battle fleet that a powerful new British task force was formed at Gibraltar on 28 June 1940. This was Force 'H': *Ark Royal, Hood, Valiant, Resolution,* two cruisers and a handful of destroyers, commanded by Vice-Admiral Sir James Somerville. Their first mission was possibly the most hateful task demanded of the Royal Navy in its entire history: the bombardment of its former ally, the French fleet in its North African ports. In the early evening of 3 July, Force H carried out a punishing gun bombardment of Mers el Kebir which blew up the old battleship *Bretagne,* damaged *Provence* and inflicted great loss of life. One of the two formidable new battle-cruisers, *Dunkerque,* was immobilised – but her sister-ship *Strasbourg* won clear and headed for Toulon with five destroyers.

Only *Ark Royal*'s aircraft could pursue *Strasbourg,* and the overload on them had already been intense: they had been called on to mine the harbour mouth as well as spot for the guns. Now they had to improvise the first-ever carrier attacks on a fast-moving capital ship (at 28½ knots, *Strasbourg* had worked up to just below her maximum speed). The first attack was launched with bomb-carrying Swordfish which had already been aloft a long time when they set off in pursuit. They showered *Strasbourg* with near-misses but scored no hits, and two had to ditch in the sea due to lack of sufficient fuel for the return flight. The second attack was a torpedo strike, coolly held back until after sundown in order to silhouette *Strasbourg* against the afterglow. Unfortunately the French ships countered by making copious smoke; the Swordfish dropped from too far out, outside the French destroyer screen, and were honestly able to claim no more than one possible hit.

It all might have ended very differently if *Ark Royal* had been able to give chase, but she was kept with Force H off Oran and Mers el Kebir, so *Strasbourg* with her gallant escorts reached Toulon without further incident. Daybreak on the 4th at Mers el Kebir revealed that the stranded *Dunkerque* was clearly not permanently disabled – but Somerville shrank from a second bombardment and turned the job over to the *Ark*'s Swordfish. A fluky hit on a boat laden with explosives and moored alongside caused severe hull damage and put *Dunkerque* out of action for a year.

Meanwhile, at Alexandria a similar tragedy was averted by British C-in-C Admiral Cunningham, who persuaded the French Admiral Godfroy to disarm his warships and agree to peaceful internment. No action was taken against the un-completed French battleship

The tragedy of Mers-el-Kebir: British shells bursting on the French fleet, as seen from the battle-cruiser *Dunkerque*. Her sister-ship *Strasbourg* successfully escaped the holocaust and won through to Toulon, despite an abortive attack by *Ark Royal*'s Swordfish

Jean Bart at Casablanca. But at Dakar there lay *Jean Bart*'s sister-ship *Richelieu*, fully armed and all but fully operational, watched by *Hermes*. On the morning of 7 July the little carrier achieved a disabling attack as successful as it was economical. In the pre-dawn dark an unsuccessful attempt was made to blow off *Richelieu*'s screws and rudders with depth-charges dumped from a fast motor-boat (an interesting anticipation of the Italian explosive speedboats and British midget submarines later in the war). *Hermes* then launched six Swordfish which caught *Richelieu*'s gunners completely by surprise, scoring one hit which immobilised the 35,000-ton battleship for a year. Added to the crippling of *Dunkerque* three days before, this attack went to show that carrier air strikes were emerging as a superior attack technique to the traditional long-range gun action – the surgeon's knife rather than the blunt axe.

War with Italy placed yet another excessive demand on the British carriers, one destined to last for the next three years. The reason was Malta, dismissed as indefensible by the Chiefs-of-Staff before the war. The gradual dawning of awareness, that Malta was not only defensible but a vital sally-port for attacks on Italy's shipping-lanes to North Africa, covered several months. By the end of 1940, however, Britain's Mediterranean naval strategy hinged on Malta's survival by frequent replenishment – with fighter and (when possible) strike aircraft, and with fuel and food for the Maltese garrison and people. To get the fighters and supply convoys through to Malta, carrier support was indispensable.

However, the world's first fleet action in which carrier aircraft attacked an enemy fleet took place when the Italian conquest of Malta still seemed only a matter of time. The convoy in question (actually two convoys) were coming *out* of Malta, with dockyard equipment considered to be of more use in Alexandria than possibly captured by the Italians in Malta; and Cunningham had taken the Mediterranean Fleet west to bring these convoys out. Meanwhile Admiral Campioni had taken the Italian battle fleet to sea on a similar mission, covering a convoy to Benghazi. The resultant collision off Calabria on 9 July 1940 saw *Eagle* valiantly trying to do the impossible with her ridiculously small air group – yet, for all that, shadowing the enemy force and launching two torpedo strikes deserving of better luck. On the way back to Alexandria after the Italians had broken away for home, *Eagle* survived 22 bombing attacks aimed at the Mediterranean Fleet by the Italian Air Force (which bombed the Italian Fleet with no

Crippled by *Hermes*, but destined later for service with the British Eastern Fleet – the French battleship *Richelieu* at Dakar in 1941

Ark Royal dodges Italian bombs on one of her innumerable western Mediterranean forays with 'Force H'

less enthusiasm or inaccuracy). The battle off Calabria was of supreme importance because it revealed the vastly encouraging defects of the Italian Air Force, and gave the Italian fleet a sense of moral inferiority which it was never quite able to shake off.

The operations leading to the Calabria battle also saw the first experiment in coordination between Force H and the Mediterranean Fleet, with Force H probing south of Minorca in a bid to divert the attention of the Italian Air Force. This succeeded all too well and revealed that Italian air strength in Sardinia and Sicily was not to be trifled with. Yet it confirmed Cunningham's belief that given adequate carrier support and concerted action between the eastern and western naval forces, the defence of the Mediterranean sealane was possible.

The first of these joint operations was Operation 'Hurry' (24 July-2 August) in which *Argus* came out from the United Kingdom with 12 Hurricanes for Malta, entering the Mediterranean with Force H on the 31st. On the evening of 1 August *Hood* and *Ark Royal* separated to carry out a diversionary bombing and mining attack on Cagliari in Sardinia, while *Argus* proceeded to fly off her Hurricanes. After the successful execution of 'Hurry', Force H returned to the UK to prepare for Operation 'Hats', a full-scale drive through the Mediterranean to reinforce Cunningham's fleet. *Ark Royal* returned for 'Hats' with a squadron of the new Fairey Fulmar fighters, still painfully slow but a vast improvement on the Skua; like the Spitfire and Hurricane, the Fulmar had a battery of eight wing-mounted machine-guns. Fulmars also provided the fighter complement in the most important unit of the 'Hats' operation: the new fleet carrier *Illustrious* with its armoured protection, plus radar – a vital tool for the early location of enemy aircraft. 'Hats' was launched on 30 August, with *Ark Royal* again hitting Cagliari with diversionary attacks before withdrawing to Gibraltar. *Illustrious*, the battleship *Valiant* and two AA cruisers joined Cunningham (1 September) south of Malta, which received its first big reinforcement in AA weaponry during the operation. Cunningham's strengthened fleet made a circuitous return to Alexandria north of Crete, with the Swordfish from *Illustrious* and *Eagle* bombing the two Italian air bases on Rhodes in the Dodecanese Islands.

Hopes for repeated joint operations in September were thwarted by the Italian invasion of Egypt (13-16 September) and the abortive

Opposite: Swordfish in flight. Above: The crippling of the Italian battle fleet in Taranto (11 November 1940) showing the Swordfish weaving gallantly through the Italian AA fire

Allied attempt to take Dakar (19-25 September). Fears for the Mediterranean Fleet base at Alexandria were allayed when the Italian advance petered out at Sidi Barrani; it was promptly countered by carrier aircraft raiding Benghazi, nodal point of the Italian supply line stretching back to Tripoli. But the depressing failure to take Dakar from the Vichy French removed Force H from Gibraltar for the entire second half of the month. The French defences at Dakar had been made far more efficient since the attack by *Hermes* in early July; *Richelieu*'s guns were the cornerstone of the French resistance to the Anglo-Gaullist invasion force. *Ark Royal*'s Swordfish failed to score a single hit on *Richelieu*, and with damage steadily mounting for no return the force retired discomfited on the 25th.

None of these setbacks, even with the addition of the unexpected Italian invasion of Greece on 28 October, caused Cunningham to abandon his plan for a joint carrier strike by *Illustrious* and *Eagle* at the six Italian battleships in Taranto. Even this was not delivered with the full force which Cunningham had envisaged, for cumulative defects made it impossible for *Eagle* to accompany *Illustrious* on Operation 'Judgement'. Five of *Eagle*'s Swordfish were transferred to *Illustrious*, but the attack force still numbered only 21 Swordfish instead of the planned 30. 'Judgement' was the climax to five days of intense naval activity from one end of the Mediterranean to the other. Force H sortied from Gibraltar, escorting more warship reinforcements for the Mediterranean Fleet which themselves carried troop reinforcements for the Malta garrison. On 9 November *Ark Royal* carried out another 'smash and grab' diversionary raid on Cagliari before Force H withdrew to Gibraltar. The warships landed their troops at Malta on the 10th. By the 11th, when the latest air reconnaissance photographs of Taranto reached *Illustrious*, the reinforced Mediterranean Fleet

was steaming north-east on its withdrawal from Malta, preparing for a cruiser raid on the Straits of Otranto – and 'Judgement'. By 9 pm on the 11th, Lieutenant-Commander K. Williamson was airborne with the first attack wave of the operation that opened a new chapter in naval history.

The two waves, striking in succession one after the other, followed the same basic ploy: diversionary bombing attacks dropping flares to assist the main force, carrying torpedoes. The defences were not caught totally by surprise: AA fire was intense, but the Italians made the mistake of not activating their smoke-screen in order not to obstruct the view of the AA batteries. These seem to have been confused by the low speed of the Swordfish – the type's best asset on many similar occasions. Above all the courage and dash of the attackers, weaving in through the barrage-balloon cables and searchlight beams, earned a rich reward. The battleships *Littorio*, *Caio Duilio* and *Conte di Cavour* were all put *hors de combat*, the first two for six months, *Conte di Cavour* for ever. In strategic terms it was a famous victory, changing an Italo-British battleship ratio of 6:5 to 3:5 for the cost of only two aircraft shot down. It was a phenomenon which, on paper, should never have happened, given the total dominance of the central Mediterranean by the Italian peninsula and its air bases. But the *moral* effects of Taranto were the most important of all. After the damage inflicted by carrier-borne aircraft at Taranto no Italian admiral dared accept battle if he suspected that there might be a British carrier within range. On the British side the Taranto raid added another legendary signal to Royal Naval history: a masterpiece of understatement. 'MANOEUVRE WELL EXECUTED', signalled Cunningham when *Illustrious* rejoined the fleet.

The moral impact of Taranto was revealed a fortnight after the raid, off Cape Spartivento in the western Mediterranean basin. It happened during another intricate collaboration between the Mediterranean Fleet and Force H, with the battleship *Ramillies* and two

Littorio, pride of the Italian Navy: rendered *hors-de-combat* (though not permanently) at Taranto. Her sister-ship *Vittorio Veneto* survived to court near-destruction at Cape Matapan
Inset: The Italian fleet base at Taranto, showing the main lines of attack used by *Illustrious*' Swordfish

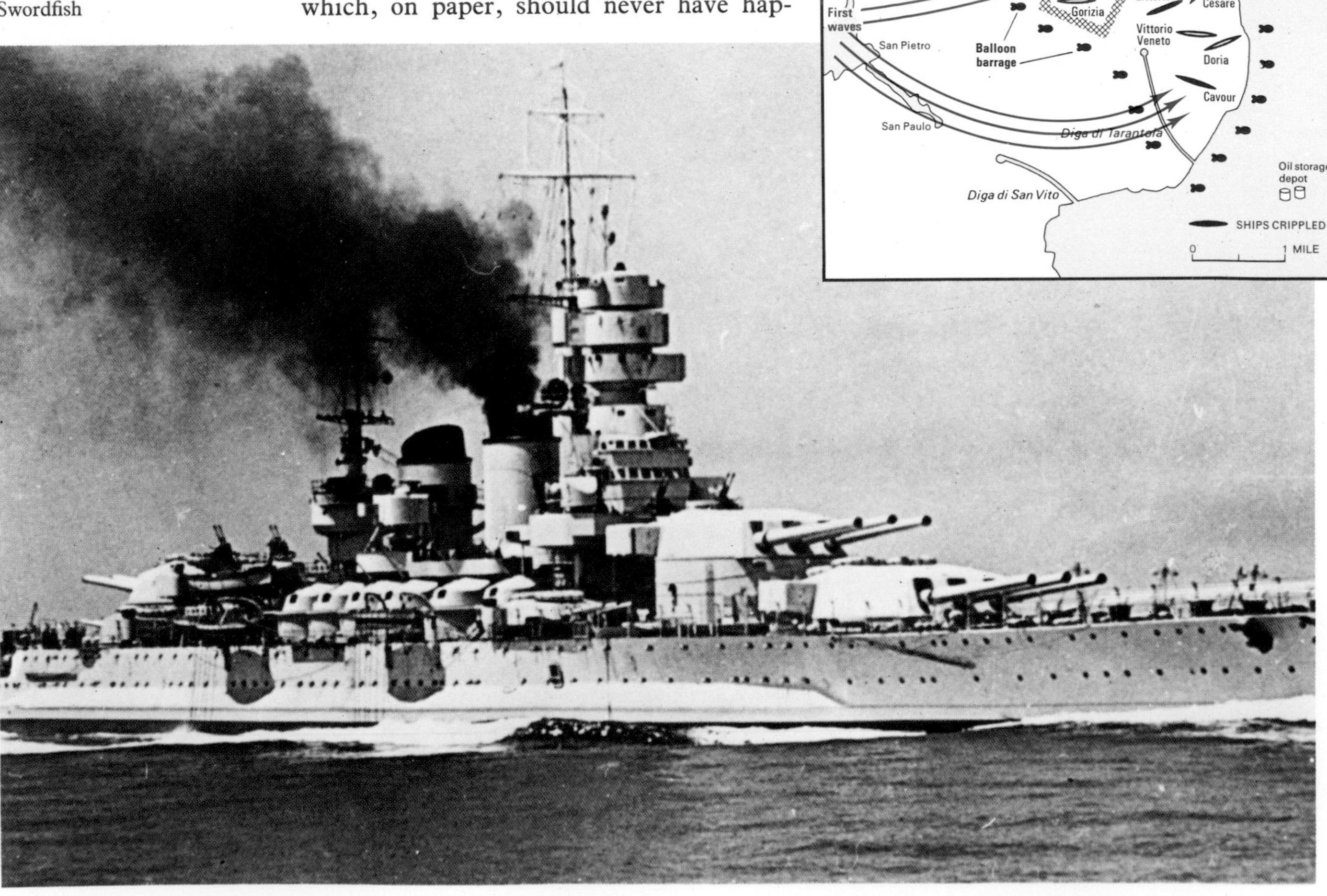

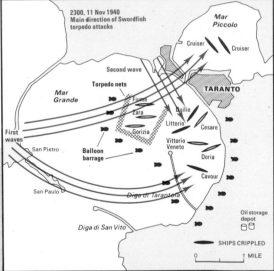

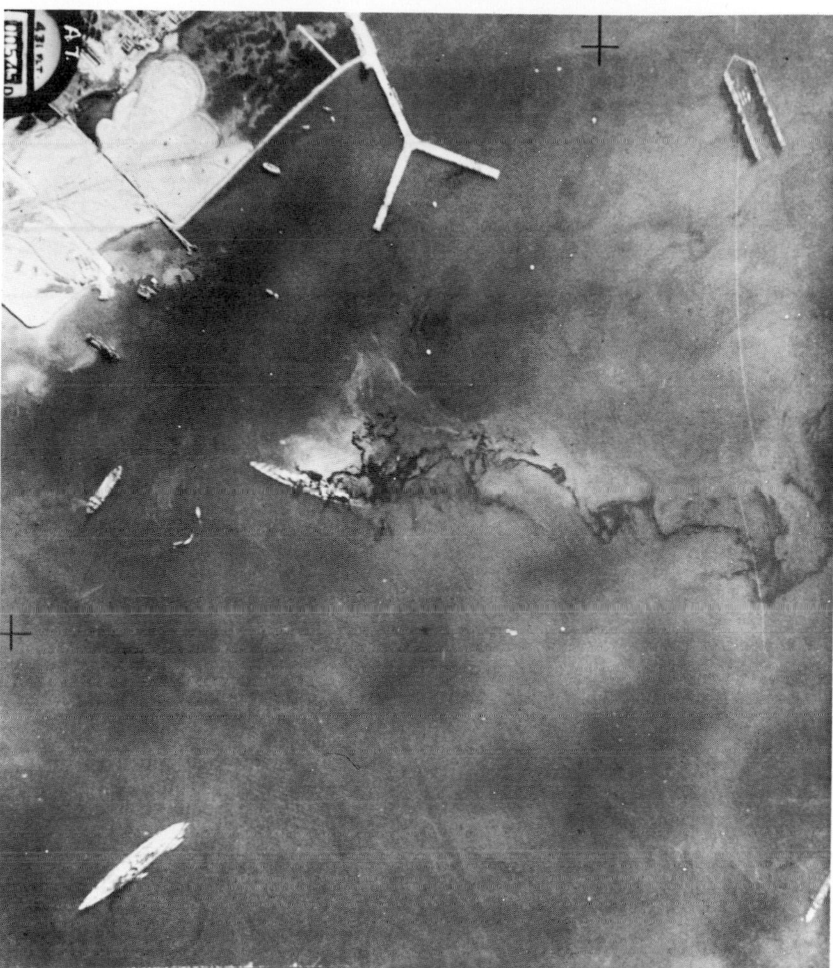

After the Taranto raid – *Conte di Cavour*, sunk by the bows, bleeds torrents of fuel oil into the harbour

cruisers being passed westward for service outside the Mediterranean. On 27 November *Ramillies* and the two cruisers had barely made rendezvous with Force H south of Sardinia when the Italian battle fleet was sighted approaching from the north: *Vittorio Veneto, Giulio Cesare,* seven cruisers and 16 destroyers. Admiral Somerville had no more than *Ramillies, Renown,* four cruisers, and ten destroyers – but he also had *Ark Royal.* As soon as Admiral Campioni heard that a British carrier was in the offing, menacing two of the last three operational battleships in the Italian Navy, he turned and ran. Eleven Swordfish from *Ark Royal* overhauled the retreating battleships, but their attacks met with no success. Unwilling to be lured too close to the Sardinian coast, mindful that he still had a convoy to see safely into the Sicilian Narrows on its way to Malta, Somerville abandoned the chase. (He was censured by court of enquiry for having broken off the action, but the court upheld his decision.) As far as what was left of the Italian battle fleet was concerned, Cape Spartivento was definitely a case of the shadow (*Ark Royal*'s) being more terrifying than the substance. But the main objective of the sortie had been achieved on the British side: another vital convoy, thanks largely to *Ark Royal*'s presence, if not prowess in attack, had got through to Malta.

Cape Spartivento was, however, the last British Mediterranean naval success before a formidable new factor entered the equation: the *Luftwaffe*. Italian defeats in Greece, the fiasco of Taranto and finally the rout in Egypt and Libya which began with the British offensive on 8 December 1940, all combined to compel Hitler to send military aid to Mussolini. First to arrive in southern Italy was X *Fliegerkorps,* the victors of Norway, whose Stukas had been installed on the airfield of Sicily by the New Year of 1941. And on 10 January 1941 they struck with devastating effect at the Mediterranean Fleet.

The *Luftwaffe* intervened at a crucial stage of Operation 'Excess', a delivery of merchantmen to Greece and to Malta. After Force H handed the merchantmen over to the Mediterranean Fleet and headed back to Gibraltar on the afternoon of 9 January, a destroyer was crippled by a mine; she was taken in tow by another destroyer and escorted to Malta by a third, with the AA cruiser *Bonaventure* in company. This dispersal of force – plus the additional detachment of the cruisers *Gloucester* and *Southampton* to escort the merchantmen of 'Excess' to Crete – left *Valiant, Warspite* and *Illustrious* with only five escorting destroyers when the German dive-bombers appeared. To make matters worse, two Italian dive-bombers were chased off by *Illustrious*' standing fighter patrol at precisely the most inopportune moment. *Illustrious* was therefore not, as she should have been, surrounded by a tight formation of escorts with pooled AA fire-power; nor did she have a standing fighter patrol overhead. The detection of the approaching German formation – between 30 and 40 Ju-87s and Ju-88s – allowed just enough time for another four Fulmars to be launched but they could do nothing to break up the Stuka formations before the latter attacked. The two battleships escaped scot-free: the Stukas concentrated on *Illustrious,* wrecking her flight-deck, setting her on fire fore and aft and destroying nine aircraft. Without her internal armour she would most likely have been lost; as it was, *Illustrious* managed to limp into Malta under her own power, having suffered seven direct hits with 126 killed and 91 wounded.

Now left completely without fighter cover, the long ordeal of the Mediterranean Fleet began. The Stukas caught *Southampton* and damaged her so badly that she had to be abandoned and sunk; *Gloucester* was also hit. As *Illustrious* lay in Malta, undergoing frantic running repairs to make her fit for escape to Alexandria, X *Fliegerkorps* did its utmost to

HMS Illustrious during German air attack while escorting a Malta convoy in January 1941.

destroy the stricken carrier, in what became known as the '*Illustrious* Blitz' (16-23 January). This caused extensive damage and loss of life; but the repairs were doggedly completed nonetheless, and well completed, enabling *Illustrious* to reach 24 knots after her stealthy departure from Malta on the evening of the 23rd. But it was impossible to complete her full scale of repairs at Alexandria, which for *Illustrious* was only the first stage on the long haul round Africa in search of prolonged convalescence. One of the first British warships to be repaired in American yards (at Norfolk, Virginia), she was not ready for action again until November 1941.

Illustrious had not even left Malta before the Admiralty had decided to replace her with *Formidable*, originally scheduled to relieve *Ark Royal* in Force H, but now sent off round Africa to join the Mediterranean Fleet by way of the Suez Canal. It was during this protracted exchange that Force H carried out two of its most aggressive attacks in the western Mediterranean. The first (2 February) was an attempt by eight torpedo-carrying Swordfish from *Ark Royal* to breach the Tirso Dam in central Sardinia. Like the famous Ruhr Valley dams, the Tirso Dam was important as the prime source of hydro-electric power in the region – but even without the vile conditions, with heavy icing obliging two aircraft to jettison, not even eight naval torpedoes striking perfectly would have done much damage. The Tirso Dam raid nevertheless represents a surprisingly early attempt to adapt naval aviation to strategic rather than purely tactical objectives – long before the aircraft and weapons capable of guaranteeing success had been developed.

Opposite: The vital sighting which led to *Bismarck*'s crippling by *Ark Royal*'s Swordfish. In this famous painting by Norman Wilkinson, the German battleship's outline sparkles with gunfire as she strives in vain to destroy the shadowing *Catalina*

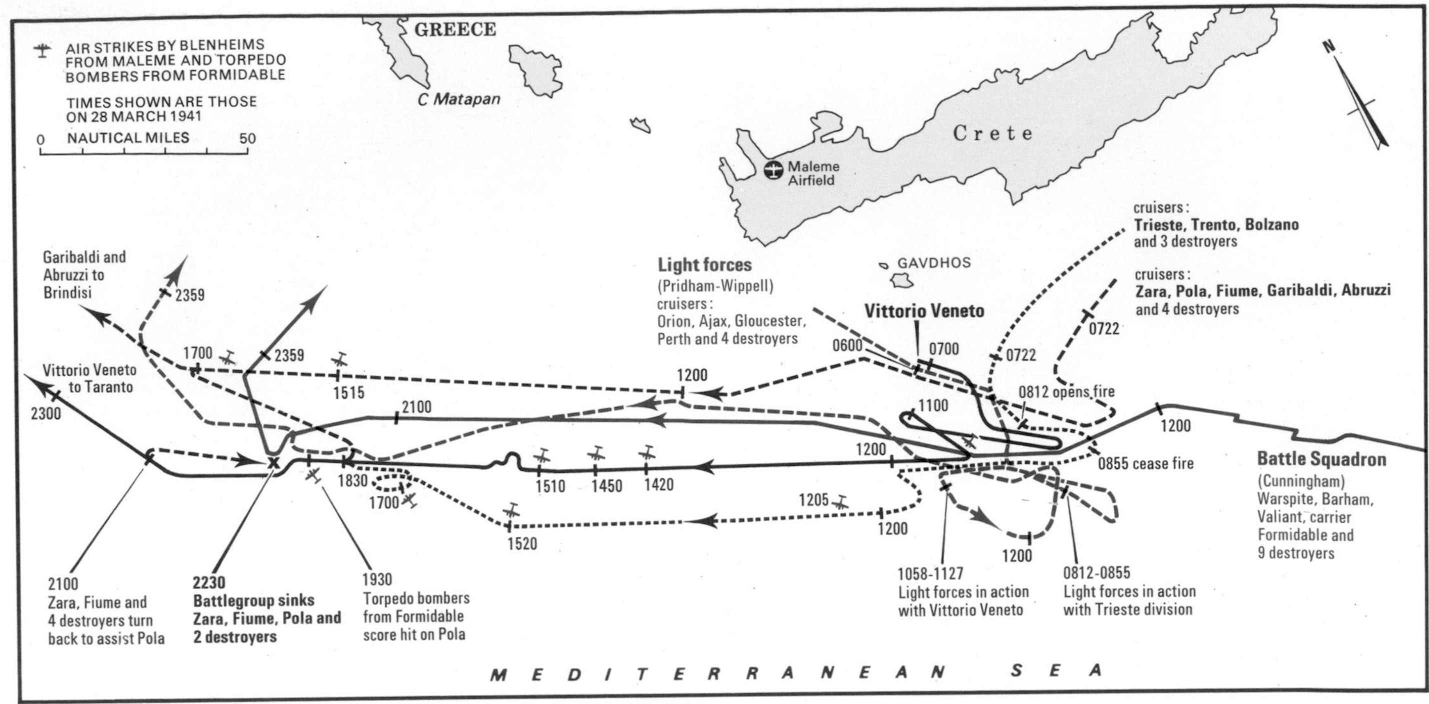

A week later came Somerville's perfectly executed bombardment of Genoa by Force H, with *Ark Royal* launching diversionary attacks on Livorno, La Spezia and Pisa. The main objective had been one of the surviving battleships from the Taranto raid, reported to be undergoing repairs at Genoa. *Caio Duilio* was indeed in dry dock at Genoa, but *Renown*'s spotter plane failed to locate her. The raid was nevertheless another resounding blow at Italian morale: a British naval foray 700 miles from base, extensive damage inflicted at four widely-separated points, and not so much as a single bomb hit on the British force in retribution. Yet the Genoa raid could have been postponed with greater profit. It coincided with a sortie into the North Atlantic by the German heavy cruiser *Hipper*, which sank seven unescorted merchant ships only 600 miles west of Gibraltar on 12 February – the day after Force H returned from the Genoa raid. For the next three months, Force H was to be increasingly diverted to the Atlantic by the increasing sorties by German heavy warships, culminating with the *Bismarck* epic in the last week of May.

Formidable's arrival in the eastern Mediterranean on 10 March was the cue for the withdrawal of *Eagle*. The old carrier now moved to the Red Sea to support operations against the Italians in Eritrea and Ethiopia. *Formidable*'s début was spectacular: on 28 March an Italian battle squadron, probing east against the British supply route from Egypt to Greece, collided with the British Mediterranean Fleet in the Battle of Matapan. Admiral Iachino with *Vittorio Veneto*, eight cruisers and 13 destroyers was opposed by Cunningham with *Warspite*, *Valiant*, *Barham* and *Formidable*, four cruisers and a similar destroyer force. In a running battle from the south of Crete northwest past Cape Matapan at the southern tip of Greece, the Italian fleet turned and ran – as at Cape Spartivento – from the presence of a British carrier. This was the first fleet action in which the rival main bodies never sighted each other, and in which carrier aircraft played a decisive part. Matapan was not a 'pure' carrier action: of the nine air attacks launched at the Italian fleet on the 28th, six were by bombers based on Greece and Crete. But it was *Formidable*'s air group which, with its second attack, scored the first carrier-launched torpedo hit on a battleship at sea, temporarily reducing *Vittorio*'s speed and raising hopes that she might be caught. A third attack at dusk was repelled by massed AA fire from the cruisers packed round *Vittorio*, but not before the cruiser *Pola* was disabled. Starved of information by the havoc wrought amid his spotter planes by *Formidable*'s fighters, Iachino made the fatal decision to send his cruisers back to support *Pola*. The upshot was a brutal series of night actions ending in the loss of the cruisers *Zara*, *Fiume*, and *Pola* and the destroyers *Alfieri* and *Carducci*. Sum total of the British loss at Matapan was the aircraft and crew of the man who hit *Vittorio:* Lieutenant-Commander Dalyell-Stead.

If Cape Matapan confirmed the carrier as a potential winner of sea battles, the performance of *Ark Royal* with Force H in February-May 1941 demonstrated the amazing range of operations of which just one carrier was capable. After the Genoa raid *Ark Royal* accompanied Force H into the Atlantic to search for the battle-cruisers *Scharnhorst* and *Gneisenau* (17-28 March), which were heading for Brest

Bismarck. During the epic chase which led to her destruction (below) she survived the strike from *Victorious* only to fall victim to *Ark Royal*'s Swordfish as Force H pounded north from Gibraltar

after a successful commerce-destroying cruise in the North Atlantic. In April the *Ark* flew off 12 fighters to Malta on the 3rd, and another 23 fighters on the 27th, before covering the vital 'Tiger' convoy (6-8 May) which delivered 238 tanks to the Army in Egypt. On 21 May, *Ark Royal* joined *Furious* to fly off another 48 fighters to Malta – and 48 hours later Force H was recalled to the Atlantic to play its part in the *Bismarck* drama.

It is a measure of the Royal Navy's commitment in May 1941 that only two modern fleet carriers were available to send against *Bismarck: Ark Royal* and *Victorious*, the third 'Illustrious' class carrier, so new that her aircrews had only been with the ship for a week. *Victorious* did not even have her full air group: her first operation was to have been a fighter supply run to Gibraltar, and the only naval aircraft she had aboard were nine Swordfish and six Fulmars. To compound the inexperience of her aircrews the weather in the North Atlantic was vile, making flying operations hazardous in the extreme. Yet when the news came in that *Bismarck* had sunk *Hood* and driven off *Prince of Wales* her Swordfish crews, led by Lieutenant-Commander Eugene Esmonde, did not shrink from attempting to cripple and slow the German battleship. The single torpedo hit which exploded harmlessly on *Bismarck*'s main armour belt was deserving of better success. Not the least of their

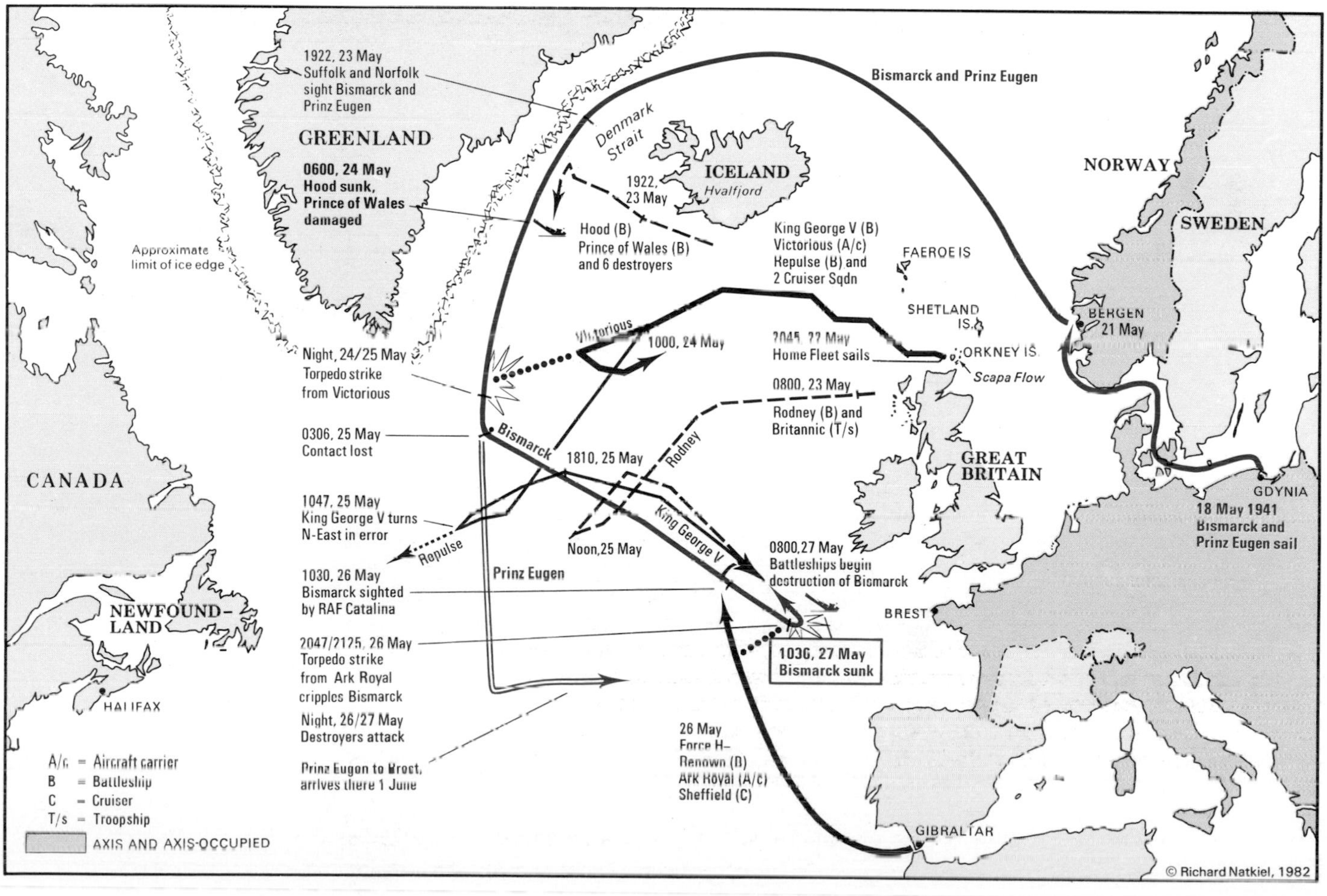

1922, 23 May
Suffolk and Norfolk sight Bismarck and Prinz Eugen
GREENLAND
0600, 24 May
Hood sunk, Prince of Wales damaged
Approximate limit of ice edge
Denmark Strait
ICELAND
Hvalfjord
1922, 23 May
Bismarck and Prinz Eugen
NORWAY
SWEDEN
Hood (B)
Prince of Wales (B) and 6 destroyers
King George V (B)
Victorious (A/c)
Repulse (B) and 2 Cruiser Sqdn
FAEROE IS
SHETLAND IS.
BERGEN
21 May
Victorious
1000, 24 May
2045, 22 May
Home Fleet sails
ORKNEY IS.
Scapa Flow
Night, 24/25 May
Torpedo strike from Victorious
0800, 23 May
Rodney (B) and Britannic (T/s)
0306, 25 May
Contact lost
Bismarck
1810, 25 May
Rodney
CANADA
GREAT BRITAIN
GDYNIA
18 May 1941
Bismarck and Prinz Eugen sail
1047, 25 May
King George V turns N-East in error
King George V
Repulse
Noon, 25 May
0800, 27 May
Battleships begin destruction of Bismarck
1030, 26 May
Bismarck sighted by RAF Catalina
Prinz Eugen
NEWFOUNDLAND
BREST
2047/2125, 26 May
Torpedo strike from Ark Royal cripples Bismarck
1036, 27 May
Bismarck sunk
HALIFAX
Night, 26/27 May
Destroyers attack
26 May
Force H–
Renown (B)
Ark Royal (A/c)
Sheffield (C)
A/c = Aircraft carrier
B = Battleship
C = Cruiser
T/s = Troopship
Prinz Eugen to Brest, arrives there 1 June
AXIS AND AXIS-OCCUPIED
GIBRALTAR

Opposite: Massive carrier air cover for the all-important 'Pedestal' convoy to Malta. *Indomitable* flies-off an Albacore, seen from *Victorious*, with *Eagle* bringing up the rear. Inset: The end at last – *Ark Royal*'s crew prepares to abandon ship after her torpedoeing by *U-81* in November 1941

achievement was finding their way back to *Victorious* and landing-on safely – though two of the Fulmar crews, sadly, were not so lucky. *Victorious* would have made a second attempt on the 25th had not radar contact with *Bismarck* been lost. By the time *Bismarck* was located again 31 hours later, it was obvious that only *Ark Royal*, pounding north from Gibraltar, had a hope of intercepting *Bismarck* before she came within range of the *Luftwaffe* based on French soil.

When it came to attacking enemy warships, *Ark Royal* had had the worst of luck ever since she had tried to sink *Scharnhorst* at Trondheim in June 1940. She had missed *Strasbourg* off Oran, *Richelieu* at Dakar, *Vittorio Veneto* and *Giulio Cesare* at Cape Spartivento; only two months before the *Bismarck* sortie, one of *Ark Royal*'s Swordfish had actually spotted *Scharnhorst* and *Gneisenau* as they headed in to France, only to be unable to pass on the vital news due to radio failure. But on 26 May 1941 only pilots of the highest calibre and determination could have lifted off *Ark Royal*'s wildly plunging flight-deck, come within an inch of sinking the cruiser *Sheffield*, returned, landed-on and re-armed – then gone out and landed the one hit that sealed *Bismarck*'s fate, jamming her starboard rudder hard over and delivering her to the guns of the Home Fleet on the morning of the 27th.

Taranto, Cape Matapan and the *Bismarck* action were the three brightest battle honours won by the British carrier arm in the Second World War. But they could not avert the Axis Mediterranean offensive of March-May 1941, which threw the British out of Greece and Crete. In its efforts to support the Army, the Mediterranean Fleet suffered immense loss from the *Luftwaffe*. *Formidable*, damaged by two bomb hits during the battle for Crete, was clearly at excessive risk in the eastern Mediterranean basin and was withdrawn through the Suez Canal in July. This left Force H and *Ark Royal* as the prime guarantors of Malta's replenishment. Aided by *Victorious* and *Furious*, *Ark Royal* flew off no less than 142 aircraft for Malta in June 1941 before covering the 'Substance' replenishment convoy of 21-24 July. The third Malta replenishment convoy of 1941, 'Halberd', followed on 24-28 September. *Ark Royal*'s final contribution to the survival of Malta, and hence to Allied victory in the Mediterranean, was 37 Hurricanes flown off with *Argus* (10-12 November 1941). She was torpedoed by *U-81* on the following day while returning to Gibraltar, and sank on the 14th. The fact that *Ark Royal* finally fell victim to a U-boat ended her splendid career in an ironic 'full circle', 26 months since those first

clumsy anti-submarine patrols of September 1939.

The outbreak of the Pacific War in December 1941 and the ensuing threat to the Indian Ocean coincided with the climax of the Mediterranean War. Between February and May 1942 the *Luftwaffe* battered Malta to the point of total defeat which, as ever, was staved off by the British carriers. With *Ark Royal* gone, the burden of fighter replenishment was taken on by *Argus* and *Eagle*; they made three ferry trips in March 1942 and flew the first Spitfires in to Malta. But attrition of Malta's aircraft by the *Luftwaffe* was so rapid that bulk fighter deliveries by a modern carrier were essential. They were provided by the American carrier *Wasp*, which on two trips into the Mediterranean (the second with *Eagle*) flew off a grand total of 111 Spitfires. *Eagle* contributed a further 17 Spitfires on 18 May before collaborating with *Argus* to provide air cover for 'Harpoon', a replenishment convoy in June.

By the end of July, however, the island was again *in extremis* and the result was the most desperate Malta convoy of them all: 'Pedestal' (9-15 August). So great was the urgency that two of the new fleet carriers, *Victorious* and *Indomitable*, were risked to join forces with *Eagle*. This was the first time in the war that three British carriers had served together on the same mission, and the reason was solely to pool their fighter protection. 'Pedestal' once more demonstrated the perils of sending carriers into enclosed waters dominated by enemy aircraft and submarines. *Eagle* was the first ship of 'Pedestal' to be lost, torpedoed by a U-boat; by the time Force H and the carriers had to withdraw, *Indomitable*'s flight-deck was inoperable and *Victorious* was the only operational carrier left. For all that, and the terrible losses suffered by the convoy (nine ships sunk out of 14) enough supplies were forced through to keep Malta going until the course of the Mediterranean war had changed for good.

Meanwhile the German invasion of Russia in June 1941 and the subsequent peremptory Soviet demands for seaborne aid had pushed the Royal Navy to the limit – particularly when *Bismarck*'s sister-ship *Tirpitz* was sent to the Arctic in January 1942 to threaten the convoys sailing for North Russian ports. Only once, on 8 March 1942, was *Tirpitz* caught at sea within range of a British fleet carrier. *Victorious*, hoping to succeed where she had failed with *Bismarck*, launched a torpedo strike which *Tirpitz*, brilliantly handled at full speed, narrowly survived without suffering a single hit (out of 12 torpedoes launched). This opportunity was never to recur; and until November 1944, when RAF Lancaster bombers finally sank her at anchor with a cascade of 6-ton bombs, *Tirpitz* acted like a malignant magnet on the movements of every British and American capital ship in the Atlantic. The real problem with the Russian convoy route, however, was its constriction between the Arctic pack ice and the Norwegian coast, where in 1942-43 the *Luftwaffe*'s strength was as unassailable as it had been in the Mediterranean in 1941-42. Not until the spring of 1944 had it waned enough for the British Home Fleet to launch a carrier strike on *Tirpitz* in her Altenfjord base. But in the deadly summer of 1942 no fleet carrier could be risked in the narrow corridor of the Barents Sea, where the bombers and U-boats lurked.

Though the fatal belief that modern warships could shoot down any hostile aircraft persisted in many quarters until December 1942, this myopia did not extend to merchant shipping. It had always been obvious that the only way to defend merchant ships against long-range shore-based bombers was a sufficiency of carrier-borne fighters. This had become an urgent need from the second half of 1940, when Focke-Wulf Fw-200 Condor bombers began to prey on British merchant shipping far out into the Atlantic. The first attempts to produce surrogate carrier protection harked straight back to the First World War. The old *Pegasus* (ex-*Ark Royal*) was converted, with three other merchant ships, as a 'fighter catapult' ship'. Some 50 other merchant ships were designated CAM-ships: catapult-aircraft merchant ships, each launching a solitary Hurricane to ditch in the sea when its fuel ran out. Another stop-gap was the MAC or merchant aircraft-carrier: a

Desperate stop-gap in the Atlantic battle – CAM-ship with Hurricane, hand-to-mouth expedient in the struggle to give convoys a minimum of air cover

The real solution – escort carrier *Biter*, photographed by one of her departing Avengers in November 1942

tanker or grain ship not dependent on derricks for loading and unloading its cargo, which could be fitted with a simple flight deck to operate four aircraft. But the only real solution was a large number of small carriers able to fly fighter and anti-submarine patrols simultaneously if need be; carriers whose main task was to protect fleets and convoys of merchant transports, not squadrons of warships capable of double the speed.

Such were the basic requirements of the ESCORT CARRIER, of which the prototype was introduced by the British with HMS *Audacity:* a conversion from a captured German prize, the *Hannover*. In a short but spectacularly successful career between September and December 1941 (when she was sunk by *U-751*), *Audacity* proved the value of the escort carrier. But it was impossible for the British, with their fully-committed shipbuilding programme, to mass-produce escort carriers. This task was performed in American yards, with the same amazing fecundity as with merchant-ship construction. By the time of the Allied invasion of French North Africa ('Torch') in November 1942 the Americans had completed six escort carriers and launched another 11; they completed no less than 39 sister-ships for the Royal Navy (which only received four).

Thus within three months of the agony of 'Pedestal' the carrier shortage in the Atlantic and Mediterranean had been resolved for good by the appearance of the escort carrier (or

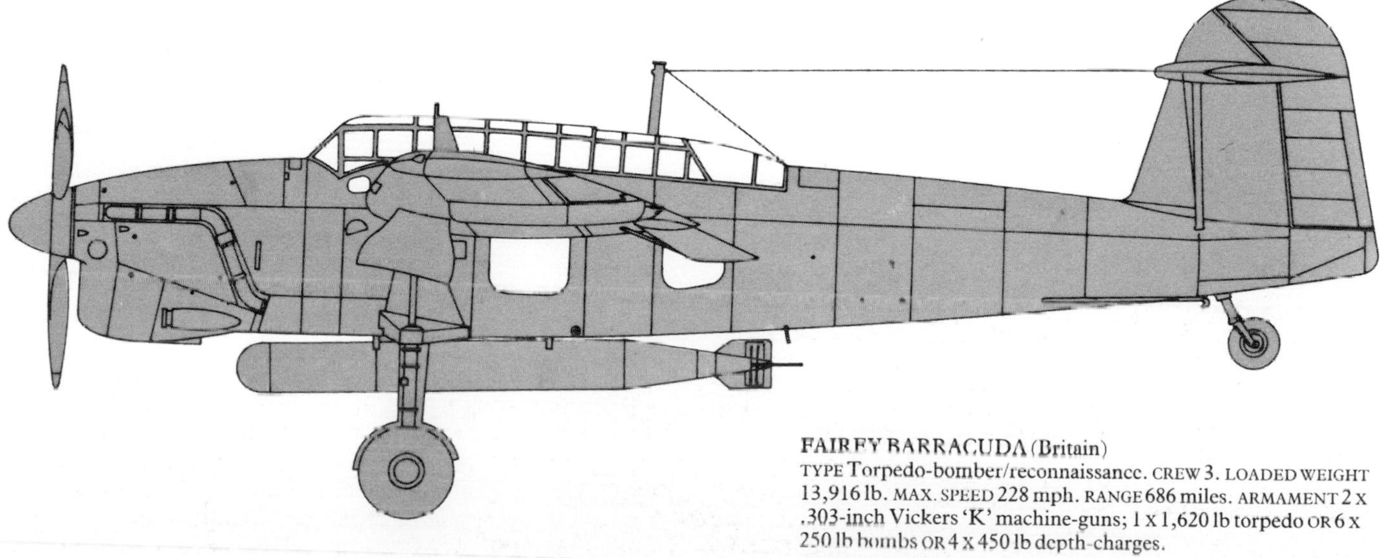

FAIREY BARRACUDA (Britain)
TYPE Torpedo-bomber/reconnaissance. CREW 3. LOADED WEIGHT 13,916 lb. MAX. SPEED 228 mph. RANGE 686 miles. ARMAMENT 2 x .303-inch Vickers 'K' machine-guns; 1 x 1,620 lb torpedo OR 6 x 250 lb bombs OR 4 x 450 lb depth-charges.

A far cry from the desperate months of 1940-1942 – Allied naval air power dominates the central Mediterranean in December 1944

CVE, in American parlance). To be sure, initial supplies were modest; the 'Torch' landings kept the escort carriers away from where they were most desperately needed, the North Atlantic, until the New Year of 1943. Yet they arrived just in time to guarantee the defeat of the U-boats in March-May 1943. There were still not enough to go round for the Russian convoy route to benefit: 1943 was the year of the great Allied amphibious invasions in the Mediterranean, of Sicily in July 1943 and Italy, at Salerno, in September. From February 1944, however, escort carriers accompanied the Russian convoys and continued to do so until the end of the war.

As briefly mentioned above, on 3 April 1944 the British Home fleet despatched *Victorious*, *Furious* and four fleet carriers against the *Tirpitz* in Altenfjord. Protected by 80 fighters (American Corsairs, Wildcats and Hellcats) 40 Barracuda strike aircraft plastered *Tirpitz* with 1,600 lb and 500 lb bombs, scoring no less than 14 direct hits and a near-miss alongside for luck. Such was Operation 'Tungsten', the last major British fleet action in Arctic waters. There had never been any real hope of sinking *Tirpitz* with bombs alone – the use of torpedoes was impossible in those narrow, well-protected waters – but the mission of 'Tungsten' was accomplished, *Tirpitz* remained unfit for sea until after the invasion of Normandy had been successfully achieved. It was all a far cry from the discomfiture of the British carriers in the same waters four years earlier.

Below: An Avenger poised for take-off from the American *Ranger* in the Mediterranean

4. CARRIERS IN THE PACIFIC, 1941-1945

Previous pages: On the flight-deck of *Enterprise*, lumbering TBD Devastators are headed by an SBD Dauntless dive-bomber

THE CARRIER WAR in the Pacific *had* to be totally different to that in the Atlantic and Mediterranean. It was only in the Pacific that carrier navy fought carrier navy, manoeuvring and fighting at distances from base undreamed-of on the other side of the world. From September 1939 to March 1945, when the British Pacific Fleet reported for duty in the Okinawa campaign, no British carrier ever spent more than a week at sea, or operated outside a week's steaming from base. But the Japanese and American navies had to learn from the outset how to operate carriers for weeks, and if need be months, without a respite. Then again, the British were still being forced to use their precious fleet carriers as aircraft ferries as late as the third year of the war, frittering away their strength in piecemeal operations against hopelessly strong land-based air power. In the Pacific the heroic defiance of daunting odds by lone carriers, though certainly not unknown in the first year, became redundant in the press of numbers. While it could never be denied that the Americans richly deserved the victories won by their carriers in the Pacific, it is equally true that those victories owed quite as much to mass production in the shipyards as to courage and skill in battle.

The Pacific War of December 1941 was the most paradoxical of all conflicts. Originally, Japan had no burning ambition to conquer the *Pacific*: since 1937 her armies had been facing the other way, fighting on the Chinese mainland. But by autumn 1941 Japan's military government had become convinced that victory in China would be impossible without the oil, rubber, tin and bauxite of what they called the 'Southern Area'; Malaya and the Dutch East Indies. That meant war with the British Empire and the Dutch government-in-exile. But as the United States, which had a strong military presence in the Philippines, would never allow the Japanese a free hand in the 'Southern Area', war would also be inevitable against the Americans. The American bomber bases in the Philippines must be destroyed at the outset, and the US Pacific Fleet destroyed at its base in Pearl Harbor, in the Hawaiian Islands. In other words, the Japanese Navy hit Pearl Harbor in December 1941 to permit the unimpeded conquest of Malaya and the East Indies, in order to ensure victory in China.

This strategy ignored all classic doctrines based on the concentration of force to attain the objective, but there was an extended, pagoda-like logic to it – *provided* the US Pacific Fleet was swept from the board at the earliest opportunity. It would plainly be impossible to accomplish this in a single attack, because of the American warships either stationed on the West Coast of the USA, undergoing refit there, or in transit between the West Coast and Pearl Harbor. These were bound to be reinforced from the Atlantic after the Japanese attack. Admiral Yamamoto's master-plan therefore catered for a second, and hopefully final encounter, with what was left of the US Pacific Fleet, about six months after the initial attack on Pearl Harbor. And the essence of the Pearl Harbor attack was that it concentrated six Japanese carriers against two, for the only American carriers in the Pacific were *Enter-*

ENTERPRISE (United States)
DISPLACEMENT 19,900 tons. DIMENSIONS 809½ ft (*overall*) x 83¼ ft x 21¾ ft. MACHINERY 4-shaft geared turbines: 120,000 SHP. SPEED 34 knots. ARMAMENT (*initial*) 8 x 5-inch (*later*) plus 40 x 40 mm AA. AIRCRAFT 100. COMPLEMENT 2,200.

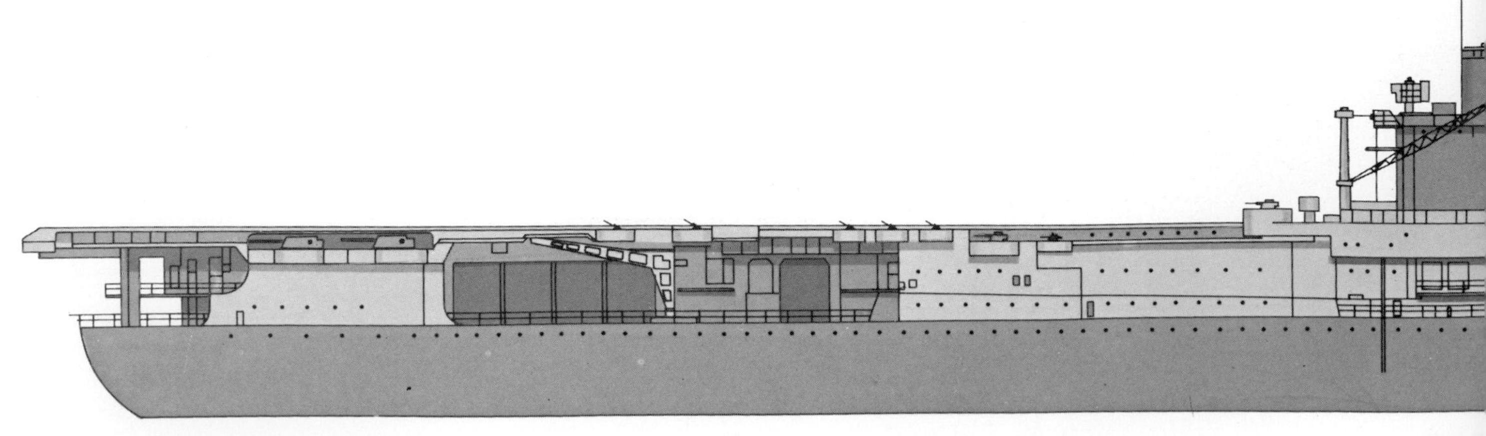

prise, *Lexington* and *Saratoga*, and *Saratoga* was on the West Coast. This meant that even if the Americans were mad enough to transfer *Ranger*, *Yorktown*, *Hornet* and *Wasp* to the Pacific in an instant mass reinforcement, the Japanese would still have six carriers against five for the final showdown.

The basic mathematics behind the Pearl Harbor attack were therefore sound enough; the application was not. Based as they were on exhaustive preparation – flight training and intensive study of photographs, maps and models – the two waves of the attack were led with skill and pugnacity. Each wave contained an admirable balance of force: torpedo, level bomber, dive-bomber, fighter cover and ground strafing. Complete surprise was achieved, and all eight battleships of the Pacific Fleet were sunk or crippled, all for the loss of only 29 out of the 384 Japanese aircraft used in the attack. Here was a victory which no conventional fleet action could have achieved – and yet it was far from complete. Admiral Nagumo's 1st Carrier Striking Force had approached its flying-off position with the foreknowledge that the American carriers were at sea, not in Pearl Harbor with the battleships. The attack plan included the freedom to search within a 150-mile radius of the island of Oahu, should the American fleet have put to sea at the last moment. Nagumo's own flight commanders urged him to order a third sortie, to find and eliminate *Enterprise* and *Lexington* and make the victory complete. They argued in vain. Nagumo, content with being the first admiral in modern naval history to have achieved the ancient objective of liquidating the enemy's line of battle, would have none of it. As soon as the last aircraft from the second wave had landed-on, he took the 1st Carrier Striking Force away to the north-west. This left *Enterprise* and *Lexington* as the core of a savagely mutilated but by no means impotent American Pacific Fleet. As far as the Japanese Navy was concerned, Nagumo's attack at Pearl Harbor had unwittingly created a Frankenstein's monster: the first fleet to measure its strength in carrier rather than battleship numbers, simply because there was no alternative.

The first fortnight of December may therefore be seen as a knife-edge in the balance of forces in the two decisive theatres of the Second World War. In Russia the German Army briefly achieved superiority in numbers over the Red Army before Moscow. In the Pacific Japan's superiority in carriers over the US Navy, which Nagumo failed to make conclusive at Pearl Harbor, was destined for gradual but relentless erosion over the coming year. Apart from the six fleet carriers which returned in triumph from the Pearl Harbor attack – *Kaga*, *Akagi*, *Soryu*, *Hiryu*, *Shokaku* and *Zuikaku* – the Combined Fleet had four light carriers available to support operations against the Philippines and East Indies. These were *Hosho*, *Ryujo*, and two belated conversions: *Zuiho* from a high-speed oiler and *Taiyo* from a liner. But the main air cover for the 'Southern Area' operations was not provided by carriers: it came from the shore-based bomber units of the Japanese Naval Air Force, which operated the best torpedo-bomber units in the world. It was these land-

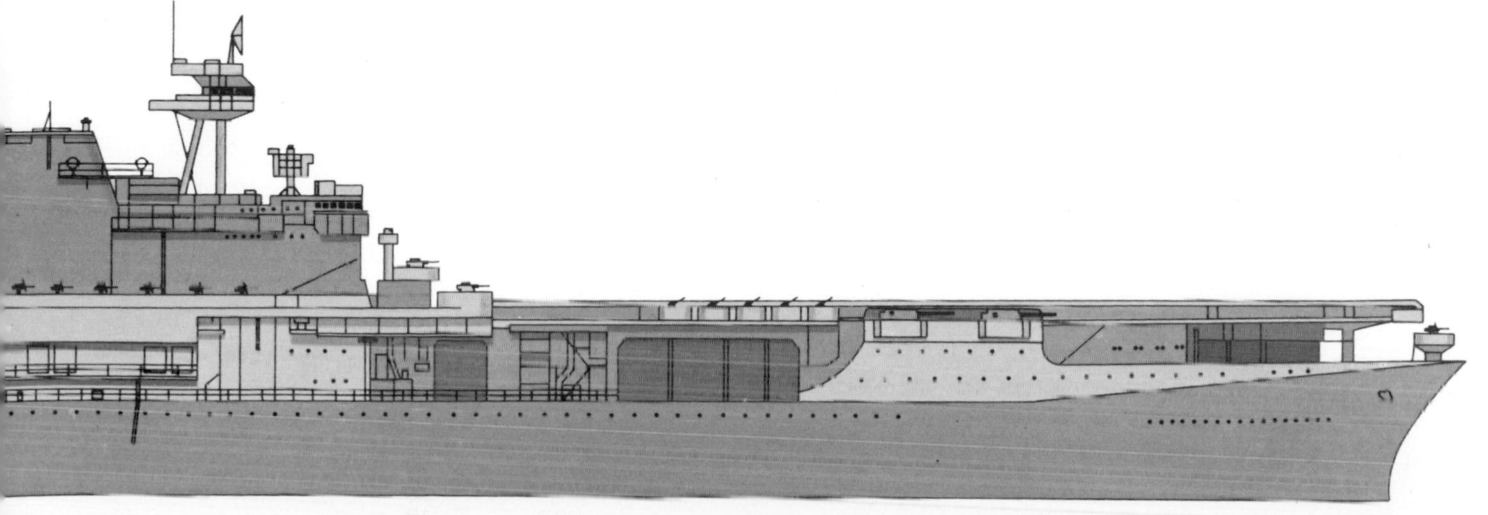

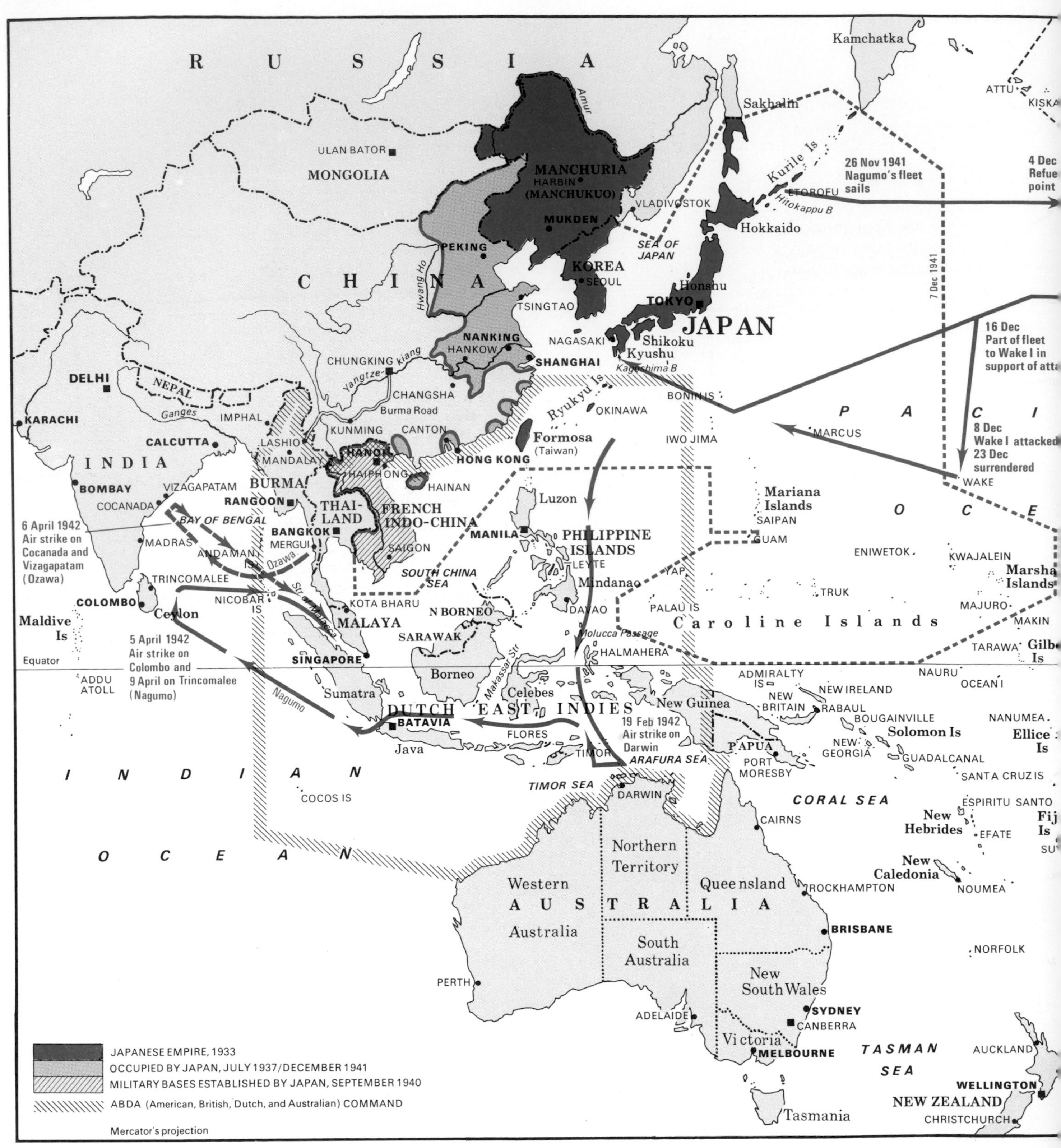

Top right: Pearl Harbor, 7 December 1941: death-knell of the line of battle. The cage-masted dreadnoughts of the American Pacific Fleet go down in ruin to the carrier strike aircraft of the Japanese Combined Fleet

based formations which overwhelmed and sank the British battleship *Prince of Wales* and battle-cruiser *Repulse* on 10 December, as they sought in vain to disrupt the Japanese invasion of Malaya.

The sinking of *Prince of Wales* and *Repulse*, coming as it did after Pearl Harbor and Taranto, was the third and final death-blow at the myth of battleship supremacy. It had never been intended to send the ships out to Malaya on their own. They were supposed to have been accompanied by the new 'Illustrious', *Indomitable*, but this was made impossible by the new carrier grounding and sustaining heavy damage while working-up in the West Indies. After this setback it was obvious that *Prince of Wales* and *Repulse*, which arrived at Singapore only six days be-

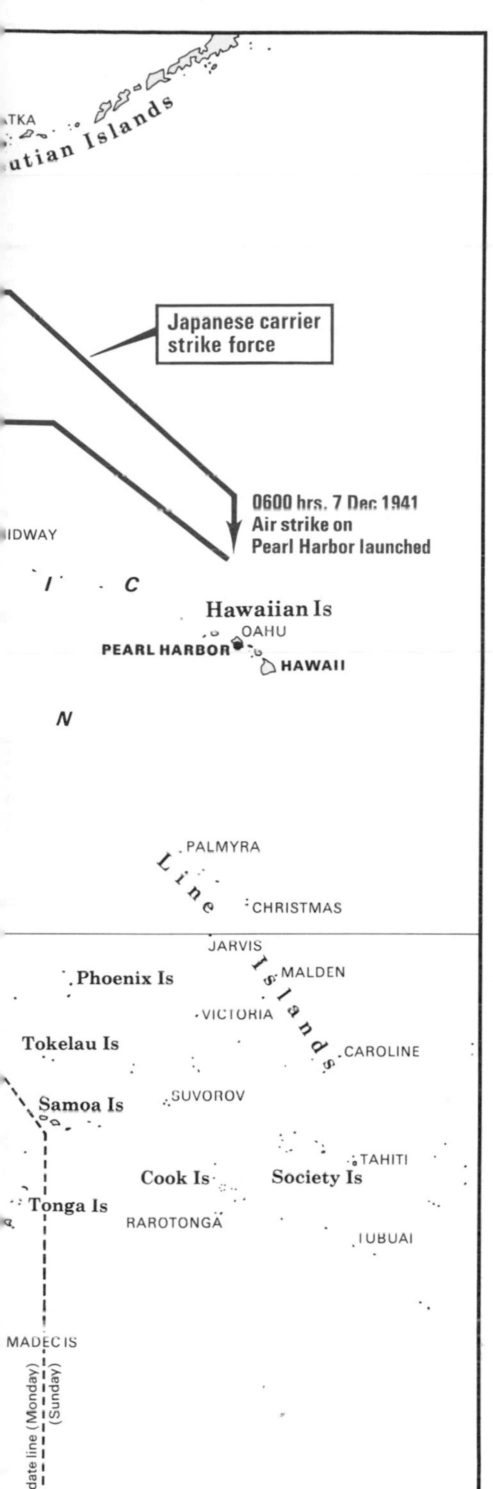

Above: May 1942. On the eve of the Midway showdown USS *Enterprise* returns for replenishment after her vain foray south to the Solomon Islands

fore the Japanese attack, must move on to Australia to fulfil their mission. This was two-fold: to act as a hopeful deterrent against Japanese aggression, and as the core of an intended British Pacific Fleet to be built up gradually from whatever units could be spared from Home Waters and the Mediterranean. *Repulse* had actually set out for Australia, only to be recalled on the news of the Japanese attack. After the Mediterranean Fleet's example earlier in the year during the campaigns in Greece and Crete, Admiral Phillips could not be blamed for trying to break up the Japanese invasion of Malaya with *Prince of Wales* and *Repulse*.

The ensuing disaster has remained a rich seedbed for debate ever since, three perennials being what would have happened if the ships

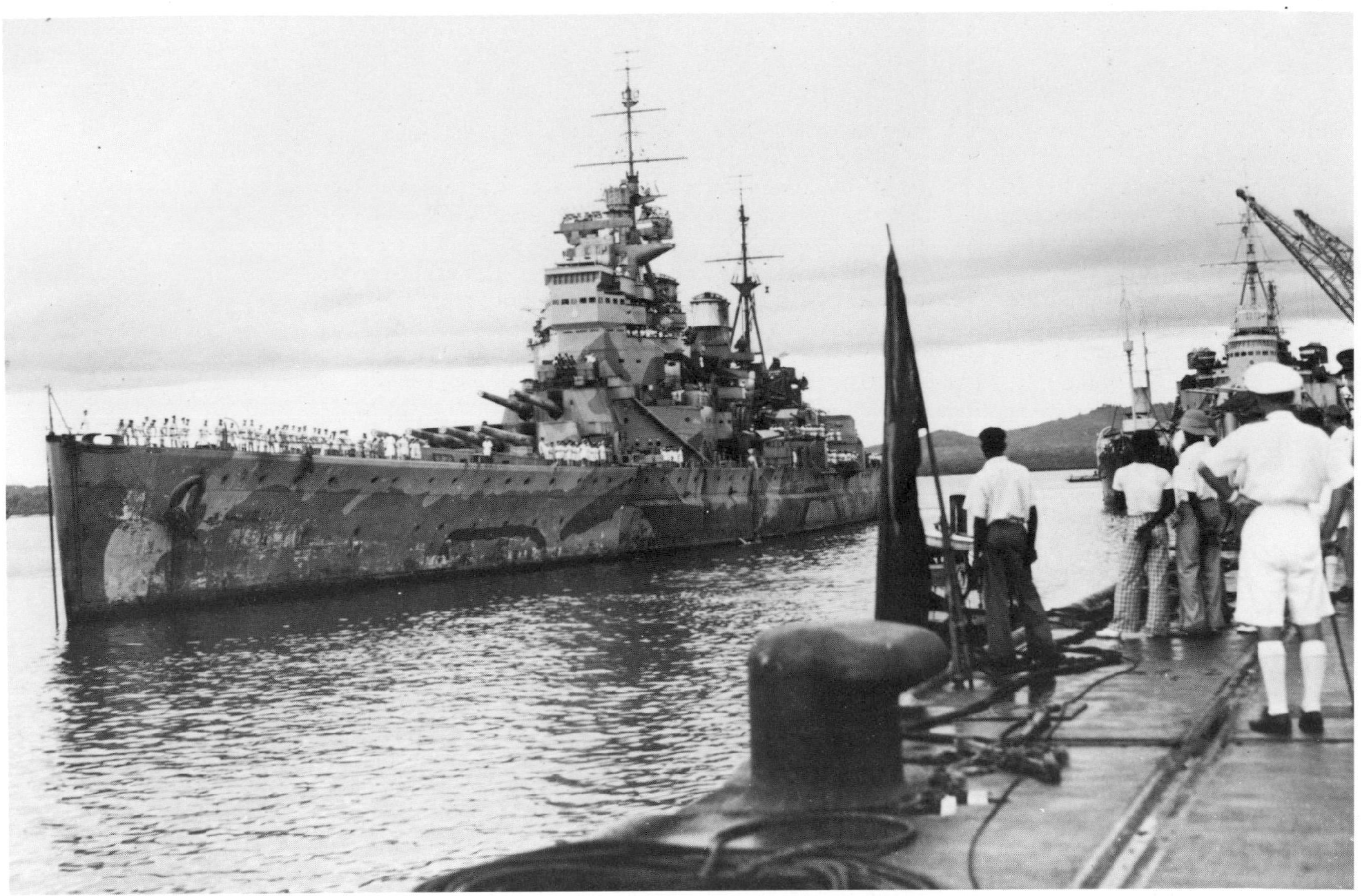

Lamb to the slaughter: HMS *Prince of Wales* arrives at Singapore in December 1941. She was destined to give horrific proof of the battleship's inability to resist intensive air attack at sea

had had proper AA armaments; what would have happened if *Indomitable* had been in company, as originally intended when the ships set out for the Far East; and what would have happened if the squadron of land-based Brewster Buffalo fighters had been called on in time, as it could have been. Certainly the AA fire of *Prince of Wales* and *Repulse* proved completely inadequate against 34 level-bombers and 52 torpedo-bombers. *Repulse* only had eight 4-inch and sixteen 2-pounder AA guns. As for *Prince of Wales*, the more modern of the two by over 20 years, the table below shows her AA armament in December 1941 with that of her sister-ship *Duke of York* three and a half years later, at the end of the Pacific War:

AA gun type	*Prince of Wales* (Dec. 1941)	*Duke of York* (July 1945)
Dual-purpose 5.25-inch	16	16
Total 2-pdr pom-pom (in 8-barrel & 4-barrel mountings)	48	88
Total 20-mm (in single & twin mountings)	7	55
Total 40-mm (in single or quadruple mountings)	1	8

Flying from their bases near Saigon, the Japanese aircraft were as devoid of fighter cover as the ships they sank; and even the modest fighter strength of *Indomitable*, with or without the assistance of the RAF Buffaloes, would have made an appreciable difference. Yet it is most unlikely that *Prince of Wales*, *Repulse*, and *Indomitable* would have survived without damage to one or more of the three; any heavy losses to *Indomitable*'s air group would have been impossible to replace, and any prolonged enforced stay in Singapore, immobilised within range of the Japanese long-range bombers, would have been no less disastrous than what actually befell. As it was, fate (the accident of her grounding) and not design spared *Indomitable*, as it had spared *Enterprise* and *Lexington* at Pearl Harbor. The British carrier eventually arrived in the Indian Ocean and ferried 50 Hurricanes into Singapore – but there was never any question of carriers sustaining Singapore as Malta had been sustained. Quite apart from the vast distances involved, there was the fact that modern fighters could only be supplied from the Middle East theatre – which could not spare them anyway. Moreover, in the Mediterranean the ups and downs of the desert war repeatedly distracted the Germans and Italians from the prospect of taking Malta. There were no such ups and downs in the Malayan/East Indies campaign of 1941-42, which was a runaway Japanese triumph from the start.

In the first three months of the Pacific War the most brilliant display of the aircraft-carrier's potential was given by Nagumo's Fast Carrier Striking Force. After returning from the Pearl Harbor strike, Nagumo detached the 2nd Carrier Division – *Soryu* and *Hiryu* – to end the heroic resistance of the US Marine garrison on Wake Island (whose guns had sunk the first Japanese warship lost in the war, the destroyer *Hayate*, on 11 December). Attacks from the two carriers eliminated the last Marine Wildcat fighter on 22 December, making possible the main troop landings on the following day. After Wake's surrender on 23 December Nagumo's carriers were used to bombard Rabaul in New Britain (20 January 1942), again as the prelude to an amphibious landing. Rabaul's capture on the 23rd gave Japan an advance base in the South-West Pacific from which attacks could be launched against New Guinea, the Solomon Islands and ultimately all Allied sea links between Australia and the Americas.

For the moment, however, Nagumo's carrier fleet was used for knocking the props from beneath the Allied attempt to defend the 'Southern Area'. An American, British, Dutch and Australian command, 'ABDA', was created on 10 January to try and hold the East Indies, denying the Japanese the island chain between Australia and the Bay of Bengal. The task of shouldering this burden, hopeless in the face of unbreakable Japanese air supremacy, fell to a gallant conglomerate force of cruisers and destroyers wiped out in the Battle of the Java Sea on 27 February 1942. By that date the Japanese had already secured the central East Indies – Borneo, Celebes and Amboina – and had outflanked Java from the west with landings on Sumatra. Before the eastern pincer closed round Java with the capture of Bali and Timor, Nagumo's carriers smashed the port area and airfield of Port Darwin (19 February), causing extensive damage against negligible opposition. This destroyed the last communications and supply link between Australia and Java, which was now totally isolated. The Fast Carrier Striking Force now moved out south of the island chain, battering the southern Javan port of Tjilatjap and preventing any substantial Allied evacuation from the island, where the last Allied land forces surrendered on 8 March. Nagumo's carriers then withdrew to Kendari on Celebes to prepare for their next foray. This was to be a sortie westward into the Indian Ocean, hopefully to do to the British Eastern Fleet at Ceylon what they had already done to the US Pacific Fleet at Pearl Harbor.

Meanwhile, east of the 'Southern Area' battle zone, the American carriers had been striving to create some kind of strategic defence with which to slow down the Japanese advance. Immediately after Pearl Harbor, *Saratoga* had been rushed out from the West Coast, embarking a squadron of Wildcat fighters for the reinforcement of Wake. With three cruisers and nine destroyers she formed a task force commanded by Rear-Admiral Frank Jack Fletcher. Both in its initial mission and overall strength, the similarity of Fletcher's task force to the British Force H in the Mediterranean is striking. Pure luck saved Fletcher's force from involuntary and what would surely have been fatal participation in the first ever carrier-versus-carrier battle. On 22 December, as the aircraft of *Soryu* and *Hiryu* softened up the defences of Wake in preparation for the troop landings, Fletcher was steaming *away* from Wake, ponderously refuelling his ships. By the time he had resumed his course for Wake on the following day the garrison had surrendered, and Fletcher was recalled after approaching to within 425 miles of the island. In the first week of January 1942 *Yorktown* arrived from the Atlantic, bringing the American carrier strength in the Pacific up to four; but this reinforcement was almost immediately cancelled out on 11 January, when *Saratoga* was torpedoed by a Japanese submarine. Though she survived the attack there was nothing for it but a return to the West Coast for repairs, which took several months.

On 27 December Admiral Chester Nimitz took over as C-in-C, Pacific Fleet (CINCPAC), his brief necessarily being little more than 'to hold what you've got and hit them when you can'. *Saratoga*'s mishap did not prevent Nimitz from carrying out his orders to secure the Pearl Harbor-Midway line, plus the South Pacific sea-lane to Australia. American troops were landed in Samoa on 23 January 1942; from their end of the Pacific, the Australians and New Zealanders reinforced New Guinea and Fiji. Eventually the link extended westward via Samoa, Tonga, Fiji and New Caledonia, providing the US Pacific Fleet with invaluable advanced bases in the South Pacific at Tongatapu and Nouméa by the late summer of 1942. Between January and May, however, the American carriers in the Pacific were restricted to widely separated pinprick raids on the Japanese outposts.

Instead of emulating the Japanese and massing their fleet carriers into a unit under centralised command, the Americans chose in

Comparatively unknown shot of 'Jimmy' Doolittle's bomber crews, mustered on the flight-deck of *Hornet* while Doolittle and Mitscher confer on the eve of the Tokyo Raid (April 1942)

this period to operate over as wide an area as possible: Admirals Fletcher in *Yorktown*, Halsey in *Enterprise*, Brown in *Lexington*. On 1 February, Fletcher and Halsey joined forces to raid targets in the Gilbert and Marshall Islands. On 20 February it fell to Brown to crack the myth of invincible Japanese air power. *Lexington*, approaching New Britain to raid Rabaul, was attacked by a force of land-based bombers eager to emulate the annihilation of *Repulse* and *Prince of Wales*. As the Japanese bombers had sortied without fighter cover the result was a field-day for *Lexington*'s fighter pilots. Very few of the attackers got back to base – but surprise had been lost and the attack on Rabaul had to be abandoned.

Four days later, Halsey with *Enterprise* bombarded Wake, following up with a similar raid on Marcus Island, 1,000 miles away to the north-west, on 3 March. Compared to what Nagumo's carriers had already achieved at Pearl Harbor and Wake, and were still achieving off Darwin and Tjilatjap, the damage done by these American nuisance raids was negligible. But the strategic impact was certainly greater; Marcus was under 1,500 miles from the Japanese home islands, and almost exactly two-thirds the distance from Pearl Harbor to Tokyo. With the American raid on Marcus, Admiral Yamamoto was given a forceful reminder of the enduring failure of the original attack on Pearl Harbor. This was that if Japanese carriers could reach Pearl Harbor from Japan, then American carriers could reach Japan from Pearl Harbor. And indeed by the time of Halsey's attack on Marcus plans were well advanced for the most audacious carrier raid of the Pacific War: the 'Doolittle Raid' on Tokyo.

The 'First Special Aviation Project', as the Doolittle Raid was code-named, had first taken shape on 10 January 1942. Captains Low and Duncan of the Chief of Naval Operation's Staff, had suggested flying-off Army B-25 twin-engined bombers for a revenge attack on Tokyo: a combination of Navy carrier range and Army bomber range. As it would be completely impossible for the B-25s to land-on again, additional kudos would be gained by having the raiders fly on to land at friendly airfields in China. Lt-Colonel 'Jimmy' Doolittle, American aviation hero of Schneider Trophy days, was picked to lead the raid, final permission being given after a demonstration launch of B-25s from *Hornet* on 2 February. Doolittle's force of volunteers then settled down to intensive practice in the art of taking-off a fully laden B-25 in under 500 feet: the length of flight-deck that would be available.

American preparations for this much-needed morale booster were still far from complete when, at the end of March 1942, Nagumo's carrier force set out for the Indian Ocean. Their new prey was the British Eastern Fleet being formed on Ceylon, command of which was given to Admiral Somerville, former commander of Force H. The Japanese objective was twofold: to destroy the Eastern Fleet and raid the Bay of Bengal sea-lane between Ceylon and Calcutta. To this end *two* Japanese carrier forces were used: Nagumo's fleet carriers (less *Kaga*) to tackle the Eastern Fleet, and the light carrier *Ryujo* with a cruiser/destroyer force, under Admiral Ozawa, for the Bay of Bengal raid. Somerville, who only took over command of the Eastern Fleet on 26 March, knew that his patchwork command stood no chance at all against the experts of the Japanese Combined Fleet. He had five old, slow battleships, the carriers *Indomitable*, *Formidable* and *Hermes*, seven cruisers and 16 destroyers. Between them, the three carriers could put up no more than 57 strike aircraft and 36 fighters. All of these were also old and slow, with no prospects of surviving attacks by the deadly Japanese Zero fighter.

But Somerville had one advantage: he was the first Allied naval commander in the Far East and Pacific to have firm intelligence that the Japanese carrier force was heading his way. What he did not know was whether or not an invasion fleet would be coming with them. If the latter were the case, the Eastern Fleet would have no option but to go down fighting in a bid to save Ceylon at all costs, for with Ceylon in Japanese hands the British would lose the vital cross-link between the Suez Canal and Australia, between India and the Cape of Good Hope. But if this turned out to be merely another Pearl Harbor-style raid, unsupported by an invasion force, Somerville was determined to avoid battle. He would resort to the age-old ploy of Fabian tactics, withdrawing from Ceylon to keep his fleet in being. To this end he withdrew the Eastern Fleet to the secret anchorage of Addu Atoll, south of the Maldives – but the intelligence estimate placed Nagumo's arrival four days early. As a result Somerville had sent his slower ships back to Ceylon to refuel, which resulted in the loss of the cruisers *Cornwall* and *Devonshire*, then *Hermes*, on 5 and 9 April respectively. With her minute air group the little carrier – the world's first homogeneous carrier design – was overwhelmed and sunk within 20 minutes by a massive Japanese strike force 90 strong, which went on to sink the escorting destroyer *Vampire*, a corvette and two tankers. At the same time Ozawa's force to the north ran a three-day rampage through the Bay of Bengal, sinking 23 ships with a total of 112,312 tons and bombing Cocanada and Vizagapatam.

These attacks, with the subsequent Japanese withdrawal from the Indian Ocean without any molestation, carried the run of Japanese victories – uninterrupted since the first day of the Pacific War – to new heights. Certainly there was little to indicate that the glory days were over. Nagumo had repeated his Pearl Harbor performance: the fleet he had set out to destroy had only been mauled and thrown badly off balance, not annihilated. Certainly the Indian Ocean raid brought the Japanese important short-term benefits. It forced the British Eastern Fleet to quit Ceylon, with the slower battleships being sent right back to Kilindini on the Kenyan coast. This new humiliating withdrawal by the Royal Navy may be seen as the battleship's formal act of homage, after Pearl Harbor, the *Prince of Wales* and *Repulse*, to the supremacy of the aircraft-carrier. The Japanese foray also panicked the British into invading Madagascar in May, the idea being to use Madagascar as an emergency base should the Japanese return in force and take Ceylon. But only ten days after Nagumo quit the Indian Ocean Doolittle's bombers hit Tokyo, momentarily eclipsing the Japanese Navy's latest flourish and demonstrating to the world that the American carrier force was still a force to be reckoned with.

The 'First Special Aviation Project' marked *Hornet*'s debut in the Pacific. She sailed from San Francisco on 2 April, laden with 16 B-25s lashed to her after flight-deck. As the parked stack of bombers rendered *Hornet* completely incapable of defending herself, she was given *Enterprise* as a consort. The resultant Task Force 16, under Halsey's command, set off

Overwhelmed: Britain's diminutive *Hermes* sinks after a shattering strike by the aircraft of Nagumo's Carrier Striking Force

Opposite: The tethered stack of B-25 bombers on *Hornet*'s flight-deck, *en route* to her historic Tokyo Raid

from its rendezvous point north of Hawaii (13 April) with a modest destroyer screen, which was to be left behind while the two carriers advanced to and retreated from the flying-off point at full speed. The raid was made all the more dramatic by the fact that Yamamoto had been expecting something like it ever since the attack on Marcus at the beginning of March. A patrol line had been extended across the most likely line of approach to Japanese waters, and the oncoming carriers were sighted and reported by one of the patrol ships on the morning of the 18th. At this point the carriers were still 720 miles east of Tokyo, some 220 miles short of the flying-off point, but the decision was taken to launch Doolittle's force at once. As a result, Yamamoto expected a conventional carrier strike on the following day; he deployed the Japanese 2nd Fleet and sent out the first of a series of bomber patrols, unaware of the fact that Doolittle's bombers were already approaching their targets and the American carriers were well on their way home.

The Doolittle Raid has too often been dismissed as a glorified publicity-stunt, if much needed as an Allied morale-booster. It was in fact the most ambitious multi-target carrier attack since *Ark Royal*'s Swordfish had attacked Livorno, Pisa and La Spezia 14 months before. Doolittle's valiant force bombed not only Tokyo but Kobe, Yokahama and Nagoya. The price to be paid for those lost 220 miles of range was the failure to reach the Chinese airfields, most of Doolittle's men bailing-out or crash-landing to be guided to safety by faithful Chinese. (Three prisoners of war were executed as war criminals by the Japanese.) The effects of the raid on Allied morale, however, were as nothing to the effect on the Japanese High Command. All efforts were now to be bent on luring the American carrier fleet to destruction in the central Pacific: to finish the job scamped at Pearl Harbor back in December. Yamamoto now planned the occupation of Midway, westernmost outlier of the Hawaiian group – a vital link in Pearl Harbor's western defences. To defend Midway, Yamamoto quite correctly estimated, the Americans would commit every warship they had left. Once Operation 'MI' (for Midway) had disposed of the American Pacific Fleet, Japan would be left as the unchallenged mistress of the Pacific.

If the Japanese High Command had approached 'MI' with the ruthless concentration of force which they had brought to every key sector of the 'Southern Area', Yamamoto's optimism would have been better repaid. But the very ease with which the

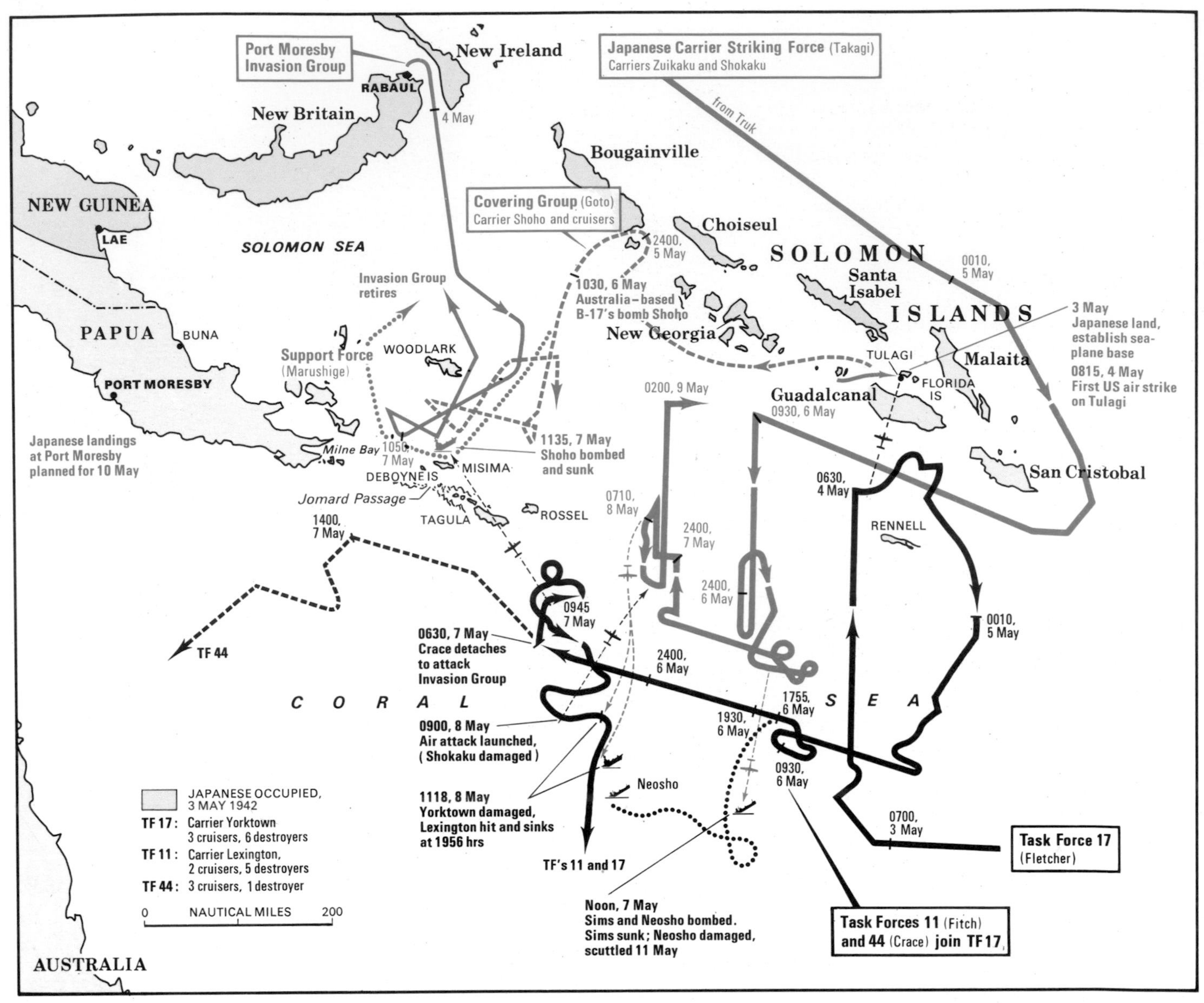

'Southern Area' had been reduced led – after the fall of Java at the beginning of March 1942 – to a delirium of what the Japanese themselves came to call 'Victory Disease'. As would soon be revealed, the gravest symptom was a readiness to dismiss Allied forces as contemptible, against which even dispersed and modest Japanese forces would be bound to prevail as before. Even after the Tokyo raid on 18 April this 'Victory Disease' persisted. Before the decisive Operation 'MI' in the central Pacific a subsidiary operation was to be completed south of Rabaul. This was 'MO', for Port Moresby: the amphibious capture of the last major Allied base in southern New Guinea, with the establishment of a new forward base at Tulagi halfway down the Solomon Islands chain. With all New Guinea and the Solomons thus built in to Japan's outer perimeter, the total isolation of Australia via New Caledonia, Fiji and Samoa could follow easily.

Yet never before had the Japanese approached such an obviously important operation with such a casual allocation of force. Close cover was entrusted to the light carrier *Shoho*, four cruisers and a destroyer – and this covering group had to serve both the Tulagi occupation force and the Moresby invasion fleet. It was hoped that American forces would rush into the Coral Sea in an attempt to intervene. Admiral Inouye, responsible for 'MO', was acting on the totally false intelligence premise that the only American carrier available for such intervention would be *Saratoga* (actually still undergoing repairs in Puget Sound on the West Coast). Thus the carrier striking force, intended to trap any American countermove, did not consist of Nagumo's entire carrier fleet this time: just the 5th Carrier Division, *Shokaku* and *Zuikaku*. But the Japanese High Command had no idea that their JN-25 code had been cracked by the Americans as early as 10 December 1941, and that the Pearl Harbor cryptanalysts were feeding Nimitz with accurate estimates of Japanese strategic intentions. Thus apprised of 'MO', Nimitz sent his southernmost pair of carriers into the Coral Sea, ideally placed to block the Japanese convergence on Port Moresby, at the end of April. The American force consisted of *Lexington* (Rear-Admiral A. Fitch, who had replaced Admiral Brown on 3 April) and *Yorktown* (Rear-Admiral Fletcher, in overall command): respectively Task Forces 16 and 17, with their forward bases at Espiritu Santo and Nouméa.

The result was the Battle of the Coral Sea, a tangle of muddle and error on both sides punctuated by occasional collisions with the enemy, in which, nevertheless, carrier fought carrier for the first time. Human error complicated the issue throughout, with each side believing that it had inflicted far more damage on the enemy than was actually the case. To excited and inexperienced pilots on both sides, destroyers looked like cruisers, tankers looked like carriers, light carriers looked like fleet carriers – and every explosion, near-miss or not, looked like total destruction. Even if they had been spared faulty data of this sort, the rival admirals had no precedent on which to base their decisions. Nor were their problems eased by the flukiest weather experienced in any of the Pacific War's carrier actions: dense rain squalls which could completely hide one group of ships, while leaving a nearby group exposed in brilliant sunshine.

So it was that on 5 and 6 May *Yorktown* and *Lexington* refuelled from the fleet oiler *Neosho* in sparkling clear weather; Admiral Takagi's *Shokaku* and *Zuikaku*, approaching from the north-east, were hidden from Fletcher's reconnaissance aircraft by overcast, but the Japanese missed the American carriers, too. On the 7th, after reports of an American 'carrier and cruiser' to the south, *Shokaku* and *Zuikaku* launched a full-dress strike which accounted for the oiler *Neosho* and attendant destroyer *Sims*. At almost exactly the same moment, *Lexington* and *Yorktown* were squandering 93 strike aircraft – launched against 'two carriers and four heavy cruisers' – on the lightweight carrier *Shoho*. Overwhelmed in less than 20 minutes by this massive 'overkill', *Shoho* sank soon after 11.35 hrs on 7 May: the second carrier to be sunk by carrier aircraft, and the first Japanese carrier lost in the war. This gave away the American carriers' position – but a late afternoon strike from *Shokaku* and *Zuikaku* missed *Lexington* and *Yorktown* in overcast and foul weather. Many Japanese pilots became so disoriented that when they *did* sight *Yorktown* they thought they were 'home' and tried to land-on.

SBD dive-bombers ranged forward on *Lexington*'s as yet unscathed flight-deck after the first strike at *Shoho* during the Battle of the Coral Sea

(This catastrophic sortie cost the Japanese 21 out of 27 aircraft for nil return.) On the morning of 8 May, each side launched major strikes at the other between 09.00 and 09.25 hrs, with *Lexington* and *Shokaku* receiving similar severe damage and *Yorktown* taking a single 800-lb bomb. With *Shokaku* unable to launch aircraft, Takagi broke off the action. Promising results from the damage-control parties in *Lexington* were, however, set at nought by a series of appalling internal explosions caused by accumulated petrol vapour. The 'Lady Lex' was evacuated and sunk by the destroyer *Phelps* at 20.00 hrs on 8 May. The battle ended very much as it had begun and proceeded: the Japanese withdrew thinking they had sunk *Yorktown* as well as *Lexington*, the Americans thinking they had sunk *Shokaku*.

Both sides, as after Jutland in 1916, could claim victory. The Japanese victory was tactical: they could well afford to lose *Shoho* in exchange for the mighty *Lexington*. The American victory was strategic: for the first time ever, a Japanese seaborne invasion had been abandoned. The Port Moresby invasion force had been withdrawn until the American carriers had been sunk, and with surprise lost for good Operation 'MO' was written off. Two Japanese fleet carriers had also been rendered unfit for the next Combined Fleet operation: *Shokaku* with bomb damage, *Zuikaku* with the chronic losses in aircraft and trained aircrew. None of these sobering facts dispelled the worst effects of 'Victory Disease': continued disparagement of the US Pacific Fleet's resources, and the over-confident tackling of too much with too little. The premature suspension of 'MO' did not stop preparations for 'MI' from being pushed ahead and receiving a deadline for the first week in June. And the over-confidence behind 'MO' was as nothing to the enormous scope of 'MI'.

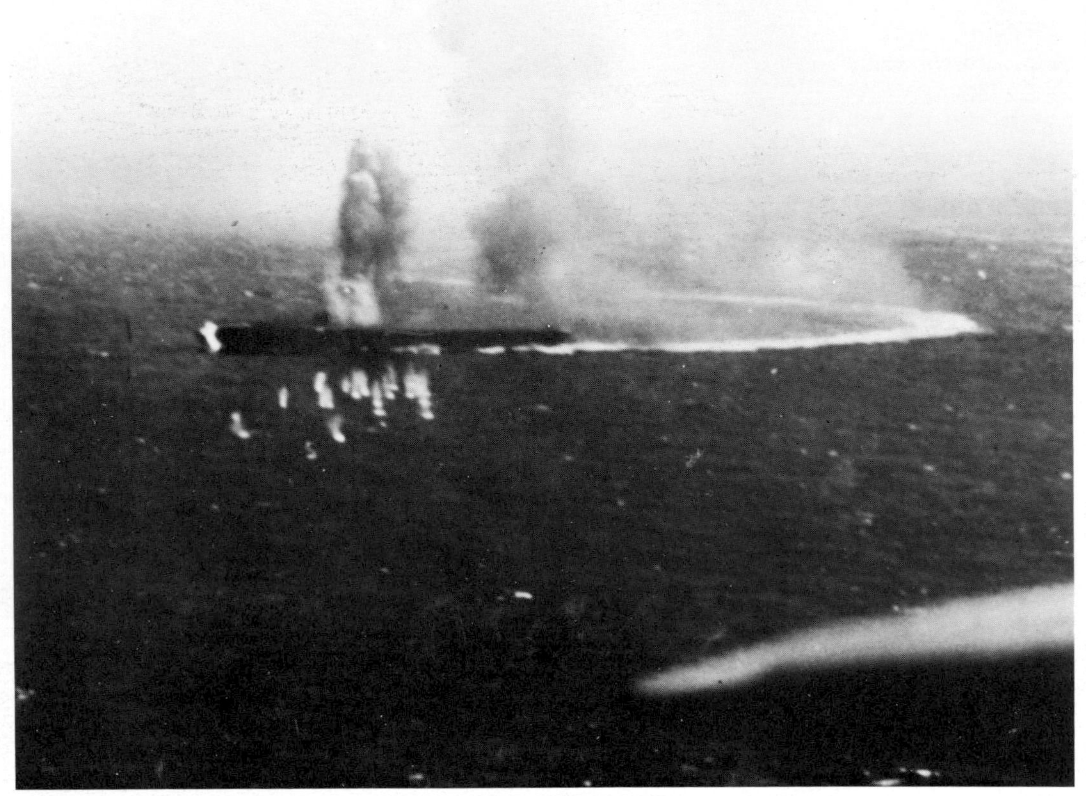

Shokaku frantically dodges American carrier aircraft during the Coral Sea attacks which shattered her bow and rendered her unfit for service in the Midway operation
Below: *Lexington*, shrouded in the smoke of her own fires, abandoned as the tragic tailpiece to the Coral Sea fight

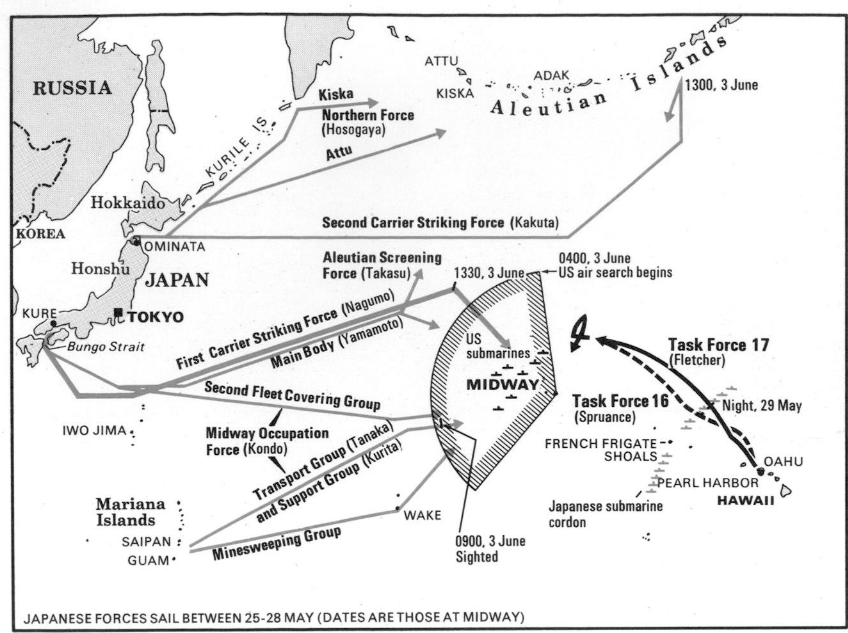

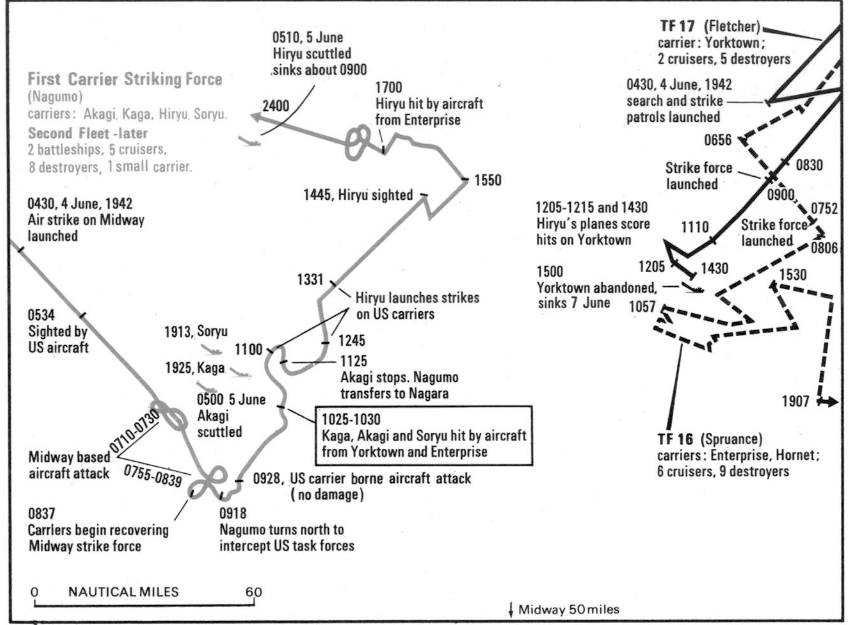

The all-important assault on Midway – the baiting of the trap into which the Americans were confidently expected to rush – was to be accompanied by the occupation of Attu and Kiska in the Aleutian Islands. The obsession with this secondary objective, over 2,000 miles from Midway, amounted to a dispersal of effort on the grandest scale. And it was particularly unwise because the light carriers *Ryujo* and *Junyo*, covering the Aleutians force, carried 100 aircraft between them and would have been most useful replacements for *Shokaku* and *Zuikaku*. As it was Nagumo's Carrier Striking Force, prime instrument of the assault on Midway, sailed for Midway at its lowest strength ever: only *Kaga, Akagi, Soryu* and *Hiryu*. This hardly seemed to matter because Yamamoto and Nagumo were expecting to encounter no more than two American carriers at most. The Japanese plan blandly assumed that *Yorktown*, with her Coral Sea battle damage, could never be repaired in time for the Midway finale. It also assumed that the Americans would do everything Yamamoto hoped they would do. But the worst Japanese assumption of them all was the assumption that the whole unfolding attack would catch the Americans completely by surprise.

In fact, down to 25 May, when the Japanese changed their JN-25 code, the superb US Navy cryptanalysts in Pearl Harbor furnished Admiral Nimitz with all important details of the forthcoming Japanese assault in the Central Pacific. This included the Aleutians operation; Midway was clearly the pivot of the whole operation, but it remained to be seen whether Midway was a 'blind' for another attack on Pearl Harbor or even, perhaps, on the American West Coast. Chilling details of the force being mustered against him enabled Nimitz to work out the best way of countering an attack on Midway launched by four carriers. First, Midway's defences were frantically 'beefed up' with more men, barbed wire, AA guns, long-range reconnaissance planes and land-based bombers, the latter to give the target the chance of hitting before it was hit. Second, the American carriers were to be posted in ambush north-east of Midway, enabling them to counter-attack either an assault on Midway or an attempt to bypass Midway and strike direct at Pearl Harbor.

Until the last moment it was doubtful how many American carriers would make it. Halsey's Task Force 16, which had been rushed down to the South Pacific to arrive too late for the Coral Sea action, arrived back at Pearl Harbor on 26 May. As *Enterprise* and *Hornet* replenished, Halsey, worn by non-stop operations since January, reported sick with a debilitating skin disease. Halsey was the 'carrier man's admiral' *par excellence*; no one had done more to restore the Pacific Fleet's morale since the shock of Pearl Harbor, and his replacement was a matter of crucial importance. On Halsey's own recommendation Nimitz appointed Rear-Admiral Raymond A. Spruance, commander of TF.16's cruiser/destroyer force, to command the entire task force in the forthcoming battle. It was to prove one of the most inspired appointments of the war. Even more urgent was the condition of *Yorktown* when Fletcher brought TF.17 back to Pearl Harbor from the Coral Sea on 27 May. Nimitz insisted that *Yorktown* must be ready for action in three days – when three weeks would have seemed barely sufficient. In an incredible saga of high-speed repair work, the Pearl Harbor dockyard

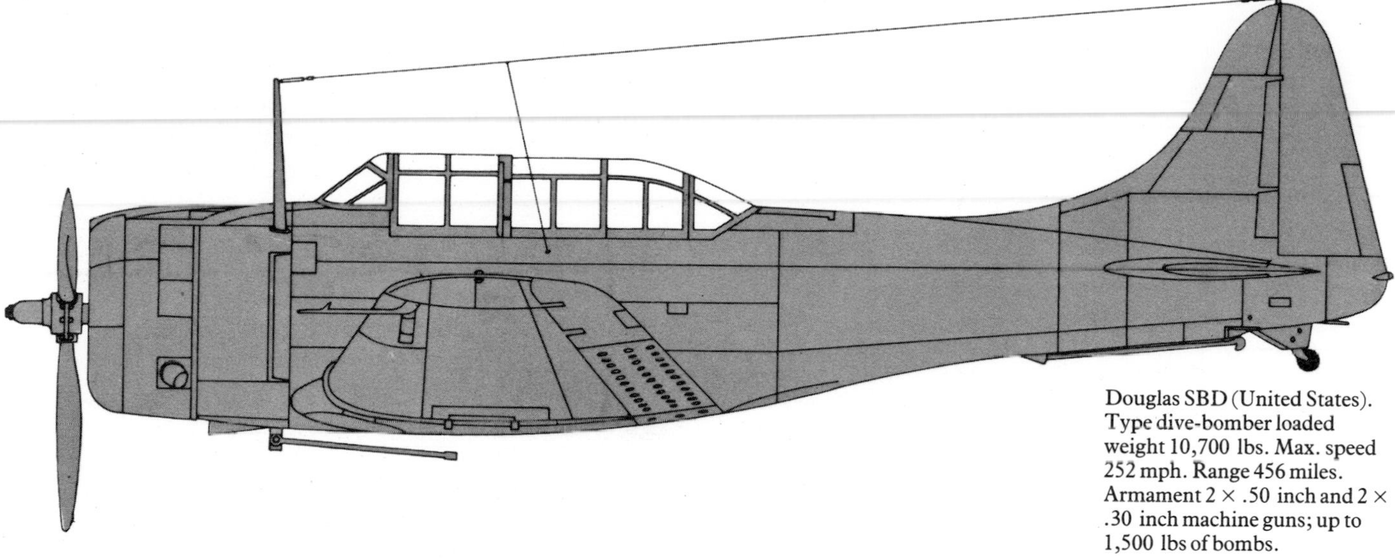

Douglas SBD (United States). Type dive-bomber loaded weight 10,700 lbs. Max. speed 252 mph. Range 456 miles. Armament 2 × .50 inch and 2 × .30 inch machine guns; up to 1,500 lbs of bombs.

teams made Nimitz's order good and *Yorktown* sailed with the rest of TF.17 on 30 May. Spruance had headed out with TF.16 two days earlier. Late in the afternoon of 2 June Fletcher caught up with Spruance at 'Point Luck', the prearranged rendezvous north-east of Midway, and assumed tactical command over the two task forces.

None of the haste was wasted. On 3 June Yamamoto's cordon of submarines had moved into position between Pearl Harbor and Midway, ready to report the US Pacific Fleet's dash to Midway's rescue – 24 hours too late. The American task forces were already in ambush; the Midway reconnaissance aircrews were already on the watch for the widely-separated elements of the oncoming Japanese armada. The Midway invasion force, 27 transports strong, was first to be sighted on the morning of 3 June. This time there were no precipitate American carrier strikes against unimportant targets, as at the Coral Sea fight; Fletcher held his hand until Nagumo's first strike was sighted heading for Midway on the morning of the 4th, and until the Japanese carriers had been located and the initial reports confirmed. While *Yorktown* tarried to recover her search aircraft it fell to Spruance to launch the first American strike of the battle: 57 aircraft from *Enterprise*, 60 from *Hornet*, followed half an hour later by another 35 from *Yorktown*. This blow was already in the air when Nagumo's search aircraft finally reported 'what appears to be an aircraft-carrier' away to the north-east.

So it was that the Battle of Midway opened with the Americans, not the Japanese, reaping the benefit of surprise. Forewarned, the land-based aircraft on Midway were sent out to attack Nagumo's force instead of being caught on the ground. Accepting that his aircraft had only wrecked an empty base, Nagumo was preparing a second strike at Midway when the sighting of the American carrier came in. By this time the Japanese carriers had had to beat off no less than five attacks by the Midway aircraft. No damage had been suffered by these attacks, but they delayed the recovery of the Midway attack force, caused the cancellation of a second strike at Midway and delayed the preparation of an anti-shipping strike at the newly-reported American force. And no sooner had Nagumo wheeled his carriers to the north-east, heading squarely towards the Americans, than the Japanese came under the first of several disjointed attacks by the air groups of Spruance and Fletcher.

Just about everything went wrong with the all-important initial American strike at the Japanese carriers. This had been tautly planned, envisaging torpedo aircraft and dive-bombers attacking in close harmony, covered by fighters to keep off the dreaded Zeros. But the slow TBD torpedo aircraft soon got separated from the faster SBD dive-bombers,

With three Japanese carriers already reduced to blazing hulks, SBD dive-bombers head out to clinch the American 'amazing victory' of Midway

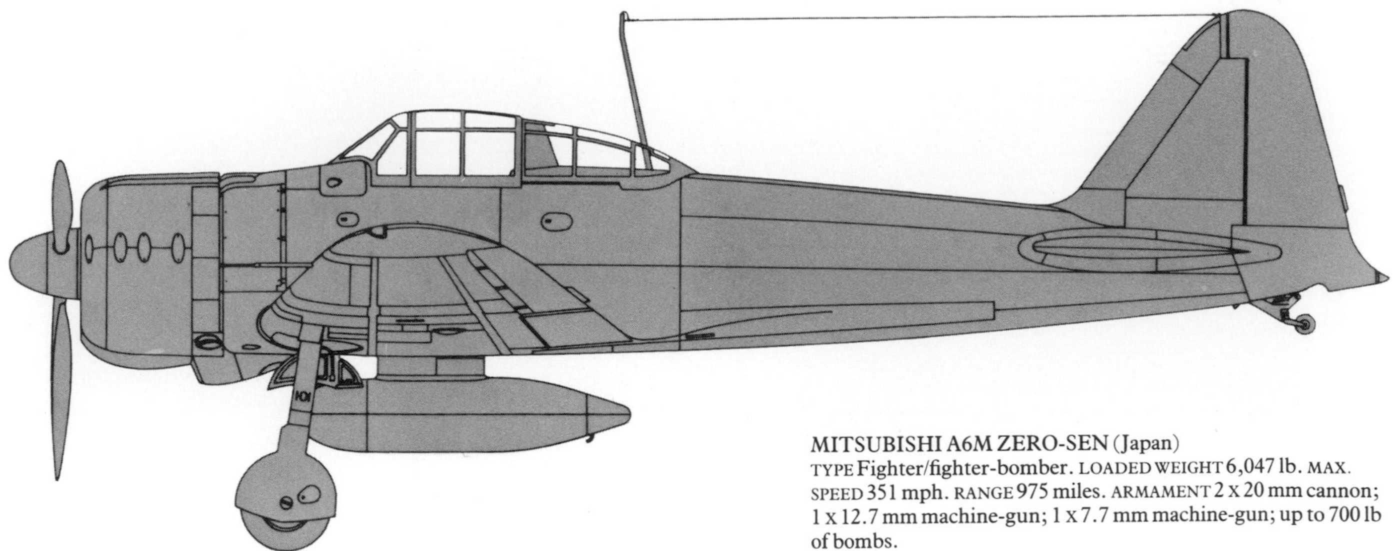

MITSUBISHI A6M ZERO-SEN (Japan)
TYPE Fighter/fighter-bomber. LOADED WEIGHT 6,047 lb. MAX. SPEED 351 mph. RANGE 975 miles. ARMAMENT 2 x 20 mm cannon; 1 x 12.7 mm machine-gun; 1 x 7.7 mm machine-gun; up to 700 lb of bombs.

and both categories became separated from their fighter escorts. Many groups, heading for the estimated point of interception with the Japanese, were foiled by the intervening Japanese turn to the north-east; others which did make contact did so with barely enough fuel to get 'home'. Attacking without fighter cover, the TBDs provided a jackals' feast for the Zeros. The American torpedo men suffered horrific losses of which the worst were incurred by *Hornet*'s Torpedo Squadron 8: all 15 aircraft shot down, and 29 out of the squadron's 30 pilots and crewmen killed. As if to add to the agony, not a single hit was scored by the Americans.

Yet the agony of the TBDs was certainly not in vain. Their valiant, disjointed attacks prevented Nagumo from launching his planned strike at the American carrier force. The TBDs also drew the Zeros down to sea level, leaving no counter to the SBDs when they arrived over the Japanese carriers, whose flight-decks were littered with fuel lines and bombs discarded when the second strike at Midway had been abandoned. At 10.22 am on 4 June, Nagumo was commanding an unscathed fleet, triumphant after beating off no less than five separate air attacks from the Midway-based bombers, then adding the scalps of the TBDs. Six minutes later *Akagi*, *Kaga* and *Soryu* were wrapped in flame and erupting with repeated explosions, wrecked

Japanese 'Kate' torpedo-bombers swarming round *Yorktown* on 4 June 1942

beyond saving by the plunging SBDs. Partial revenge for the holocaust was exacted by *Hiryu*, which survived untouched for 6½ hours. Two successive strikes by *Hiryu*'s aircraft crippled *Yorktown* and forced her crew to abandon ship, before aircraft from *Enterprise* and *Yorktown* found *Hiryu* and completed the annihilation of Nagumo's crack carrier force.

On abandoning *Yorktown*, Fletcher wisely passed tactical command to Spruance in *Enterprise*. Spruance thereby became the man who could, despite the liquidation of four enemy carriers, still have lost the Battle of Midway – and the Pacific War. This was, remember, his first battle as a carrier task force commander. On the morning of the 4th his acceptance of advice from Captain Browning, the chief-of-staff inherited from Halsey, had launched the all-important first strike at the Japanese two hours earlier than he, Spruance, had originally planned. Now, with the last Japanese carrier out of the fight, Spruance overrode the pleas of his 'Halseyite' staff officers for an all-out pursuit of the Japanese. The overwhelming Japanese strength in battleships and cruisers was still untouched and he had no intention of running blindly into a night action in which all the tactical cards would be held by the Japanese. Spruance won the battle when he prudently withdrew on the night of 4-5 June, returning the following morning to cover Midway or attack the Japanese fleet as need might require. In so doing he almost certainly spared his fleet a night gunnery action which it had little chance of winning. For his part Yamamoto, calling off the occupation of Midway at 02.55 hrs on 5 June, had come to grief because of the consistent refusal of the American

Yorktown sags in the water after the Japanese dive-bomber attack at Midway which inflicted mortal damage to her furnace air-uptakes and prompted the first 'abandon ship'

Right: Damage-control crewmen struggle for a foothold on *Yorktown*'s listing flight-deck
Below: Midway tailpiece – the battered hulk of the Japanese heavy cruiser *Mikuma*, finally sunk by strike aircraft from *Enterprise* on 6 June 1942

carrier admirals to do what he had expected them to do.

Fate handed both victors and vanquished a bitter postscript to the battle. The Japanese heavy cruisers *Mikuma* and *Mogami*, peremptorily recalled from a planned bombardment of Midway, collided with each other. As they limped away to the west, bereft of friendly air cover, the exultant American carrier planes struck and sank *Mikuma; Mogami* barely escaped. Far more poignant was the case of *Yorktown*, abandoned after *Hiryu*'s attacks and left to drift throughout 5 June. *Yorktown* was still afloat on the 6th, when American repair parties boarded her and began the long task of nursing her back to Pearl Harbor under tow. This would surely have been accomplished without the prowess of Lt-Commander Tanabe of the Japanese submarine *I-168*. In one of the classic submarine attacks of the war, Tanabe gave *Yorktown* her death blow with a final pair of torpedoes. A third blew in half the destroyer *Hamman*, secured alongside *Yorktown* to supply power for the repair crews. *Yorktown* and *Hamman* were the only American ships lost at Midway: one fleet carrier and a destroyer, plus 147 aircraft and 307 dead. Japanese losses amounted to four fleet carriers, one heavy cruiser, 332 aircraft and 3,500 dead.

This time there could be no haggling over the technicalities of winning and losing, as after Coral Sea. Midway was a shattering defeat for Japan – her first at sea in 350 years. It was the first of the great 'turning-point' battles of 1942-43, soon to be followed by Alamein, Stalingrad and Guadalcanal. And the essence of the battle was Japan's instantaneous loss of supremacy in fleet carriers. It gave the US Pacific Fleet carrier parity even before the great machine of American war production

Right: Japanese 'Betty' bombers streak in for a low-level daylight attack on the American transports swarming off the Guadalcanal beaches

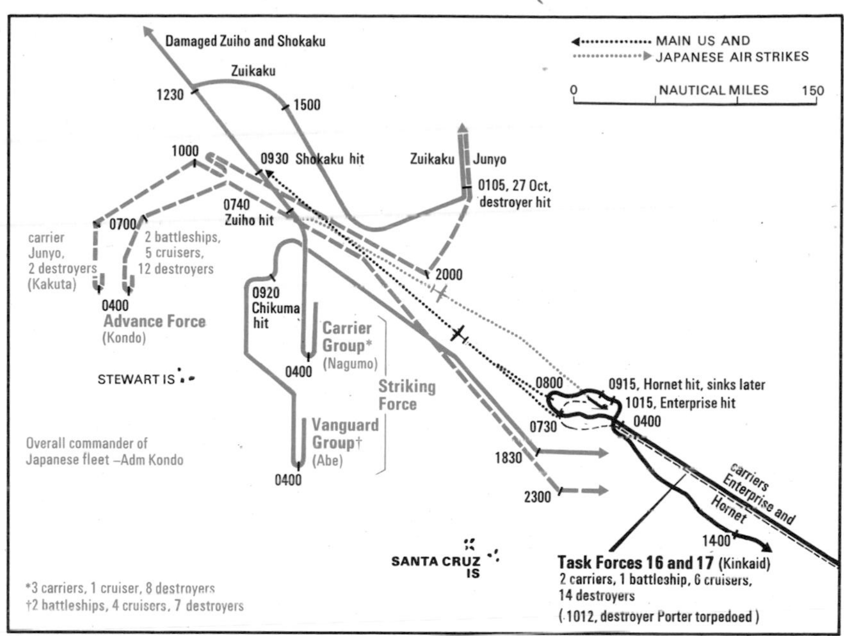

had fairly begun to roll. But the undoubted high drama of Midway was rapidly followed by the long attrition-battle of Guadalcanal (August 1942-February 1943), the most demanding land/sea/air battle of the war. And the key to understanding Guadalcanal is that it was a battle of trained manpower and *matériel* – the type of battle which the Japanese, for all the losses and human agony they might inflict, were bound to lose in the long run.

The US Marines landed on Guadalcanal (7 August 1942) because the Japanese were building a large airfield there, clearly destined for what might have been a decisive southeasterly shift of Japanese air power from Rabaul. Having taken the first trick and lodged the Marines on Guadalcanal, halfway between the Japanese base at Rabaul and the Allied base at Nouméa, the US South Pacific Command dared not keep the fleet in close support, in the confined waters of the Solomons Islands chain. This left the Japanese free to land their own troops to recover Guadalcanal, blissfully unaware that there were already 17,000 US Marines on the island against the bare 3,000 Japanese who could be spared from the parallel battle raging in New Guinea. The first Japanese troops landed on Guadalcanal on 17-18 August – and for the next 3½ months the Pacific War turned on whether the Japanese, supreme at night fighting despite American radar, could run in enough reinforcements and supplies by night to offset the American reinforcements and supplies by day.

The land battle was focussed on the airfield (named 'Henderson Field' after the Marine Corps major who died leading the first Midway-based air attacks on Nagumo's fleet on 4 June). The Japanese threw in successive reckless attempts to capture Henderson Field, while Yamamoto's Combined Fleet waited to fly in fighters the moment the field was in Japanese hands. Japanese strategy included the use of warship bombardment to render Henderson Field unusable by the Marines, who were naturally dependent on replacement fighters flown in from the American carriers. Hoping to succeed in this new naval confrontation where he had failed at Midway, Yamamoto moved the Combined Fleet down to Truk and watched for a decisive engagement. For a while, due to one-sided losses inflicted by submarines, the attrition in carriers ran against the US Navy and carried the Japanese to the brink of victory on Guadalcanal – until the nightly losses of the cruiser/destroyer 'Tokyo Express' proved decisive. And the indecisive carrier engagements of the Eastern Solomons (24 August) and Santa Cruz (25-26 October) merely served to keep the crucible of the land battle on the boil. They certainly did not – as they could have done – provide Yamamoto with revenge for the humiliation of Midway.

The Eastern Solomons fight of 24 August was a real stand-off. Fletcher, with *Saratoga*, *Enterprise* and *Wasp*, became the first carrier admiral to have the benefit of the AA firepower of a modern battleship: *North Carolina*, with twenty 5-inch, sixteen 1.1-inch, forty 20-mm and twenty-six 0.5-inch machine-guns. Fletcher was up against his old opponents of the Coral Sea: *Shokaku* and *Zuikaku*, plus the seaplane carrier *Chitose* and with the light carrier *Ryujo* pushed forward as a 'sacrificial goat'. Fletcher was not favoured by a return of the luck he had enjoyed at Midway. Having prematurely detached *Wasp* to refuel, he then launched a strike at *Ryujo* before *Shokaku* and *Zuikaku* had been located; attempts to switch the attack to *Shokaku* and *Zuikaku* failed because of bad atmospherics. Like *Shoho* at the Coral Sea, *Ryujo* was overwhelmed and sunk; *Chitose* was damaged – but despite the 'stack' of fighters held back by Fletcher and the prodigious AA umbrella thrown up by *North Carolina*, *Enterprise* suffered three bomb hits. Well 'buttoned up' as she was, with all fuel drained below and fuel hoses filled with carbon dioxide, she was operating aircraft from a patched-up flight-deck within the hour, but after the battle petered out there was nothing for it but emergency repairs at Pearl Harbor. *Hornet* was despatched to the South Pacific in exchange.

Three weeks after the Eastern Solomons, *Hornet* was the only operational carrier in the Guadalcanal area. *Saratoga* was again crippled by submarine attack on 31 August and on 15 September *Wasp* blazed to spectacular destruction after taking three torpedoes from *I-19*. In the same attack *I-15*, narrowly missing *Hornet*, crippled *North Carolina* instead. On the nights of 13 and 14 October, Henderson Field was neutralised by the pulverising fire of 14-inch gun battleships and 8-inch gun cruisers. By nightfall on the 15th, before the Japanese cruisers returned to hammer the airfield again, 4,500 Japanese troops had been landed with impunity and the overall Japanese strength on Guadalcanal raised to within 1,000 of the American. This was the nadir of American fortunes on Guadalcanal, with supplies for the hard-pressed Marines reduced to a trickle and even daylight command of the sea apparently lost to the Japanese. But Halsey was appointed South Pacific C-in-C on 18 October; the hastily-repaired *Enterprise* was rushed south to rejoin *Hornet*, and under Halsey's aggressive standing order of 'ATTACK REPEAT ATTACK' Rear-Admiral Thomas C. Kinkaid moved out to bring on the Battle of the Santa Cruz Islands (25-26 October 1942).

Santa Cruz was the only carrier action in which the stronger side – in this case the Japanese, after the loss of *Wasp* and crippling of *Saratoga* – was *not* primarily seeking a decisive battle. Never since Pearl Harbor had the Japanese fleet found itself so hamstrung by a land battle. The Japanese carriers at Santa Cruz had put to sea with one overriding mission: to give General Hyakutake's soldiers an

Last minutes of USS *Hornet*, ravaged by 'Val' dive-bombing attacks in the battle of Santa Cruz (26 October 1942)

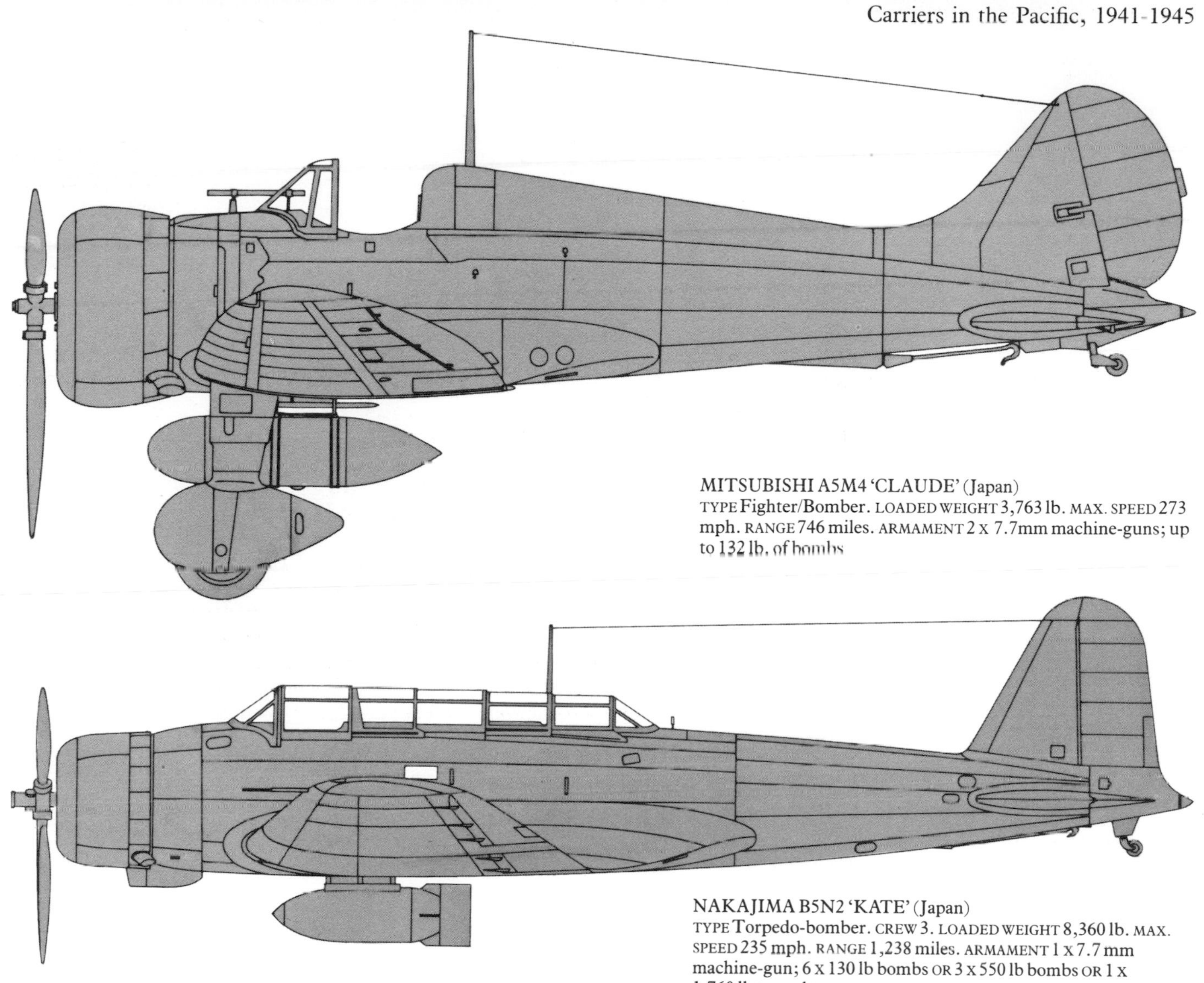

MITSUBISHI A5M4 'CLAUDE' (Japan)
TYPE Fighter/Bomber. LOADED WEIGHT 3,763 lb. MAX. SPEED 273 mph. RANGE 746 miles. ARMAMENT 2 x 7.7mm machine-guns; up to 132 lb. of bombs

NAKAJIMA B5N2 'KATE' (Japan)
TYPE Torpedo-bomber. CREW 3. LOADED WEIGHT 8,360 lb. MAX. SPEED 235 mph. RANGE 1,238 miles. ARMAMENT 1 x 7.7 mm machine-gun; 6 x 130 lb bombs OR 3 x 550 lb bombs OR 1 x 1,760 lb torpedo.

instant air force, flying-off their aircraft to operate from Henderson Field the moment the latter had been wrested from the Americans. Admiral Kondo's fleet had been hovering in the wings, vainly awaiting the fall of the airfield, for four days before Kinkaid attacked on the 26th. To oppose *Hornet* and *Enterprise*, Kondo had four carriers: *Shokaku* and *Zuikaku*, the light carrier *Zuiho* and the new *Junyo* (a 24,150-ton conversion from a luxury liner). Yet even after the bitter experience of the Aleutians/Midway deployment in June, the Japanese fleet was still operated as a loose bundle of separate groups. *Junyo* was detached to operate away from Nagumo's striking force, which was thus deprived of the crushing superiority it could have had.

At Santa Cruz tactical victory again went to the Japanese, who sank the *Hornet* and sent *Enterprise* back to Nouméa for more repairs. Kinkaid's aircrews had done no more than inflict heavy damage on *Zuiho* and *Shokaku*; he had no option but withdrawal after the action. But this was a battle where victory or defeat was measured in aircraft, not ships – and the air fighting of the 26th was crippling to the Japanese carrier arm. On top of the 90 Japanese aircraft lost at the Eastern Solomons, Santa Cruz clawed down another 100. Though the Marines on Guadalcanal were now temporarily deprived of any carrier support at all, the Japanese only had about 100 aircraft to divide between *Hiyo* and *Junyo*. As the US Marines held on to Henderson Field, and as the American air strength operating from Henderson was equal to the combined air strength of the only two operational Japanese carriers left, it was stalemate.

By the end of October 1942 the rival carrier navies in the Pacific had fought each other to a standstill. The desperate sea battles of November 1942, in which the US Navy finally wrested control of the approaches to Guadalcanal from the 'Tokyo Express', were night surface gunnery and torpedo clashes. In these actions the only role for carrier aircraft was to pick off the cripples with the coming of daylight. Attacks of this nature sealed the fate of the first Japanese battleship lost in the war:

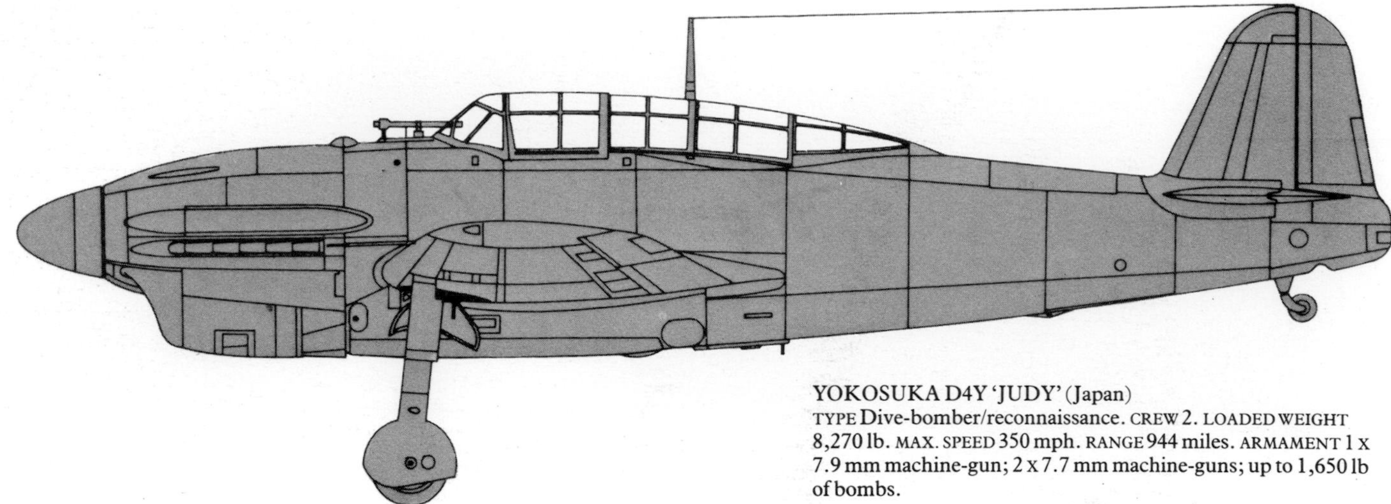

YOKOSUKA D4Y 'JUDY' (Japan)
TYPE Dive-bomber/reconnaissance. CREW 2. LOADED WEIGHT 8,270 lb. MAX. SPEED 350 mph. RANGE 944 miles. ARMAMENT 1 x 7.9 mm machine-gun; 2 x 7.7 mm machine-guns; up to 1,650 lb of bombs.

Hiei, abandoned and scuttled after attacks from Henderson Field and *Enterprise* on 13 November.

The Solomons remained the centre of Pacific operations after the eventual Japanese withdrawal from the island in February 1943. Covered at every step by the massive airfield complex built up at Henderson Field, the Americans advanced doggedly up the island chain. Neither carriers nor battleships played any part in the fierce but sporadic sea fighting during the Solomons campaign, which ended with the American landings on Bougainville at the beginning of November 1943. For the Japanese as for the US Navy, 1943 was a year for recovery and replenishment after the losses of May-November 1942. Prowess in combat now yielded second place to industrial production – a contest in which, as Admiral Yamamoto had always warned, Japan was a non-starter. In 1943, for example, her steel production (2 million tons short of target) came to no more than 7.8 million tons; American steel production for 1943 was 90 million tons. By the first anniversary of Midway, American yards had already completed four 'Essex' class fleet carriers and five 'Independence' class light carriers to replace *Lexington*, *Yorktown*, *Wasp* and *Hornet*. Seven converted escort carriers were already serving in the Pacific and

American light fleet carrier *Independence* leaving San Francisco, July 1943

Casablanca, first of the mass-produced American escort carriers (1943), which turned the tide in both the Atlantic and Pacific theatres

were due to be joined by the four 'Sangamons' from the Mediterranean. On top of all this, the first homogeneous escort carrier design was already in mass production in the Kaiser yards, birthplace of the freight-carrying 'Liberty Ships' whose mass production had done so much to beat the U-boats in the Atlantic. The first five of these new escort carriers, the 7,800-ton 'Casablanca' class, had already been launched, and another 20 had followed by the end of the year.

In dismal contrast, Japan had lost six carriers in 1942 to the US Navy's four. Six 17,150-ton 'Unryu' class carriers, intended to carry a maximum of 65 aircraft, were laid down in 1942-43 – but only two had been launched by the end of 1943, and none had been completed before the destruction of the Japanese fleet air arm in June 1944. The 29,000 *Taiho* was the only homogeneous Japanese fleet carrier built during the war to see action. Launched in April 1943 after a lagging 20 months on the stocks, *Taiho* was not completed until March 1944. After Midway the hull of the third 'Yamato' class super-battleship, *Shinano*, was taken in hand for completion as a maintenance carrier; but *Shinano* was not completed until November 1944. The only other Japanese carriers completed by the end of 1943 were conversions, not one of which could even carry the 45 aircraft boasted by the lightweight American 'Independence' class, let alone the 100 aircraft carried by the 'Essex' class. These were *Chuyo* and *Unyo* (27 aircraft); *Ryuho* (31 aircraft); *Chitose* and *Chiyoda* (converted from seaplane-carriers to carry 30 aircraft each); *Kaiyo* (24 aircraft); and *Shinyo* (33 aircraft). By the end of 1943, therefore, Japan was hopelessly outmatched both in carrier construction and in the carrying capacity of the ships actually completed. Japanese aircraft production was outstripped five-fold by the Americans in 1943, and this disadvantage was qualitative as well as quantitative. Against the new American Lightning, Hellcat and Corsair fighters only an expert could hold his own in the once-invincible Zero – and after the losses of 1942 the supply of such experts was fast running out. Saburo Sakai, one of the most prominent Zero aces, records that in December 1941 he had gone to war in a fighter wing 150 strong, of which, by the end of January 1943, less than 20 were still alive.

All these deficiencies meant that the Japanese 'First Mobile Fleet', as reorganised for the defence of the Central Pacific in summer 1944, had more carriers but was actually weaker in aircraft than the Carrier Striking Force which had hit Pearl Harbor in

December 1941. The six Pearl Harbor carriers had mustered 450 aircraft between them; the nine Mobile Fleet carriers of June 1944 could put up only 432. A telling symptom of the Japanese carrier starvation was the conversion of the batleships *Ise* and *Hyuga* as battleship-carriers, the aft two 14-inch turrets being removed and a flying-off deck built to operate bomber seaplanes. These hybrids have justly been condemned as classic examples of the Japanese reaction to modern lessons by harking back to the First World War; the seaplanes were to be hoisted back aboard by crane after landing alongside. Given anything the Americans had in 1944-45, *Ise* and *Hyuga* were a bad joke. Yet they are overdue for analysis in the light of post-war developments, as another example of Japanese far-sightedness in naval aviation. *Ise* and *Hyuga* were the first recognisable attempt at the blend of surface-to-surface fire-power with the potential of a small air group, as finally achieved 24 years later in the Soviet Navy in the era of the helicopter and V/STOL aircraft (see p. 177).
Another experimental innovation in *Ise* and *Hyuga* was an admittedly primitive battery of 180 rocket missile launchers for use against aircraft, the missiles being tipped with phosphorus and fitted with trailing wires. Though hardly more successful than the abortive British experiments with AA rocketry in 1940-41, here again was a genuine anticipation of modern practice: an attempt at a complete system of shipboard surface-to-air missiles for AA defence.

Above left: American fighter mainstay of the Pacific War's decisive months: the superb Grumman F-4F Wildcat
Below left: Curtiss SB2C Helldiver dive-bombers
Above: Superb all-rounder – Chance Vought F4U-1D Corsair fighter/strike aircraft aboard USS *Bunker Hill*, 1944

Frantic Japanese expedient after excessive carrier losses: the battleship *Ise*, with her after-turrets removed to create an improvised flight-deck

None of this was of any practical avail to the Japanese Mobile Fleet. In overwhelming contrast Admiral Spruance's US 5th Fleet operated 15 carriers by June 1944, grouped as 'Task Force 58' under Vice-Admiral Marc Mitscher. TF.58 was itself made up of four carrier task groups (three of four carriers, one of three), plus a battle group of seven new battleships all completed or launched since Pearl Harbor. The beauty of the task group structure was its flexibility; the groups could be detached to carry out individual missions as well as serving together in invincible strength. Together, the carriers of TF.58 could put up 900 aircraft – and that was without the 5th Fleet's expeditionary force, Task Force 51, protected by 12 escort carriers operating over 300 aircraft. To go with more and better carriers went improved communications and control systems – longer-ranged radars, crisper radio links to avoid the fumble and confusion so prevalent in 1942. In short the US 5th Fleet was poised to give the Japanese Navy its first object-lesson in how overwhelming naval strength, with carrier versatility as its cutting-edge, should be used.

Though grossly under-estimating the odds against them, the Japanese naval planners accepted that they had no chance in a straight carrier-versus-carrier engagement. They never intended to fight one, but persisted in the delusion that the Americans could be lured into a suitable killing area between the hammer of the Japanese Mobile Fleet and the anvil of Japanese shore-based attacks. This was the 'A-GO' plan, intended to reverse American carrier supremacy as Japanese carrier supremacy had been reversed two years before. Admiral Toyoda had replaced Yamamoto after the latter's death in ambush by fighters from Guadalcanal in April 1943. It was on Toyoda's order that 'A-GO' was set in motion when the Americans landed on Saipan in the Marianas on 15 June 1944. Admiral Ozawa accordingly led the Mobile Fleet eastward across the Philippine Sea, confident that the land-based aircraft in the Marianas (on Saipan, Tinian, Rota and Guam) were already at work whittling the American carrier forces down to size. According to the 'A-GO' plan, these initial land-based attacks were supposed to inflict one-third casualties at the very least, enabling the Mobile Fleet to force a battle on even terms.

Never was wishful thinking more brutally punished. By the time Ozawa put to sea on the 15th, American air supremacy over Saipan and Guam had been secure for 48 hours. Japan's air strength in the Marianas had been so reduced that Spruance confidently de-

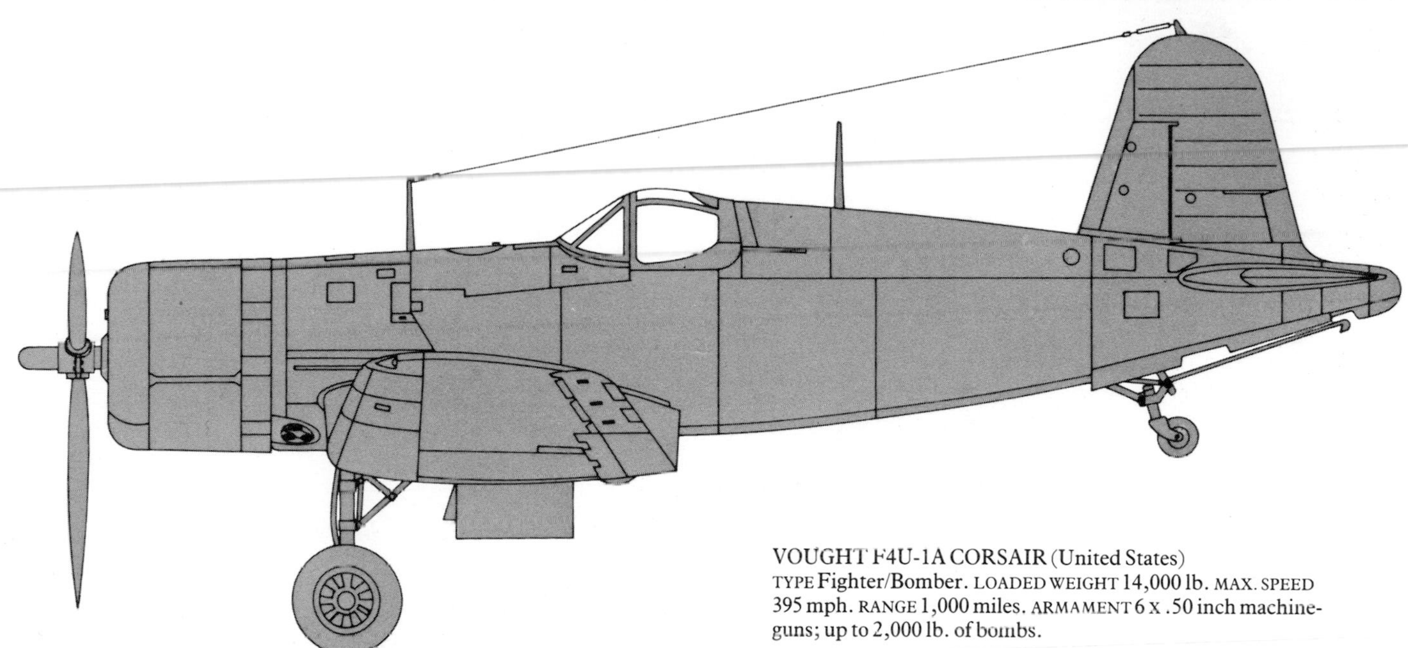

VOUGHT F4U-1A CORSAIR (United States)
TYPE Fighter/Bomber. LOADED WEIGHT 14,000 lb. MAX. SPEED 395 mph. RANGE 1,000 miles. ARMAMENT 6 x .50 inch machine-guns; up to 2,000 lb. of bombs.

tached half the carrier task groups of TF.58 to bombard Iwo Jima and Chichi Jima, 650 miles to the north. This effectively prevented Iwo from being used as an air staging-post for Japanese aircraft attempting to reinforce the Marianas from the home islands. While Iwo was being bombarded, American submarines alerted Spruance to the approach of the Japanese fleet. Spruance coolly permitted the bombardment of Iwo to go ahead, ordering the two task groups to return for a rendezvous with the rest of the fleet 180 miles west of Tinian on the 18th. Ozawa found himself with only one lucky card: the superior range of the Japanese scout planes, which located the 5th Fleet before Spruance had received any up-dated intelligence on the Japanese position. If he headed too far west in his search for Ozawa, Spruance knew that there would be a good chance of the smaller Japanese fleet ducking past the 5th Fleet and savaging the swarming transports lying off the Saipan beaches. Taking as his prime objective the safeguarding of the Saipan beach-head and invasion fleet, Spruance therefore stood firmly on the de-fensive between Saipan and the oncoming enemy, refusing to dissipate the overwhelm-ing fighter strength of Mitscher's carriers in vain sweeps over empty ocean.

The result was the virtual destruction of the Japanese Naval Air Force in the Battle of the Philippine Sea (19-20 June 1944), which the Americans sardonically called the 'Great Marianas Turkey Shoot'. Well they might. Ozawa's carrier strikes headed straight into the mincing-machine, being overwhelmed by the massed fighters waiting for them. The 'hammer-and-anvil' strategy of 'A-GO' never stood a chance: the 5th Fleet pre-invasion bombardments and sustained fighter domina-tion during 19-20 June meant that Japanese shore-base aircraft in the Marianas (Guam and Rota) never rose above 50. It was a field day for the American fighters. Total Japanese aircraft losses on the 19th were about 315 – out of the 373 launched by the Japanese carriers during the day – against a total American aircraft loss of 29. Apart from a torpedo aircraft crashing into the battleship *Indiana* (without the torpedo exploding) and splinter damage from near-misses alongside *Belleau Wood* and *Wasp*, Spruance's carrier armada escaped untouched. Still Ozawa refused to give up,

Left: The 'Great Marianas Turkey Shoot' – a Japanese aircraft plunges into the sea during the unavailing assault on Spruance's 5th Fleet in the Battle of the Philippine Sea

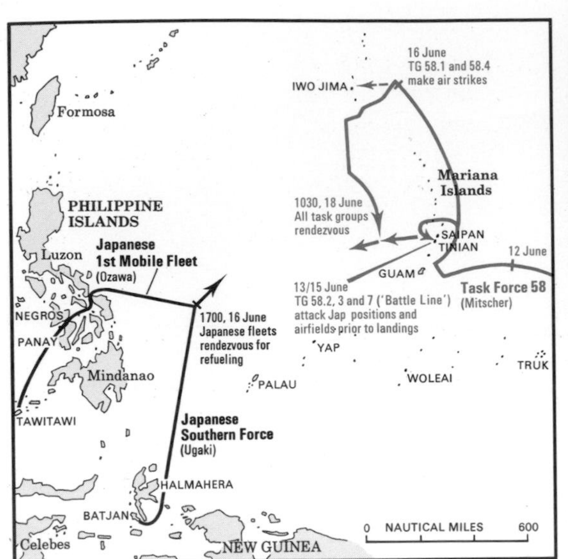

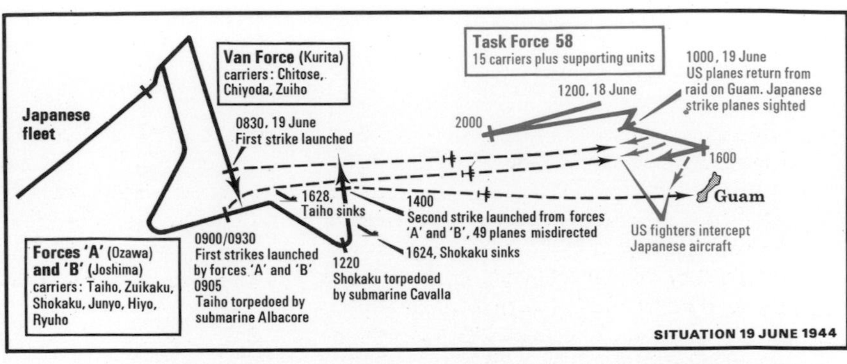

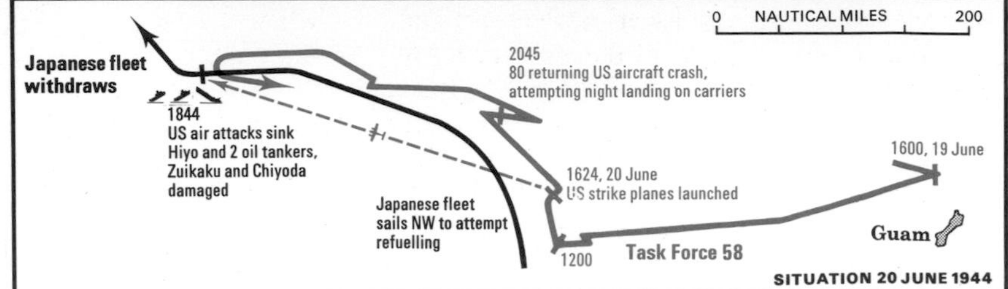

hoping that the land-based strike units – from which he had heard nothing – had fulfilled their role in the 'A-GO' plan and inflicted commensurate loss on the American carrier planes. He began on the 20th with 100 serviceable Japanese aircraft but by the end of the day, with only 35 aircraft remaining to the entire Mobile Fleet, even Ozawa accepted that there was nothing for it but withdrawal.

Ozawa's tenacity was all the more remarkable because of the disasters which had befallen the precious Japanese fleet carriers on the 19th. As *Taiho* (Ozawa's flagship) was launching her first strike wave, the American submarine *Albacore* fired six torpedoes at her. One was detonated by the heroism of Sakio Komatsu, a pilot from *Taiho* who had just taken off; spotting the incoming torpedo, Komatsu dived on it and blew himself up along with the missile. This did not save *Taiho* from a single torpedo hit which, while permitting flight operations to continue, started a deadly leak of fuel fumes. Four hours later *Shokaku* was torpedoed by another submarine, *Cavalla*; after a three-hour death agony featuring the familiar cycle of explosions, spreading fumes and more explosions, *Shokaku* sank an hour before *Taiho* erupted in flame. Since the explosion of *Albacore*'s torpedo the fumes had continued to spread; an ill-judged decision to ventilate the ship merely spread the fumes from one end of *Taiho* to the other. The resultant inevitable explosion lifted the flight-deck and ripped the hull sides and bottom beyond salvation. Shortly after Ozawa shifted his flag to the cruiser *Haguro*, *Taiho* sank with immense loss of life: about 1,650 out of her complement of 2,150.

The heaviest American losses were suffered during Mitscher's attempt to destroy the Mobile Fleet late on the 20th. Escorted by 85 fighters, a total of 131 American strike aircraft came up with the Mobile Fleet as the sun was setting. Results were poor: only the carrier *Hiyo* was sunk, with *Zuikaku* and *Chiyoda*, the battleship *Haruna* and the cruiser *Maya* suffering varying degrees of damage. The most important fruit of the attack was the reduction of Ozawa's remaining aircraft strength by 65 for the loss of only 14 American aircraft. The American pilots then had a 300-mile flight 'home' and the ordeal of a night deck landing. Mitscher reduced the latter by ordering TF.58 to illuminate the flight-decks, regardless of the help this would be to any prowling Japanese submarine. Even with the lights no less than 80 aircraft were written off – some crashing, others going down in the sea as their fuel ran out – but expert rescue work cut the loss of aircrew life to 49.

The Philippine Sea battle was the last of the great carrier-versus-carrier engagements which had begun with the Coral Sea action of May 1942. Spruance's victory must be considered one of the least-flawed exploitations of naval aviation on record. The battle shows that provided a fleet is secure in the air it can not only go where it likes and hit whatever targets it likes: it can – in defiance of every lesson of naval warfare since Salamis – deliberately abandon the initiative to the enemy and *still* win a crushing victory. In the aftermath of the Philippine Sea battle, however, it was far from obvious on the American side that a crushing victory had been won. It was many months before the true value of Japan's air losses, rather than warship losses, became apparent; before this awareness dawned it was easy to criticise Spruance for having let a mauled but helpless enemy escape. Such criticisms were voiced especially by admirers of the aggressive Halsey, who had yet to command in a fleet action. He was soon to get his chance – with near-disastrous results.

After the conquest of the Marianas command of the Pacific Fleet passed in rotation from Spruance to Halsey, each commanding for a specific operation before handing over to the other. On being relieved, each admiral withdrew to Pearl Harbor with his staff to plan the next operation. The ships and task forces at sea remained the same, with only a change of number, from '5th Fleet' under Spruance to '3rd Fleet' under Halsey. Similarly, Mitscher's carrier task force, 'TF. 58' when under Spruance, became 'TF.38' under Halsey. It therefore fell to Halsey to command 3rd Fleet during the next major Pacific advance after the Marianas: the invasion of Leyte in the Philippines in October 1944. This would be carried out by the US 6th Army, landed and provided with close cover by the 17 escort carriers and powerful battleship/cruiser force of Admiral Thomas C. Kinkaid's 7th Fleet. The main task of Halsey and the 3rd Fleet, while helping the Army Air Force beat down the formidable Japanese air strength in the Philippines, was to crush any attempt by the Japanese surface fleet to intervene.

After the loss of the Marianas the Japanese High Command knew that failure to retain the Philippines would cut the Japanese Empire in two; and the need to fight an all-or-nothing battle produced an all-or-nothing plan. With only four Japanese carriers seaworthy, able to put up 52 fighters and 64 strike aircraft between them, there was no question of a viable role for Ozawa's carrier force, as on the eve of the Philippine Sea battle. On the other hand, the mere *presence* of the Japanese carriers was correctly estimated as a bait which no

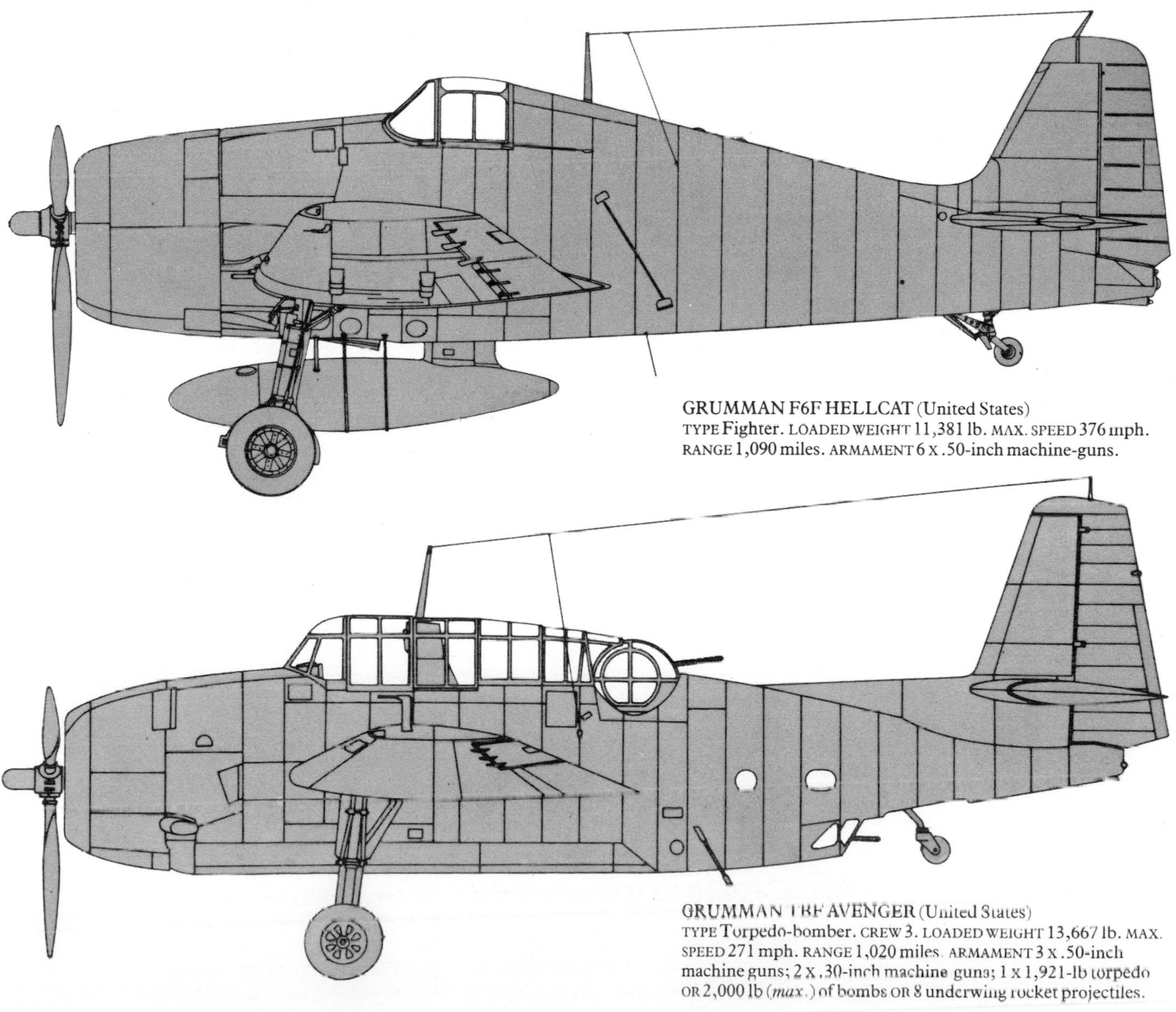

GRUMMAN F6F HELLCAT (United States)
TYPE Fighter. LOADED WEIGHT 11,381 lb. MAX. SPEED 376 mph. RANGE 1,090 miles. ARMAMENT 6 x .50-inch machine-guns.

GRUMMAN TBF AVENGER (United States)
TYPE Torpedo-bomber. CREW 3. LOADED WEIGHT 13,667 lb. MAX. SPEED 271 mph. RANGE 1,020 miles. ARMAMENT 3 x .50-inch machine guns; 2 x .30-inch machine guns; 1 x 1,921-lb torpedo OR 2,000 lb (*max.*) of bombs OR 8 underwing rocket projectiles.

American admiral could ignore. In 'SHO-GO', the plan to crush the Americans in their beach-head on Leyte, Ozawa's carriers were to approach from the north and lure away the American fast carrier task force. While Ozawa was taking as long as possible in getting sunk, as he was bound to be, two Japanese battle squadrons would approach from the south-west, thread the narrow straits through the central Philippine archipelago, and finally converge on Leyte Gulf in overwhelming strength. Meanwhile Japanese land-based aircraft in the Philippines would add to the attrition of the American task forces operating offshore.

The obvious objections to 'SHO-GO' (after, that is, the sacrificial nature of the whole venture had been accepted and set aside) were that even if the Americans did fall for Ozawa's decoy they still had abundant strength to eliminate him *and* block the approach of the battle groups to the south; that the latter were unlikely to get anywhere near Leyte Gulf without being detected and attacked from the air; and that if the Marianas experience was anything to go by, the contribution of the land-based aircraft was hardly likely to be decisive. All these objections were proved perfectly sound by the course of events. And yet 'SHO-GO' came within an ace of inflicting a crushing tactical defeat on the Americans. If Spruance in the Philippine Sea action demonstrated how air/naval superiority should be exploited with maximum economy, Halsey in the three-day Battle of Leyte Gulf (23-25 October 1944) showed that such superiority can be diverted and dissipated only with maximum risk.

Down to 20.00 hrs on 24 October, everything seemed to be going Halsey's way. Task Force 38 had opened the Leyte campaign on 10 October with the first of a breathtakingly ambitious series of attacks on the Japanese air bases able to reinforce the Philippines. Okinawa was hit on the 10th, Aparri (northern Luzon) on the 11th; the airfields of Formosa from the 12th to the 14th. By the 16th, the combined Japanese air strength in the Philippines and Formosa had been reduced to under 200 machines, and the Luzon airfields continued to be hammered down to the 19th – the day before the Leyte landings went in. Meanwhile, Admiral Toyoda had issued the 'SHO-GO' executive order on 18 October and by the 23rd the two battle squadrons had begun the penetration of the Philippine archipelago via the Sibuyan and Sulu Seas. As in the Philippine Sea action, first blood went to the American submarines, with USS *Darter* and *Dace* sinking the cruisers *Atago* and *Maya* on the morning of the 23rd.

Halsey had sent one carrier group from TF.38 away to refuel; he now recalled it, and moved the other three groups further west to search for the oncoming Japanese forces. This exposed them to heavy air attacks from the Luzon airfields on the morning of the 24th. All were beaten off without loss, bar one – a lone dive-bomber which landed a 55-lb bomb fair and square on the flight-deck of the 'Independence' class light carrier *Princeton*. Exploding on the hangar deck, the bomb created an inferno of blazing aviation fuel which devoured six TBF Avengers armed with torpedoes, all of which exploded in turn. The cruiser *Birmingham* came to *Princeton*'s aid only to suffer terribly when *Princeton*'s bomb store exploded – 233 men killed outright and over 400 wounded. Finally abandoned and sunk by torpedoes, *Princeton* was the first American carrier lost since *Hornet* at Santa Cruz two years before.

The *Princeton* tragedy was, however, offset by the sinking of the 'Yamato' class super-battleship *Musashi* in the Sibuyan Sea. Nothing testifies more to the immense strength of these mighty ships than the fact that it took no less than four carriers to sink her, with a total of 18 torpedoes; and that she still took some seven hours to go down. Other hits were claimed on the four other battleships and eight cruisers doggedly advancing towards San Bernadino Strait through the Sibuyan Sea. There could be no denying its strength, and Halsey concentrated the battleships and cruisers of TF.38 to form 'Task Force 34', under Admiral Lee. Half an hour after taking this precaution, however, Ozawa's decoy force was finally sighted away to the north. Halsey thereupon chose to regard Ozawa's carriers as his main objective, as the 'SHO' plan intended he should. Halsey cannot be blamed for not knowing that the Japanese carriers were a paper tiger, and for wishing to annihilate them in overwhelming force. But he was to blame for not leaving the battleships and cruisers of Task Force 34, covered as they could have been by a single carrier task group, to block San Bernadino Strait. This elementary precaution seemed so obvious that Admiral Kinkaid of 7th Fleet did not confirm TF.34's whereabouts when Halsey set off in pursuit of Ozawa at 20.00 hrs on the 24th.

Certainly the 7th Fleet had nothing to spare with which to guard its northern flank; all available battleships and cruisers were massed off the mouth of Surigao Strait, ready to engage the Japanese battleships spotted advancing on Leyte Gulf through the Sulu Sea. The resultant Battle of Surigao Strait in the early hours of 25 October 1944 was the last battle-

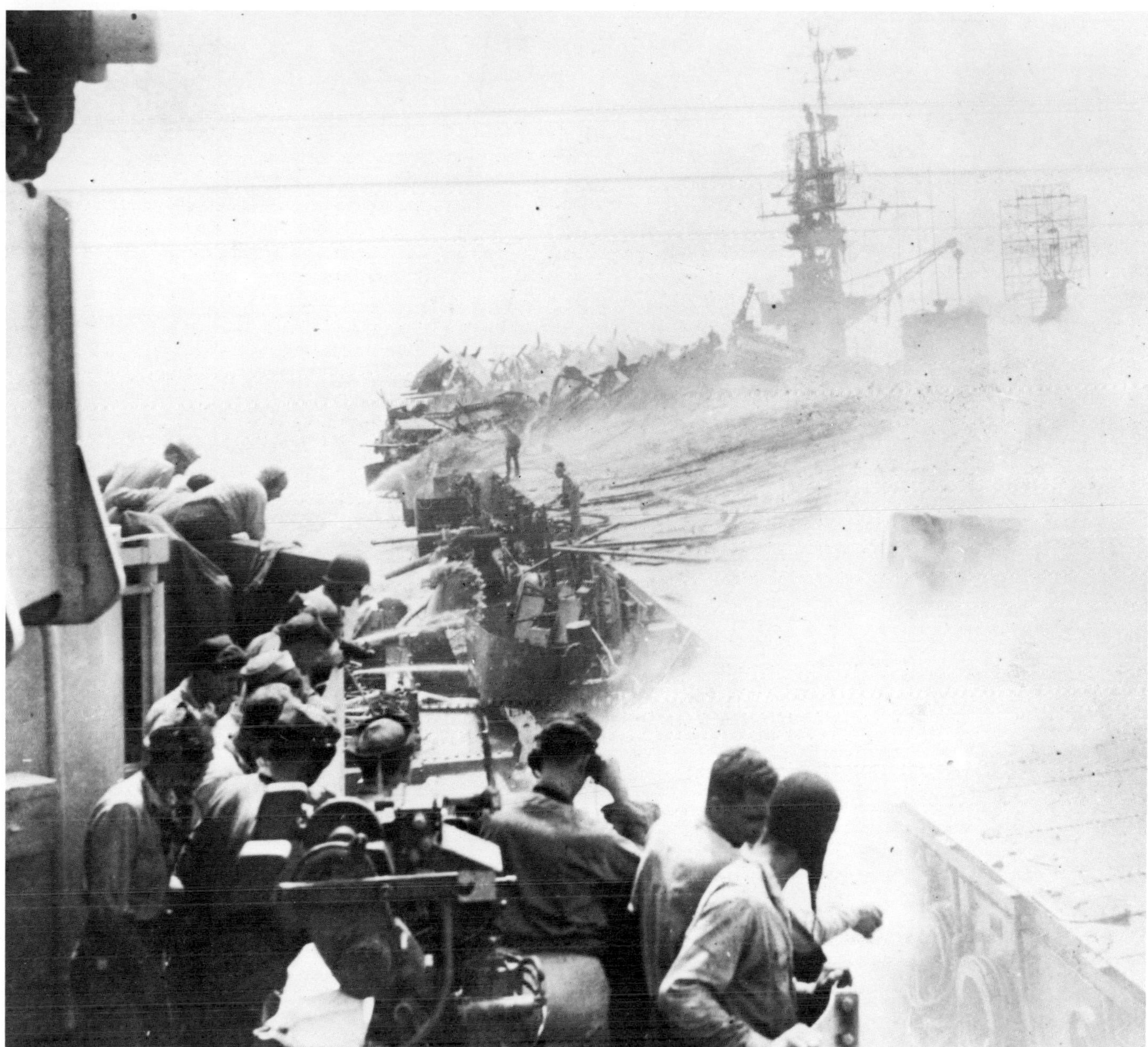

The blazing wreck of *Princeton*'s flight-deck, seen minutes before the final devastating explosion during the Battle of Leyte Gulf (25 October 1944)

ship-versus-battleship action, and a resounding victory for the Americans: it completely destroyed the southern prong of the 'SHO' assault on Leyte Gulf. Almost at once, however, at 07.00 hrs on the 25th, unbelievable news came from the north. Rear-Admiral Clifton Sprague, commanding the six escort carriers of Task Group 77.4's Unit 3, reported themselves as under enemy battleship fire. Because of his belief that Halsey had left TF.34 to screen 7th Fleet's northern flank, the 7th Fleet's commander now found himself helplessly presiding over imminent disaster. There was nothing to send to the immediate aid of Sprague's escort carriers. Halsey was too far to the north; the victors of Surigao Strait were too far to the south, and short of ammunition to boot. For only the second time in the war (the loss of *Glorious* to *Scharnhorst* and *Gneisenau* being the first) battleships had surprised and were attacking carriers.

That any of Sprague's carriers escaped was due, he claimed, 'to the definite partiality of Almighty God' – aided and abetted by the selfless devotion of Sprague's destroyer men, and the mistakes made by the enemy. Admiral Kurita, commanding the Japanese battle force, had been shaken when he sighted carrier silhouettes on the southern horizon instead of helpless transports. Instead of taking the time to deploy a methodical team attack, Kurita signalled a 'general chase' – a devil-take-the-hindmost scramble into action, with much involuntary obscuring of targets in the process. The built-in confusion of the Japanese pursuit was compounded by the gallantry of the seven destroyers screening the escort carriers. Torpedo attacks from Sprague's destroyers crippled the cruiser *Kumano* and forced the mighty *Yamato* to take

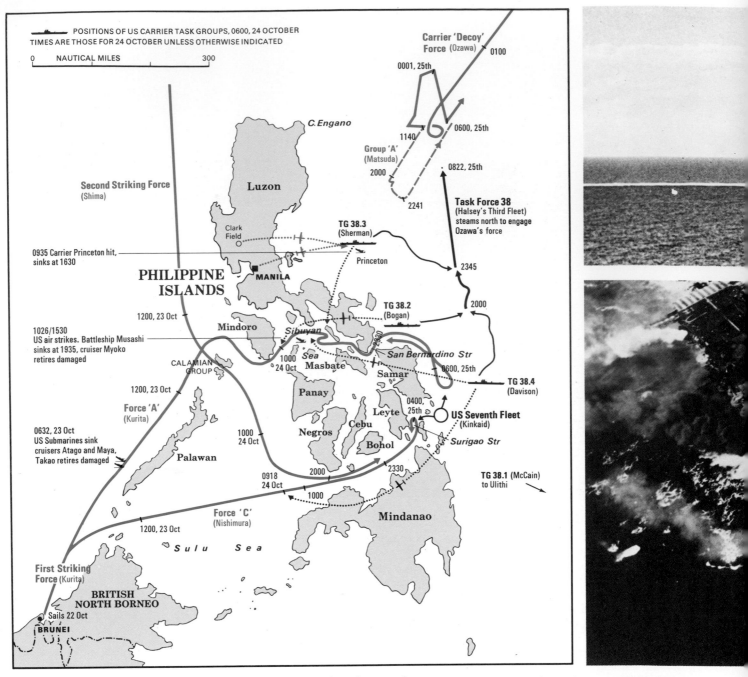

POSITIONS OF US CARRIER TASK GROUPS, 0600, 24 OCTOBER
TIMES ARE THOSE FOR 24 OCTOBER UNLESS OTHERWISE INDICATED
0 NAUTICAL MILES 300
Carrier 'Decoy' Force (Ozawa) 0100
0001, 25th
C. Engano
1140
0600, 25th
Group 'A' (Matsuda)
2000
0822, 25th
2241
Second Striking Force (Shima)
Luzon
Task Force 38 (Halsey's Third Fleet) steams north to engage Ozawa's force
Clark Field
TG 38.3 (Sherman)
0935 Carrier Princeton hit, sinks at 1630
Princeton
2345
PHILIPPINE ISLANDS
MANILA
2000
TG 38.2 (Bogan)
1200, 23 Oct
Mindoro
1026/1530 US air strikes. Battleship Musashi sinks at 1935, cruiser Myoko retires damaged
Sibuyan Sea
1000 24 Oct
San Bernardino Str
CALAMIAN GROUP
Masbate
0600, 25th
Samar
TG 38.4 (Davison)
1200, 23 Oct
Panay
0400, 25th
Force 'A' (Kurita)
Leyte
US Seventh Fleet (Kinkaid)
0632, 23 Oct US Submarines sink cruisers Atago and Maya, Takao retires damaged
1000 24 Oct
Negros
Cebu
Bohol
Surigao Str
Palawan
2000
2330
0918 24 Oct
TG 38.1 (McCain) to Ulithi
1000
Force 'C' (Nishimura)
Mindanao
1200, 23 Oct
Sulu Sea
First Striking Force (Kurita)
BRITISH NORTH BORNEO
Sails 22 Oct
BRUNEI

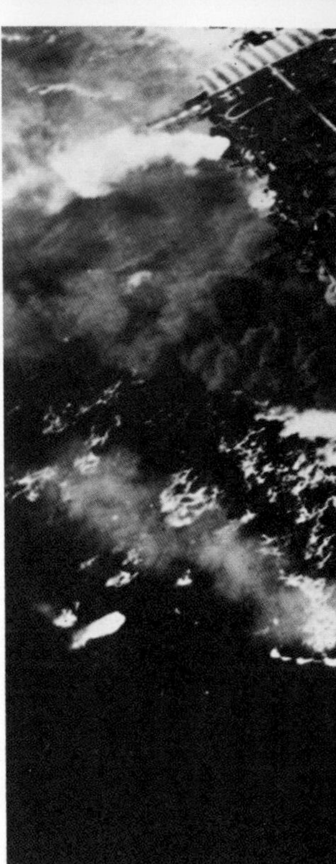

such violent evasive action that she ran clean out of the battle, gaining time for the little carriers to run east into wind and fly off all operational aircraft. This done, Sprague's force turned down wind and ran for it at its maximum speed of 17½ knots. In the ensuing two-hour running battle down the coast of Samar Japanese gunfire sank the rearmost escort carrier, *Gambier Bay*, with destroyers *Hoel*, *Johnston* and *Roberts*. Aircraft from the fleeing carriers, aided by Admiral Stump's Group 2 to the southward, disabled the cruisers *Chikuma*, *Chokai* and *Suzuya*, all of which were sunk. But by 09.00 the Japanese cruisers, with their 15-knot speed advantage, had remorselessly lowered the range. The latter was down to 10,000 yards and the foremost Japanese cruisers were actually passing the rearmost carriers when, at 09.15, Kurita suddenly ordered his force to withdraw to the north. The likeliest explanation for this premature retreat is the effect on Kurita – after the battering air attacks of the 24th – of sighting yet more flight-decks to the south (Stump's Unit 2).

Halsey meanwhile had persisted with his quest for Ozawa's carriers, despite the agonised pleas for assistance coming over the air from 7th Fleet. As far as the 3rd Fleet carriers were concerned there was little Halsey or Mitscher could do: their aircraft were already committed to the first sortie against Ozawa. To make matters worse, Ozawa's ships had been reported as being 120 miles closer to TF.38 than was actually the case, which spelled further delays. But Halsey

Left: The distinctive plume of smoke from a torpedo strike wreaths the Japanese heavy cruiser *Kumano* during the battle off Samar
Below left: Last view of *Zuiho*'s distinctive deck camouflage as, defenceless, she braves the American strike aircraft off Cape Engaño

could have detached TF.34, the battleship/cruiser force, as soon as Sprague raised the alarm. Instead he did not do so before Nimitz himself had testily interposed a blunt message from Pearl Harbor, demanding to know TF.34's whereabouts. When Halsey finally reversed his decision and detached TF.34, the latter set off too late to intercept Kurita and too soon to participate in the destruction of Ozawa. After the aircraft he had flown off to assist the land-based strikes at 3rd Fleet on the 24th, Ozawa had been left with no more than 19 Zero fighters. The massive 3rd Fleet carrier attacks on the 25th sank *Chitose*, *Chiyoda*, *Zuihaku* and *Zuiho*; *Ise* and *Hyuga*, the hybrid battleship-carriers, struggled back to Japan, to be sunk in port within four days of each other in July 1945.

This execution of the last Japanese carrier task force to put to sea was dignified as the 'Battle of Cape Engaño', from the nearest point of land (the north-eastern extremity of Luzon). The date of 25 October 1944 was not merely the last occasion when one carrier fleet attacked another, nor was the engagement and destruction of Ozawa's force the final act of the Leyte Gulf epic. Admiral Sprague's escort carriers were still recovering their aircraft after Kurita's providential retirement when they came under an entirely new form of attack: Zero fighters, armed with bombs, deliberately diving on selected targets. These were the *kamikaze* ('Divine Wind') special attack forces, so mistakenly described in Western phraseology as mere 'suicide attacks'. A Zero smashed clean through *St Lô*'s wooden flight-deck and exploded in the hangar, ripping the ship apart and sinking her in 30 minutes; *Kitkun Bay* and *Kalinin Bay* were narrowly clipped by near-misses. Though attacks of this nature appeared the height of insanity when measured by Western standards the word 'suicide', with its connotations of hopelessness and despair, hardly applies. A *kamikaze* pilot, affirms Saburo Sakai, had faith in his country, not despair: 'It was a cheap price to pay: one man, perhaps, against the lives of hundreds or even thousands . . . Every one of these men who gave up his life did not really die. He passed on life to those who remained.'

Descending from the metaphysical to the purely tactical level, suffice it to say that the *kamikazes* heralded the modern era of tactical naval warfare: the age of the missile. For that is how the *kamikaze* pilots thought of themselves: manned missiles, plunging down through the AA fire to select their victim's most vulnerable spot, and score a hit where a bomb would be more likely to miss. The 'Catch 22' of *kamikaze* tactics was that they came into being because the expert Japanese pilots were mostly dead. It was a bid to use unskilled pilot reserves to the best possible

Opposite: Inferno on the after flight-deck of *Belleau Wood* after a *kamikaze* strike off Leyte in the Philippines
Inset: A 'Betty' poised for departure on a *kamikaze* mission, with an *Ohka* manned missile slung beneath the fuselage

advantage – and yet actually to intercept and ram a carrier where it hurt most demanded pilot skills of the very highest order. This was true of the bomb-carrying Zeros used in the first *kamikaze* attacks and was even more true of the specially-designed MXY-8 *Ohka*. Fitted with a high-explosive warhead 775 lb heavier than Germany's V-1, this piloted bomb, which entered service in September 1944, had to be carried by a 'mother' plane to within 60 miles of the American fleet. Normally released at about 27,000 feet, it would then glide steeply for about 50 miles, reaching about 230 mph, until there were only about 5 miles to go. The pilot would then ignite three rockets in the tail, accelerating to around 570 mph in a final death dive at 50 degrees.

The actual performance record of the *Ohka*, custom-built for the immolation of American carriers, was somewhat less impressive than any description of the weapon is bound to be. The first batch of completed *Ohkas* were loaded aboard the new super-carrier *Shinano* for delivery to Formosa, the intended base of operations. For *Shinano*, at 64,800 tons the biggest carrier ever built until the American 'Forrestals' of the 1950s, this delivery run to Formosa doubled as a shake-down cruise. But there was no strategic future for *Shinano*. Scattered around the naval bases of the Japanese home islands lay seven carriers, none of which was to be rendered fully battle-worthy, and for which neither aircraft, trained pilots nor fuel oil could be found. On 28 November 1944 *Shinano* was not even 24 hours out of Yokosuka, let alone out of sight of land, when she was hit by four torpedoes from the submarine USS *Archerfish*. Execrable damage-control work and the unneccessary maintenance of far too high a speed caused the flooding to spread rapidly. Instead of being nursed back to port, or even beached, *Shinano* sank seven hours after being torpedoed. She took with her the only available batch of *Ohka* piloted bombs, and the type was not tried in earnest until March 1945. Of the 18 *Ohkas* which set out, none even approached a viable target and all their 'mother' planes were shot down. The only two successful *Ohka* attacks – out of a total of some 800 built – took place on 12 April 1945. Eight *Ohkas* were launched of which two hit, sinking one destroyer and damaging another.

The biggest problem with the *Ohka* was that the 'mother' plane – usually the twin-engined Mitsubishi G4M 'Betty' – was totally incapable of defensive manoeuvre while carrying an *Ohka*. This vulnerability cancelled the intended 'one man, one warship' economy of the *Ohka* by resulting in the additional loss of the 'Betty', with its crew of seven, for no result. Only 74 *Ohkas* were despatched on missions, and of these 56 were either dropped short or shot down with their 'mother' plane. They were a spectacular offshoot of *kamikaze* tactics but a negation, not an enhancement, of its potential.

Kamikaze attacks by conventional aircraft, however, were a very different matter. The next amphibious pounce after Leyte was the main Filipino island of Luzon, invaded after the usual softening-up attacks by the carriers and battleships of the 3rd Fleet, on 9 January 1945. By the end of January Philippine-based *kamikazes* had flown 421 sorties against 3rd Fleet, and the results were impressive. Sixteen ships had been sunk, including the escort carrier *Ommaney Bay* (sunk on the eve of the Luzon landings). Another 87 warships, transports and troopships had been damaged, including 22 fleet, light, and escort carriers. The 'Essex' class *Franklin* and 'Independence' class *Belleau Wood*, having suffered the joint loss of 158 men killed and 45 aircraft destroyed, were both forced to quit the fleet for repairs. But this was just a foretaste of the ordeal in store for *Franklin*. During the bloody fight for Iwo Jima (19 February-25 March 1945) *Franklin* was hit off Kyushu by a low-level bomber; two bombs sliced through her flight-deck and set off an inferno amid the fuelled, armed planes in the hangar. *Franklin* burned like a torch, her crew suffering 832 killed and 270 wounded. Heroic fire-fighting brought her fires under control but *Franklin* was so badly damaged that she was never returned to service. In the same wave of attacks, other *kamikazes* hit *Enterprise*, *Wasp* and *Yorktown*. These attacks followed the most effective single *kamikaze* strike of the campaign: a 32-plane attack on 21 February, which sank the escort carrier *Bismarck Sea* and damaged *Saratoga* along with four other warships. It was the increasing effectiveness of the *kamikaze* attacks, mounting in intensity as the Americans approached the Japanese home islands, which helped strengthen the case for using the atomic bomb in order to hasten the end of the war.

The zenith of the *kamikazes* must be accounted the battle of Okinawa (1 April-2 July 1945) in which the massed-attack or *kikusui* predominated: ten in all, apart from individual and smaller group attacks, expending 1,465 aircraft. But by now the initial target for *kamikazes* was no longer carriers and battleships: the Japanese had learned of the new defensive ploy of studding radar-warning 'picket' destroyers round the approaches to the fleet. Having to concentrate on the picket

86

The end of *Yamato*, overwhelmed and sunk in the East China Sea by massive 3rd Fleet air strikes on 7 April 1945

destroyers undeniably took the pressure off the American carriers – and yet 12 of them were damaged during the Okinawa campaign, forcing Spruance (back in command since the end of January) to redeploy TF.58 as three task groups instead of four. But in the end this modest Japanese success was of no avail: it was instantly made good by the arrival of the newly-formed British Pacific Fleet, which served with the US 5th Fleet as 'Task Force 57'. The Americans were deeply impressed by the ability of the four British fleet carriers, with their armoured flight-decks, to shrug off *kamikaze* attacks. All four British carriers were hit, yet none was obliged to quit the battle and withdraw for repairs.

Though Washington meanly insisted that the British Pacific Fleet was not to be given any chance of sinking the surviving units of the Japanese Fleet (to make revenge for Pearl Harbor an all-American affair), the British force more than justified its presence. It had to struggle with the vast distances of the Pacific, enjoying little or none of the lavish seaborne supply facilities built up by the US Navy. For all that, Spruance was glad to accept the offer of the British seaborne commander, Admiral Rawlings, for TF.57 to stay with 5th Fleet for an additional week instead of breaking off for replenishment as scheduled. So slow was the conquest of Okinawa, against more fanatical Japanese resistance than ever, that not enough land-based air strength could be based on the island during the battle. Air cover, despite the intensity of the *kikusui* attacks, must be provided by the carriers, and the presence of the four toughest carriers in the Pacific, operating separately, helped dissipate the Japanese attacks and take the load off the flimsier American ships.

The US Navy nevertheless claims the honour of having launched the last carrier attack on an enemy 'fleet' at sea. This occurred on 7 April 1945: the 'Battle of the East China Sea'. Crammed with ammunition and just enough fuel for a one-way voyage, *Yamato*, the light cruiser *Yahagi* and eight destroyers sailed from Japan to go out in a blaze of glory, all guns blazing at the Americans landing across the Okinawa beaches. Sighted in ample time, none of the Japanese ships even sighted Okinawa; *Yamato, Yahagi* and four of the destroyers were pounded to destruction by 380 strike aircraft launched by TF.58. The American aircrews met negligible opposition,

Near-miss – this *kamikaze* Zero attacking the battleship *Missouri* crashed in the sea without making contact

Instrument of victory: carriers lead the battleships and cruisers as Halsey's 3rd Fleet cruises majestically off Japan in August 1945

for the major Japanese air effort was concentrated in that day's *kikusui* attacks. The only successful Japanese attack on the 7th was a *kamikaze* hit on the American carrier *Hancock*.

Yet after fruitless wastage (estimated at between 60 and 90 per cent) during the Okinawa campaign, the *kamikaze* fury had to weaken. Though *kamikaze* attacks continued to the last day of the war they could not prevent the American and British carriers from battering the Japanese home islands as they chose. Halsey had taken over from Spruance on 27 May, and on 1 July he led the replenished 3rd Fleet out from Leyte to begin the next phase of softening-up bombardment attacks. These were aimed squarely at the Japanese homeland, in preparation for Operation 'Olympic': the invasion of Kyushu scheduled for 1 November 1945. The wheel had indeed come full circle over the past three and a half years, when Halsey and his fellow admirals had been capable of no more than hit-and-run raids with single carriers. He was now wielding the mightiest naval weapon the world has ever seen, which had as its cutting edge 14 fleet carriers (four of them British) and six light carriers, putting up a combined strength of 1,450 aircraft.

Halsey's carriers were not, to be sure, the only instrument of air power working towards Japan's inevitable defeat. Japan was already exposed to regular strategic bombing from the Marianas, and massive base facilities were being created amid the ruins of Okinawa for medium-range Army Air Force operations against Japan. It was from Tinian in the Marianas, not Halsey's carriers, that the atomic raids on Hiroshima and Nagasaki were carried out on 6 and 9 August 1945. But it was the remorseless accuracy and intensity of the carrier-borne attacks, launched unpredictably and at such short ranges as to guarantee invincible fighter cover for the strike aircraft, which sank the last remnants of the Japanese Fleet where they lurked at anchor. In Halsey's three-day blitz in the last week of July 1945, only one of the 'Unryu' class fleet carriers, *Amagi*, was caught in water deep enough to allow her to sink. The other four, with *Kaiyo*, *Ryuho* and *Ibuki*, were all surrendered inoperative or as constructive total losses.

Only one unit of Japan's once-mighty carrier fleet could be regarded as operative at the time of the Japanese surrender (agreed on 15 August and signed on 2 September). This was the little *Hosho*, Japan's first-ever carrier, which had provided the Imperial Japanese Navy with so many lessons in the potency of naval aviation – lessons either discounted, or no less fatally ignored.

5. BALANCE SHEET, 1945: THE CARRIER TRIUMPHANT

Previous pages: Escort carrier *Searcher*, built for the British in the American Seattle-Tacoma yards. After the war, when the British disposed of their entire escort-carrier fleet, *Searcher* was returned to the USA to begin civilian life as the merchant ship *Captain Theo*

IN SEPTEMBER 1945 few of the original doubts over the role of the aircraft-carrier remained. The most celebrated of these doubts, the battleship-or-carrier debate, had certainly been laid to rest. After the six-year lesson of the Second World War, not even the wildest gambler would have seriously considered pitting a squadron of battleships against a carrier task group. The undisputed heyday of the battleship was over; surface-to-surface gunnery by giant, breech-loading rifles was no longer the ultimate medium for the resolution of battle at sea. It had given place perforce to air-to-surface bombardment by carrier-launched bombers, torpedo-carrying aircraft and, in the last year of the war, by a new weapon: their air-to-surface rocket missiles. No longer was an intact battleship 'fleet in being' a guarantee of security by sea. Wherever enemy carrier aircraft ruled the skies, no battleship could count itself secure, no matter how formidable the defences of its anchorage might be.

This the British had convincingly demonstrated in the Mediterranean, at the expense of the Italian battle fleet. The exploits of the British carriers in the Mediterranean, culminating in the near-destruction of *Vittorio Veneto* at Matapan in March 1941, finally convinced Mussolini that he had been wrong to oppose the development of Italian fleet carriers. In July 1941 work began on one of the most interesting carrier conversions of the war, from the liner SS *Roma* to the armoured carrier *Aquila*. She would have been the first Axis carrier to incorporate wartime experience. *Aquila*'s hull was given massive reinforced-concrete bulges as protection against torpedoes, and she was designed to carry as many as a hundred and four 37 mm AA guns and up to 51 Reggiane Re 2001 fighters. If she had only been started two years earlier *Aquila* would have been an invaluable asset to the Italian battle fleet. But by the time she was ready for sea trials in September 1943 the Axis powers had been expelled from North Africa, Sicily had been invaded and conquered, the Italian fleet had been deprived of all freedom of action and Italy driven to the brink of surrender. It was a classic instance of the perils of not seeing the light in time; also of the impossibility of remedying years of neglect with an emergency building programme, no matter how well conceived, AFTER the outbreak of war.

When all this is admitted, the carrier's undoubted triumph in 1945 was nevertheless far from being unmitigated. The dominance of carrier power had not rendered the battleship totally redundant, as has so often been sweep-

Belated fruit of the Matapan battle – Italy's unfinished carrier *Aquila*, converted from the former liner *Roma*

British battleship *Warspite*, veteran of two world wars, giving 15-inch fire support to the troops ashore in the battle for Normandy. The unique economy of the fire-support role was to save the battleship from total obsolescence in the post-war era

ingly claimed. Even at the end of the war, the battleship still had many advantages which the most modern carrier could not hope to match. Ship for ship, discounting fighter protection aloft, a battleship had far more anti-aircraft fire-power than the most modern fleet carrier afloat. The battleship was also better protected against bombing attacks, being proof against low-level bomb hits that could turn a carrier into an inferno. Though no such phenomenon as a torpedo-proof hull had been developed, battleships were also demonstrably capable of surviving more torpedo hits than carriers. The battleship could operate and even fight in weather conditions which would make carrier air operations impossible, and by the same token was far less susceptible to weather damage.

When it came to supporting the troops ashore in foul or thick weather which made low-level air sorties dangerous or impracticable, the sheer economy of radar-guided battleship gunfire was virtually impossible to emulate – or to endure. During the Battle of Normandy in June-July 1944, German armour attempting to crush the Allied beach-head was repeatedly broken up by battleship gunfire as far as 20 miles inland. Indeed, as an *all-weather* platform for gun and missile fire-power the battleship has never been surpassed, as Korea and Vietnam were to prove. It should have come as no surprise when in January 1982 the world's strongest carrier navy, still that of the United States, announced that its four 'Iowa' class battleships were to be broken out of mothballs to serve again – nearly 40 years after launch.

However, when all is said and done, the carrier's decisive advantage over the battleship outweighed every other disadvantage. This was the advantage in range. The big gun had been specifically developed to enable battleships to fight and win, safely outside the range of enemy torpedo craft. But whereas a battleship's big guns could reach over 20 miles, a carrier's torpedo-bombers could reach over 300. The deadly results of this simple fact were demonstrated at Leyte Gulf in October 1944 and again, most brutally of all, in the crushing of *Yamato* five months later.

As with nearly every weapon of the Second World War, the aircraft-carrier of 1945 had many revolutionary features denied its predecessor of only six years before. The carrier was no longer entirely dependent on the human eye to detect the approach of an enemy, or to find and attack the enemy from the air. The radar revolution had introduced

Above: Corsair with underwing rockets. The air-to-surface rocket missiles introduced in the Second World War gave the naval strike aircraft the fire-power of a cruiser
Right: British fleet carrier *Indefatigable* showing her fully-enclosed or 'hurricane' bow – one of the many British carrier features adopted by the Americans after the Second World War

Much-loved veteran of the entire Pacific War – *Enterprise*, with massed Hellcats ranged on deck

not merely surface-to-surface radar to locate enemy ships, but surface-to-air to locate enemy aircraft. The biggest boon came with air-to-surface radar which a reconnaissance aircraft could carry, adding the long probe of radar to the long radius of aircraft, and thus transforming the carrier's built-in range advantage. The timely provision of these new radars, plus a rapidly-learned expertise in operating them, made possible the massed precision carrier operations of 1944-45. It was all a far cry from the groping, mauling carrier engagements of 1942.

Though a carrier's fighters remained her best anti-aircraft defences, they could only be kept aloft on defensive patrolling at the cost of depriving the strike aircraft of adequate fighter escort. For this reason the carrier, like every other warship type, had added mightily to its AA gun armoury by the end of the war. Thus Britain's *Ark Royal*, completed in 1938, had a (then lavish) AA battery of sixteen 4.5-inch guns and forty-eight 2-pdrs, plus thirty-two .5-inch machine-guns. *Illustrious*, completed in late 1940, had the same basic armament plus eight 20 mm rapid-firers; *Indefatigable*, three years later, had the 'hose-pipe' rapid-fire of the 20 mm raised to thirty-four. It was the same story with the Americans. *Yorktown* had gone to war with only eight 5-inch AA guns; she fought her last fight at Midway with an additional 'lash-up' of over 30 spare machine-guns from the aircraft; her sister-ship *Enterprise* ended the war with forty 40 mm, while the 'Essex' class carriers mounted up to sixty-eight 40 mm. Significantly (from their successes in 1941-42) the Japanese had never needed telling. The old *Akagi* had had twelve 4.7-inch and twenty-eight 25 mm AA guns; *Hiryu*'s twelve 5-inch and thirty-seven 25 mm AA guns were still insufficient to save her at Midway; *Taiho*'s 25 mm AA armament numbered 51 guns (in seventeen triple-gun mountings). Pride of

Left: Shape of things to come – Henschel Hs-293 air-to-surface guided missile, the first successful type introduced in the Second World War
Below: Incredible veteran – Swordfish in its anti-U-boat role, with underwing rockets, coming in to land on the escort carrier *Tracker* in autumn 1943

place was held by *Shinano*, with no less than sixteen 5-inch and *one hundred and forty-five* 25 mm. No matter the navy, the lesson was the same: no carrier could be fitted with enough AA fire-power to make it immune from air attack. The distinctive circular screen of the carrier task group, still used in the modern missile age for the same purpose, serves to pool its individual anti-submarine and anti-air defences that the carrier may survive, strike and triumph.

Of one novel form of air attack, the rocket missile, carriers emerged from the Second World War innocent of experience. Carrier-borne aircraft were *armed* with unguided rocket missiles, launched with devastating effect in underwing salvoes; rocket-armed Swordfish launched from escort-carriers proved one of the deadliest foes to the U-boats in the Atlantic. Unguided rocket missiles were in widespread use on both sides, in the air-to-air as well as the air-to-surface role. Germany produced the first true guided missiles in the form of the 'Fritz X' (which sank the Italian battleship *Roma* in September 1943) and the rocket-boosted Henschel 293. Both depended on radio guidance from the mother plane, and Anglo-American electronics proved easily capable of neutralising such weapons by radio jamming. The less advanced Japanese had no

A radar-guided Bat air-to-surface missile is hoisted into position under the starboard wing of a US Navy PBY4-2 Privateer

Escort carrier *Khedive* with bristling radar array, at the close of the Pacific War. An undoubted war-winning weapon, the escort carrier was only retained in post-war service with the US Navy

such luck against the American radar-guided 'Bat' which, on its debut in April 1945, sank a Japanese destroyer at its maximum range of 20 miles. After some belated experiments with missile rocketry the Japanese fell back on the manned rocket missile in the form of the *Ohka* (*for the weaknesses of which see* p.108), and on manned, power-diving conventional aircraft for their *kamikaze* attacks. Though, as we have seen, *kamikaze* strategy using 'manned missiles' was inherently counter-productive as far as the supply of skilled pilots was concerned, the failure of the *kamikazes* nevertheless left two worrying lessons for the future. Though the vast majority of the 'manned missiles' were shot down or deflected to crash in the sea, enough still got through – sometimes with devastating results – to suggest that far faster, unmanned guided rocket missiles would have done even better.

In 1945, however, there could be no doubt that the fleet aircraft-carrier would continue into peacetime service as the dominant heavy warship type. The same could not be said of the escort carrier, that frantically-contrived stop-gap conjured into being for one purpose: the protection of Atlantic convoys. After ensuring victory on the Atlantic and Arctic convoy routes, the escort carrier was used to provide cover for the invasion fleets, as the Allies took the offensive in the Mediterranean and the Pacific. They were the second-echelon carriers, purely defensive, providing economy-sized helpings of air/sea cover in order to free the big fleet carriers to take the offensive elsewhere. In 1944-45, as the British fleet carriers moved east to Ceylon and the Pacific, it was the escort carriers which left the British Home Fleet with an air-strike capability in Home Waters. But when it was used as the core of an anti-submarine hunter/killer group, the escort carrier really came into its own. This did not occur until after the supreme effort of the U-boats (January-May 1943) had been met and broken by conventional escort flotillas and long-ranged shore-based aircraft. In January-May 1943 so few escort carriers could be spared that their kills were inevitably low; their aircraft accounted for no more than four U-boats in

those months. Over the succeeding 12 months, however, escort carrier aircraft claimed credit for no less than 43 U-boats sunk. But what could not be quantified was the numbers of frustrated U-boat attacks which the escort carriers caused by their mere presence. A U-boat forced to remain submerged by a patrolling carrier aircraft, even if not located and attacked, was a U-boat which could not stalk, intercept or attack. In short, the mass-produced 'Woolworth' carrier had made an invaluable contribution to Allied victory at sea – but with the total defeat of the Axis submarine fleets there was no apparent peacetime role for the escort carrier.

One particular consideration was clearly about to have a profound effect on post-1945 carrier design: the continuing rise in aircraft sizes, weights and speeds. Ever-improving construction techniques and greater ingenuity in wing-folding helped keep the size problem under control. Far more serious was the rise in weight and speed, both of which had taken a giant upward leap during the war:

Type *Fighter*	Country of Origin	Date	Max. Speed	Max. Loaded Weight (armed)
Gloster Sea Gladiator	Britain	1940	246 mph	4,646 lb
Grumman F4F Wildcat	USA	1941	330 mph	7,002 lb
Grumman F6F Hellcat	USA	1943	376 mph	11,381 lb
Chance Vought Corsair	USA	1943	393 mph	12,039 lb
Strike				
Fairey Swordfish	Britain	1940	138 mph	9,120 lb
Douglas SBD Dauntless	USA	1942	252 mph	10,352 lb
Grumman TBF Avenger	USA	1943	271 mph	15,667 lb

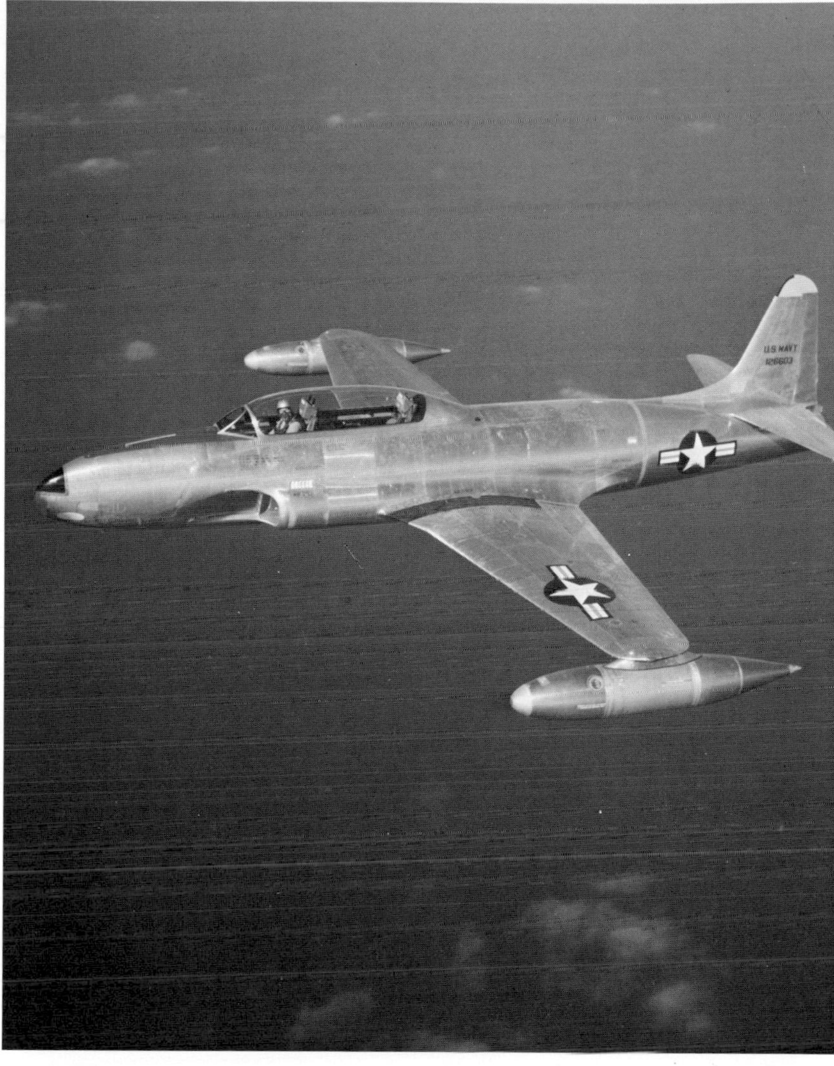

First essay in jet-age naval aviation: a Lockheed T-33 Sea Star of the US Navy. The massive leap in aircraft speed and weight which accompanied the new era was to pose formidable new problems for the aircraft-carrier

Despite these formidable increases in aircraft deadweight and flying-speed, carrier operations of the Second World War had just escaped the need to catapult-launch each loaded and armed aircraft. But in September 1945 aircraft development had by no means reached a plateau; on the contrary, it was soaring onward and upward. The new land-based jet aircraft – Britain's Gloster Meteor (475 mph and 12,500 lb loaded) and the USA's Shooting Star (558 mph and 14,000 lb loaded) were the obvious equivalent of the first streamlined monoplane fighters barely ten years before. That particular breakthrough had brought about the total obsolescence of the biplane in less than five years. Sooner or later, if it wished to avoid a slump into the obsolescence into which it had lapsed between the world wars, naval aviation must surely adopt jet aircraft.

It remained to be seen how long the piston-engined aircraft of 1945 could stave off the challenge of the jets. It also remained to be seen whether traditional carrier design could be adapted to cope with the aircraft of the post-war era, and the awesome weapons they could now carry.

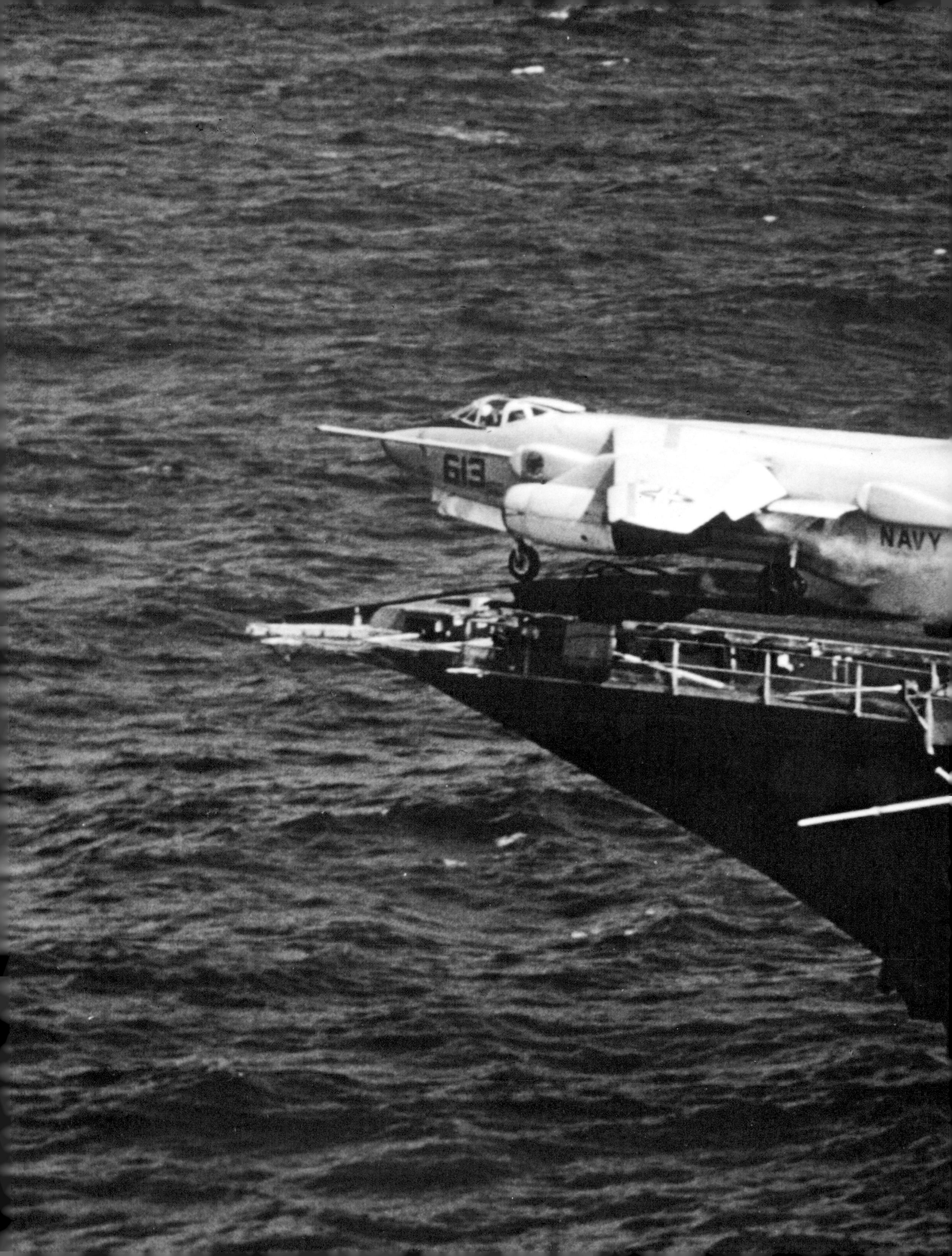
613
NAVY

6. THE JET AND THE BOMB, 1945–1962

Previous pages: A Douglas A-3 Skywarrior screams off from the catapult of the 'Midway' class heavy carrier *Coral Sea*

ALTHOUGH THE US NAVY dwarfed the Royal Navy in September 1945, the victorious Anglo-American carrier navies had two characteristics in common. Both were still expanding rapidly and were caught by surprise when Japan surrendered; both were thereupon required to reverse the process, undergo massive demobilisation and 'slim down' to the most modest possible peacetime establishment. There the similarities ended. After six years of war Britain was exhausted, financially bankrupt and completely dependent on American financial aid for survival. The United States was by contrast the world's paymaster – to wartime friends and former enemies alike. Until a dollar loan was negotiated by Britain's new Labour Government the American termination of Lend-Lease, the wartime supply arrangement which had supplied Britain with American *matériel*, to be returned or paid for when the war ended, threatened Britain with complete financial disaster. And this underlying financial crisis, coupled with the termination of Lend-Lease, explains why Britain's 1945 carrier fleet was demolished at a far greater pace than that of the US Navy.

With the coming of peace the abrupt ending of co-operation on weapons between Britain and the United States may have been inevitable but it was certainly a tragic waste of time, money and resources. It prevented a peacetime standardisation of equipment and operating techniques that would have been wholly beneficial – especially after the signing of the North Atlantic Treaty in 1949 – without imperilling national independence. Anglo-American co-operation on post-war jet propulsion and atomic weaponry would have been particularly valuable. As it was, British

compliance with the return-clauses of Lend-Lease in 1945-46 led to the US Navy being saddled with a surplus of ships and aircraft which it did not want. Much of this was wastefully dumped at sea without even being delivered to the scrapyard. By the end of 1946 Britain had cleared her entire wartime fleet of escort carriers, 35 ships in all; most were converted back into merchant ships. Only one ex-British escort carrier of American construction, HMS *Biter*, went to the French Navy as *Dixmude*. Of the four escort carriers of British construction, HMS *Nairana* went to the Royal Netherlands Navy as *Karel Doorman*; the other three reverted to merchantmen. There was, at the end of 1946, no way of knowing that those lost 33 escort carrier hulls would be desperately missed by the NATO navies in 35 years' time.

As for the British fleet carriers, the extremely ambitious carrier fleet expansion programme of 1945 was also abruptly curtailed with the coming of peace. By VJ-Day, Britain's four 'Illustrious' class and two 'Implacable' class fleet carriers (23,000 tons and 26,000 tons respectively) were rapidly being joined in the Pacific by the first of a new line of light fleet carriers. These were the ten ships of the 'Colossus' class, rapidly followed by the six 'Majestic' class light fleet carriers. The 'Colossus' class displaced 13,190 tons and could operate 48 aircraft (with the exception of *Perseus* and *Pioneer*, which were completed as maintenance carriers for the British Pacific Fleet). Only four of them, with *Perseus* and *Pioneer*, had reached Australia by VJ-Day, none of them in time to see action. The six 'Majestics' displaced 14,000 tons but carried no more than 34 aircraft. These two classes were a purely British wartime expedient, the best the British could do towards building a sizeable indigenous carrier fleet. By any

Escort carrier *Biter* displays her modest dimensions – one obvious reason for the type's early demise in the jet age

standard of their own day, they were too small and too slow. Yet one of them, the 'Colossus' class HMS *Ocean*, claims the honour for receiving the first deck landing by a jet-engined aircraft: a Vampire I fighter (65 mph faster but 4,320 lb lighter than the Meteor) on 3 December 1945.

Three other classes of British aircraft-carriers were in hand at the end of the war, and all three were viciously curtailed. The 'Audacious' class, four ships in all, were to have followed the 'Implacables'. They were basically an expanded version of the 'Illustrious/Implacable' format, with thicker deck armour and an air group of 100 aircraft. Two of them were cancelled outright but *Audacious* and *Irresistible* survived, to be

Left: *Victorious*, the only British wartime fleet carrier to serve through to the late 1960s (scrapped 1969)

Left: *Implacable*, one of the earlier victims in the post-war shrinkage of the British carrier arm (scrapped 1955)

Below: British light fleet carrier *Colossus* in RN service, before her 1951 transfer to the French Navy as *Arromanches*

Albion in 1958, in her last commission before being converted to a commando carrier

completed years later as *Eagle* and *Ark Royal* (36,800 tons). The 'Gibraltar' class, at 45,000 tons, would have been the equivalent of the American 'Midways', though with better protection and probably less aircraft. All three had been cancelled before the first anniversary of VJ-Day. This decision must be regarded as the biggest blow at Britain's air/sea security before the notorious Wilson/Healey Defence White Paper of 1966 (*see below*, pp. 162-66). Finally there were the eight carriers of the middleweight 'Hermes' class (18,300 tons) of which only four were completed: *Albion*, *Bulwark*, *Centaur* and *Hermes*. Originally designed to operate 50 aircraft, *Bulwark* and *Albion* were converted to commando carriers in 1960 and 1962.

Only two of Britain's pre-war carrier fleet had survived the war: *Furious*, transferred to the Reserve for the last year of the war after good and faithful service with the Home Fleet; and *Argus*. With the temporary abundance of new carriers both in service and completing, there could be little objection to the early scrapping of *Argus* and *Furious* (1946 and 1948). But between 1946 and 1953 no fewer than nine of the new British carriers were sold or scrapped. *Magnificent* and *Warrior* were transferred to the Royal Canadian Navy in 1946; two years later *Venerable* went to Holland as the new *Karel Doorman* (freeing the ex-*Nairana* for re-conversion to a merchant ship) and *Terrible* was transferred to the Royal Australian Navy as *Sydney*. In 1951 France received *Colossus* as *Arromanches*; in 1952 *Ocean* was scrapped, *Vengeance* transferred to Australia and *Powerful* to Canada. The scrapping of *Formidable* followed in 1953.

This rate of depletion was completely uncompensated by any new fleet carriers joining the Fleet; nor did it occur in what, by the remotest stretch of the imagination, could be described as peacetime. Quite apart from the momentary lurch towards war with the Soviet Union in 1947-48 caused by the Soviet blockade of Berlin, the British Far Eastern Fleet was repeatedly shot at during the Chinese Civil War, and was finally involved in the United Nations' defence of South Korea from the invading Communists of North Korea. Despite the undoubted cost of Britain's commitment to the Korean War (June 1950-July 1953) with land, sea and air forces, neither the Labour nor Conservative Governments of 1950-53 treated the war *as* a war. Governmental doubletalk represented it as large-scale police action in peacetime – one of the most distasteful phrases used to introduce the British Defence Estimates during the Korean war was 'the largest ever presented *in peacetime*'. Apparently this made the continuing depletion of the carrier fleet quite in order. In any event, Britain had had ten fleet carriers and eleven escort carriers serving in the Pacific on VJ-Day. Less than five years later, her only contribution to the UN Fleet off Korea was a

Bulwark (later converted with *Albion*) in her fleet carrier days, with Sea Hawk fighters ranged forward (1958)

solitary light fleet carrier – and remained so throughout the war.

It was in the skies over Korea that the last-generation British piston-engined naval fighters came up against the Soviet MiG-15 fighter. High pilot skill and the excellent handling qualities of the British Sea Furies and Fireflies prevented total catastrophe, but the experience made it crystal clear that the British Fleet Air Arm must have jet aircraft of its own. Another revelation to the British in Korea was the value of the new-fangled helicopters on 'plane guard' duties: rescuing air-crew from crashes alongside during launch or recovery. But the greatest single lesson of Korea was that the atomic bomb had not rendered conventional land, sea, or air warfare obsolete. And it was while the Korean War was dragging on that Britain was deprived of its last excuse for slimming-down the Royal Navy. The Soviet Union began an immense submarine and cruiser construction programme, the avowed intention of which was to make the Soviet Union a front-rank naval power.

The American response to the lessons of Korea and the prospect of a Soviet ocean-going navy was to modernise and recommission ten wartime 'Essex' class carriers to add to the already impressive American carrier fleet. Britain proceeded to scrap *Indomitable*, and *Implacable* in 1955; hand over *Majestic* to the Australian Navy in the same year; and scrap *Illustrious* and *Indefatigable* in 1956. This raised the number of British fleet carriers disposed of since the end of the war to 14. Small

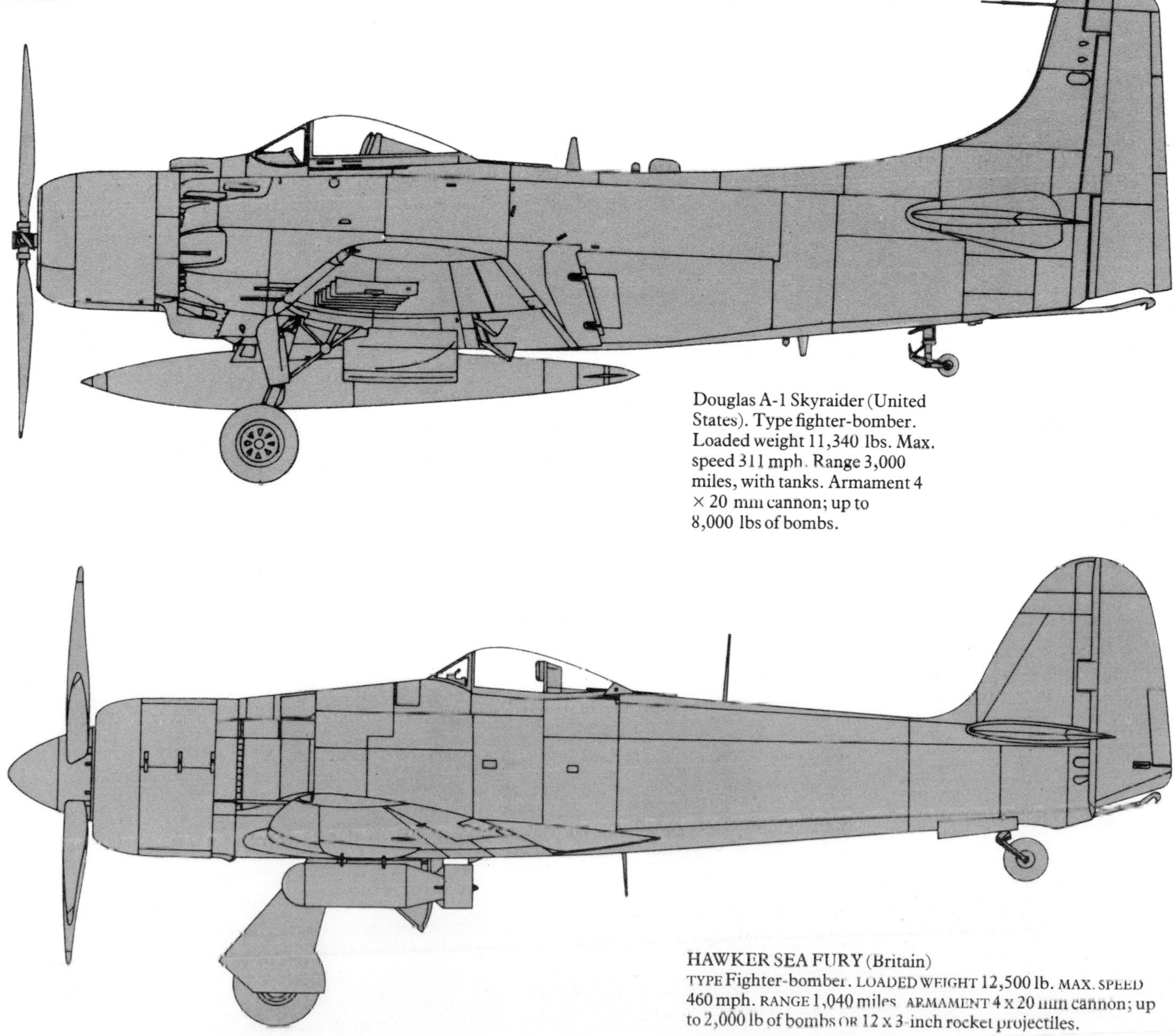

Douglas A-1 Skyraider (United States). Type fighter-bomber. Loaded weight 11,340 lbs. Max. speed 311 mph. Range 3,000 miles, with tanks. Armament 4 × 20 mm cannon; up to 8,000 lbs of bombs.

HAWKER SEA FURY (Britain)
TYPE Fighter-bomber. LOADED WEIGHT 12,500 lb. MAX. SPEED 460 mph. RANGE 1,040 miles. ARMAMENT 4 x 20 mm cannon; up to 2,000 lb of bombs OR 12 x 3-inch rocket projectiles.

July 1952 – British light fleet carrier *Ocean* in Korean waters. The fighters ranged on deck are Second World War Fireflies, expressive of the obsolescent slump of British naval aviation in the first post-war decade

wonder that when the British and French Governments attempted to occupy the Suez Canal zone in November 1956, the Royal Navy could only deploy three fleet carriers for the job of neutralising the Egyptian airfields AND patrolling the Canal, to prevent the Egyptians from blocking it with so much as a rowing-boat. The British carriers therefore concentrated on the airfields first; the Canal was blocked before it could be seized by the troops put ashore; and the operation failed. Far more important, 'Suez' plunged Britain into a fog of international opprobrium and self-recrimination which has obscured the nation's true defence priorities ever since.

The US Navy had emerged into peacetime with the course of its carrier force already set. Where the British had produced the slow, lightweight 'Colossus' and 'Majestic' classes, the Americans had produced the three imposing 'Midway' class 'battle carriers' (CVB): *Midway*, *Franklin D. Roosevelt* and *Coral Sea*, 45,000 tons, 33 knots, 137 aircraft and a mighty 113 ft across the beam. Though these ships arrived too late for the Pacific War, they were invaluable operational test-beds for the first generation of American carrier-borne jets. The first of these, the McDonnell FH-1 Phantom, made its first take-off from *Coral Sea* in July 1946. With the three 'Midways', the pride of the fleet, the US Navy still had 20 carriers in active service by 1948, including eight 'Essex' class and two 'Independence' class, plus seven escort carriers. The vital difference to the British experience was the fact that the US Navy had the funds to mothball their surplus carriers instead of selling them or breaking them up.

In the first peacetime atomic bomb tests at Bikini in 1946, surplus warships of every class were collected to make a target fleet on which the effects of atomic bombardment could be tested and assessed. The American carriers expended in this test were the old *Saratoga* and *Independence*. Much was learned: it took two

MIDWAY (United States)
DISPLACEMENT 45,000 tons (1945); 51,000 tons (1982). DIMENSIONS 986 ft x 113 ft x 32¾ ft (1945); 979 ft x 121 ft x 35¼ ft (1982). MACHINERY 4-shaft geared turbines: 212,000 SHP. SPEED 33 knots. ARMAMENT 18 x 5-inch AA; 84 x 40 mm AA (1945); minus 5-inch guns, plus 3 x 20 mm Mk 15 CIWs guns, ALSO 2 x BPDMS Mk 25 Sea Sparrow missile launchers and 2 x Mk 115 Missile FC systems (1982). AIRCRAFT 137 (1945); approx. 75 (1982). COMPLEMENT 4,085 (1945); approx. 4,415 (1982).

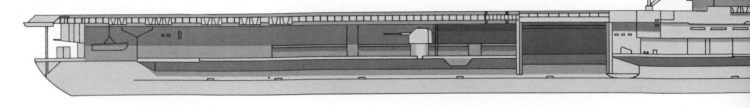

'Midway' class carrier *Coral Sea*, showing her enclosed 'hurricane' bow and angled flight deck – both features of British derivation

American thriftiness in getting as many years' service as possible out of wartime ships was in stark contrast to the stream of British disposals after 1945. This is *Bennington*, of the 'Modernised Essex' class (launched February 1944) in 1967

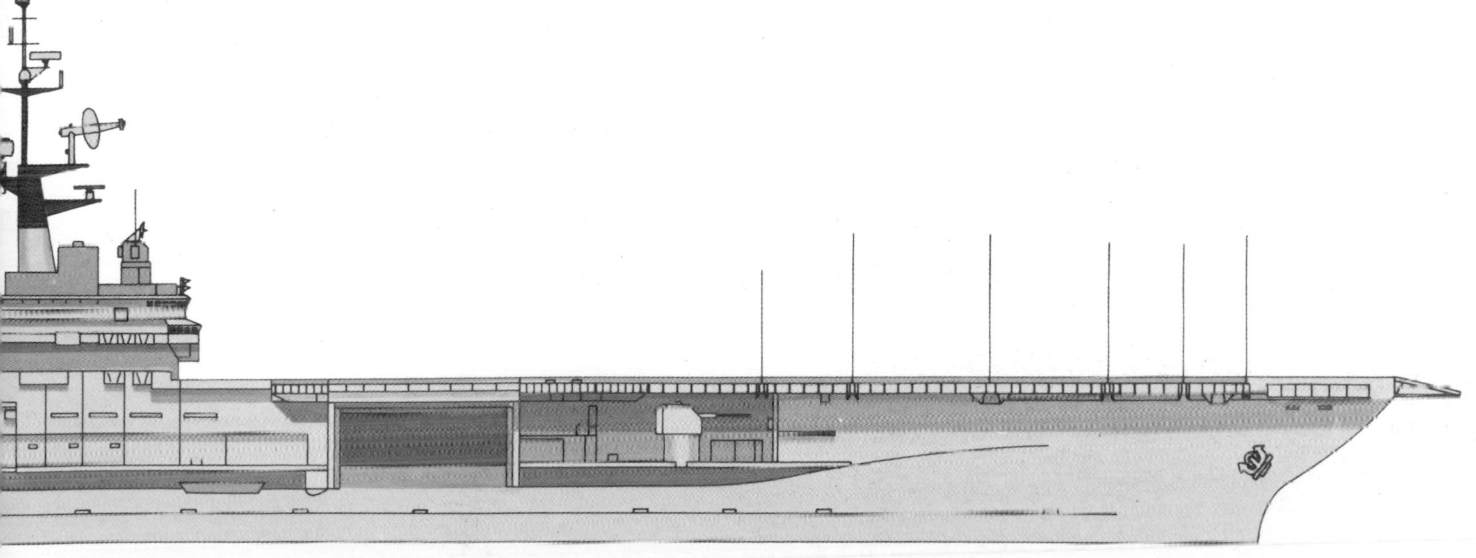

602
603

Right: F-4B Phantom from USS Midway, supporting ground forces against the Vietcong in November 1965
Below: A-7A Corsair poised for launch on a similar mission, Gulf of Tonkin, August 1968

atomic bursts to sink the immobile *Saratoga*, which indicated that a carrier task force dispersing at top speed would have an excellent chance of surviving a nuclear attack. These tests were the prelude to a bitter battle between the US Navy and Air Force over whether or not the latter should have the monopoly of delivering nuclear weapons, the real point at issue naturally being the biggest slice of the military appropriations pie. Two pressing arguments shelved this conflict when the Navy was already planning a giant carrier for the launching of long-range nuclear strikes: the detonation of the first Soviet nuclear device in 1949, followed by the conventional prior demands of the Korean War.

Happily, work had already started on an ambitious modernisation programme aimed at fitting the 'Essex' class fleet carriers for the jet age. This programme, designated SCB 27, began with the carrier *Oriskany* in 1948. The salient points were strengthening the flight-deck to take the massive impact of heavy jets when landing; widening and strengthening the flight-deck lifts; and increasing aircraft fuel stowage and pumping capacity while adding an improved fire-fighting system to the hangar deck. In addition the island was tidied up to create more taxying space on the flight-deck, by removing the old 5-inch gun turrets and concentrating the automatic AA guns. When it was all over, *Oriskany* went back to sea and promptly notched up a stunning 32½ knots on her trials before sailing for Korea. It was a standing rebuke to the British, with their reckless disposal of so many carrier hulls of similar vintage. In the light of Korean experience, ten more 'Essex' carriers were earmarked for the SCB 27 treatment and all had recommissioned by the end of the Korean War.

And yet it was Britain, and not the United States, which produced the three features essential to the jet-age carrier. These were the angled flight-deck; the steam catapult; and the mirror-landing system, all appearing in the early 1950s.

The angled flight-deck solved the problem, which had become crucial by the late 1940s, of multiple flight-deck crashes caused by landing and take-off accidents. The lighter and slower aircraft of earlier years could fail to pick up an arrester-wire and career into the elastic crash barrier with only minimal damage. But over 10,000 lb of uncontrollable aircraft, arriving at speeds first approaching, then surpassing 100 mph, were too much for any crash barrier; the normal result was a hideous smash into the aircraft ranged forward, with appalling damage being caused from exploding fuel and

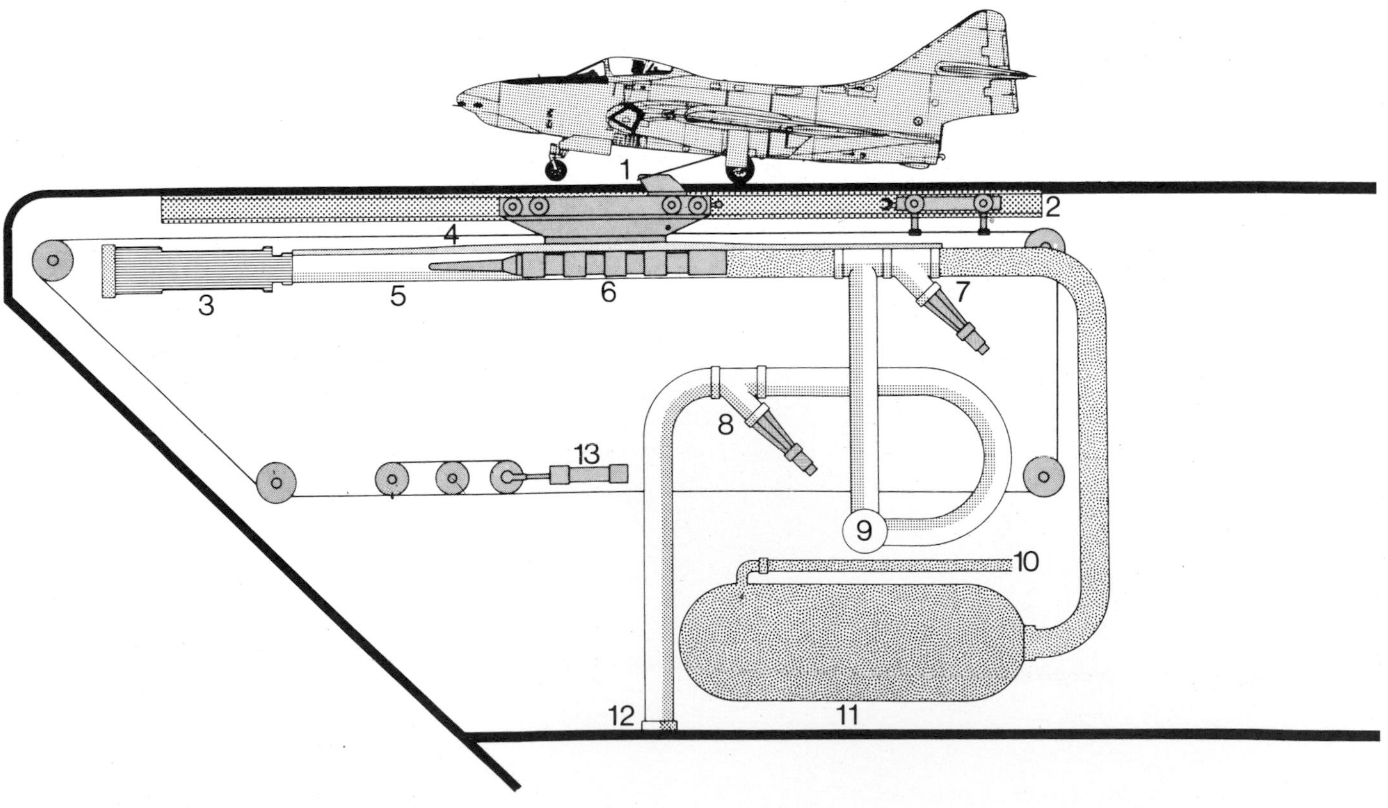

1 Towing strop
2 Shuttle return grab
3 Retardation cylinder
4 Cylinder seal
5 Twin cylinder tubes
6 Piston and shuttle assembly
7 Launch valve
8 Exhaust valve
9 Exhaust collector box
10 High pressure steam supply
11 Steam receiver
12 Exhaust steam
13 Hydraulic jigger and pulley sheave assembly operates return grab via cables to retrieve shuttle and pistons after launch

Britain's *Centaur*, test-bed for the angled flight-deck, in 1954

weaponry. The angled flight-deck, first experimented with in the light fleet carrier HMS *Triumph* (1951-52) was beyond price as an enhancer of safety. Instead of following the line of the ship's keel, the flight-deck is 'skewed' out from the port side at an angle varying from 5° to 10°. As a result, an incoming aircraft missing an arrester-wire merely has to open the throttle, go round and try again. Nor are aircraft which lose power and crash into the sea on take-off inevitably trampled under by the carrier's bow. Quite apart from the safety factor, the angled flight-deck has transformed the problem of ranging aircraft on deck during launch and recovery operations.

The US Navy was still appraising the angled flight-deck when, in late 1951, HMS *Perseus* arrived in US waters to demonstrate another vital new British carrier innovation. This was the steam catapult, which needed no separate power source to drive it but drew its tremendous energy direct from the ship's boilers. A launching valve, regulated by the weight and correct take-off speed of the aircraft, selects the head of steam required per launch. The beauty of the steam catapult is its simplicity: power on demand and power to spare. A carrier fitted with four steam catapults, two in the waist amidships and two forward, can launch aircraft virtually at the rate of one every

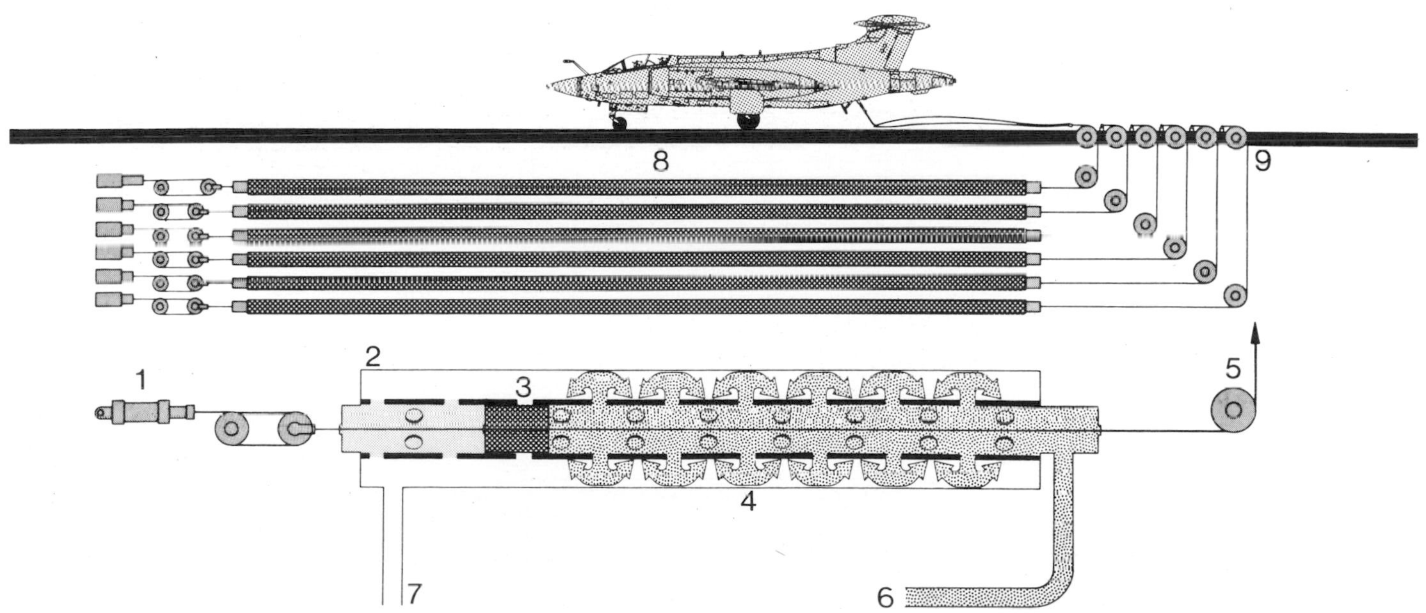

1 Cable resetting mechanism multi-sheave pulley system with hydraulic jigger
2 Spray containment tube
3 Piston
4 As piston is pulled along cylinder fluid is forced out of small holes in cylinder wall at increasing pressure to provide braking effect
5 Cable drawn out by landing aircraft
6 Continuously cycling replenishing fluid
7 Fluid return to reservoir
8 Braking cylinders (both sides of ship beneath flight-deck)
9 Six arresting cables strung across deck. Pulley sheaves guide cables up and across flight-deck

Occasionally an aircraft misses the arrester cables. If it cannot go round again, it is then stopped by a barrier of wire rope and webbing.

Essex, converted to the anti-submarine support role, in November 1968

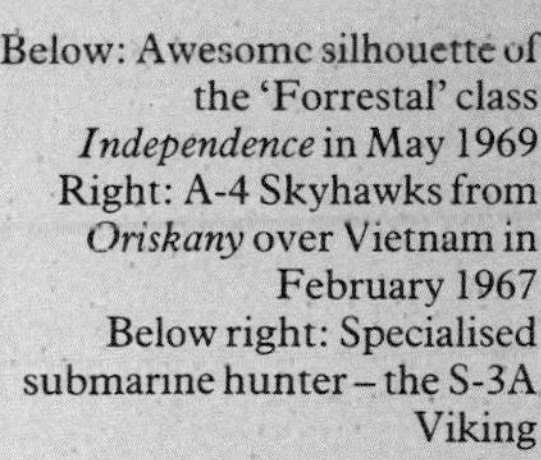

Below: Awesome silhouette of the 'Forrestal' class *Independence* in May 1969
Right: A-4 Skyhawks from *Oriskany* over Vietnam in February 1967
Below right: Specialised submarine hunter – the S-3A Viking

Advance of the giant carrier: *Forrestal*, serving with the 6th Fleet in the Mediterranean, August 1975

20 seconds. Thirty years since the steam catapult's adoption, there seems no limit to the deadweight of the aircraft it can launch. A modern naval fighter such as the F-14 Tomcat needs a mile of runway from which to get airborne ashore; the steam catapult does the job in barely 300 ft, hurling the fighter's 30-ton deadweight down the flight-deck at 170 mph in a marvellously controlled explosion of pure energy.

The third British contribution was really a rediscovery of the experimental Japanese work done aboard *Hosho* back in the 1920s: the mirror-landing system. This, too, was enforced by the increasing approach-speeds of the new post-war aircraft. The old-style 'batsman', mimicking the approaching aircraft's attitude with his bats and signalling appropriate corrective action for the pilot to take, was clearly a dangerous anachronism in the jet age. The sheer speed of approach left insufficient time for the message to travel from deck to cockpit – the reflexes of deck officer and pilot could not function at sufficient speed. But the mirror-landing system, cutting out the deck officer and leaving the approach to the pilot to judge, was yet another enormous safety gain. A pattern of lights is shone into a mirror on the carrier's deck. When the pilot has judged his approach correctly, he sees the correct pattern while looking naturally forward at the flight-deck instead of having to watch a gesticulating officer. Within 20 years of their adoption, American assessment set the accident reduction achieved by the adoption of the angled flight-deck and mirror-landing sights at 50 per cent.

All these improvements were built into Britain's last two fleet carriers, *Ark Royal* and *Eagle*; and into *Victorious*, the only one of Britain's wartime carriers to be given a comprehensive refit. And they were adopted with almost indecent haste for the first homogeneous carriers designed and built after the Second World War: the 79,500-ton giants of the American 'Forrestal' class. The speed with which the 'Forrestals' were brought into service in the late 1950s is attributable to the progress made with the Navy's projected giant carrier *United States*, aborted in 1949. The motive was the same. *Forrestal*, *Saratoga*, *Ranger* and *Independence* were conceived and rushed into service to carry the American seaborne nuclear deterrent. The 1950s had come in with the American deterrent firmly in the hands of the long-range land-based bombers. By the late 1950s, however, the opening rounds of the space race were already honing a formidable new armoury of intercontinental missiles. To such weapons the eternal mobility of the aircraft carrier task group was the obvious answer. With enough Soviet missiles to hand, every American nuclear bomber base

FORRESTAL (United States)
DISPLACEMENT 59,060 tons. DIMENSIONS 1,086 ft x 129½ ft x 37 ft. MACHINERY 4-shaft geared turbines: 260,000 SHP. SPEED 33 knots. ARMAMENT 2 x BPDMS Sea Sparrow missile launchers (*4 x 5-inch guns removed 1967*). AIRCRAFT approx. 70. COMPLEMENT approx. 4,940.

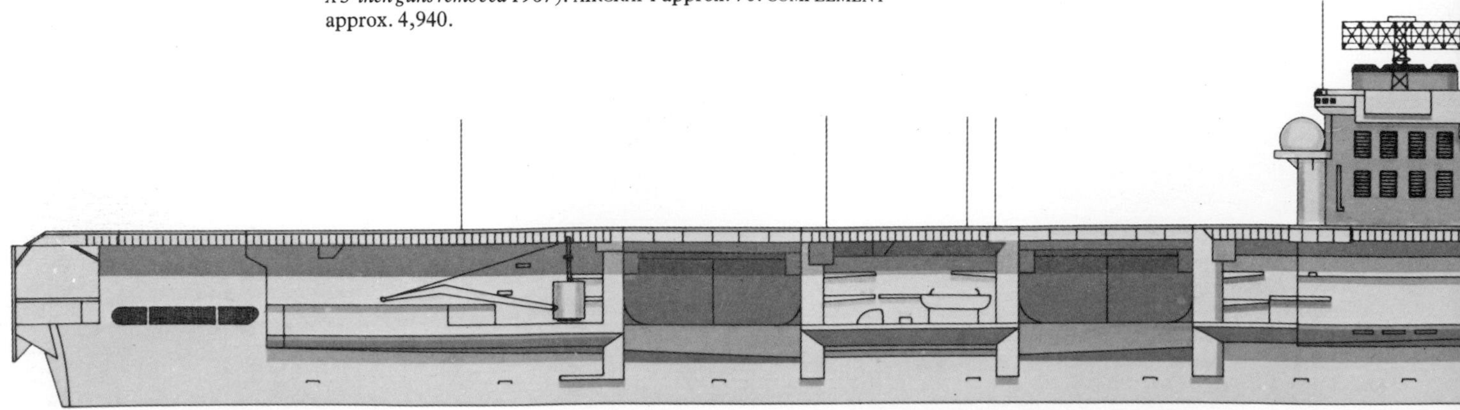

Steam wreathing from the catapult tracks of *Independence*, fanned by a UH-2B Seasprite helicopter (June 1969)

could be 'taken out' as a pinpointed, immovable target – which the fast-moving carrier task group at sea could never be.

Perhaps never again will a superpower ever indulge in so much hoped-for security, in so many forms, in so short a time. To the long-range nuclear bombers of Strategic Air Command, the American defence chiefs added the carrier menace of the 'Forrestals'. But before the first of these great ships had even entered service, the first ballistic missile submarine was already taking shape on the stocks. America's Polaris programme, so proudly announced as the 1960s opened, had deprived the carrier arm of its main strategic function at the outset.

The only other indigenous carrier navy established during the 1950s was that of France. In its vain attempt to hold French Indo-China against Ho Chi Minh's Vietminh, the post-war French Government needed every carrier it could get to ferry aircraft out to the Far East. The elderly *Béarn* and the discarded ex-British escort carrier *Dixmude* proving woefully inadequate, Britain obliged with the loan of HMS *Colossus* in August 1946. After five excellent years 'on approval', *Colossus* was finally bought by the French Navy as *Arromanches* in 1951. She was joined the same year by the former American 'Independence' class light carrier *Langley* sold to the French Navy as *Lafayette* in June 1951.

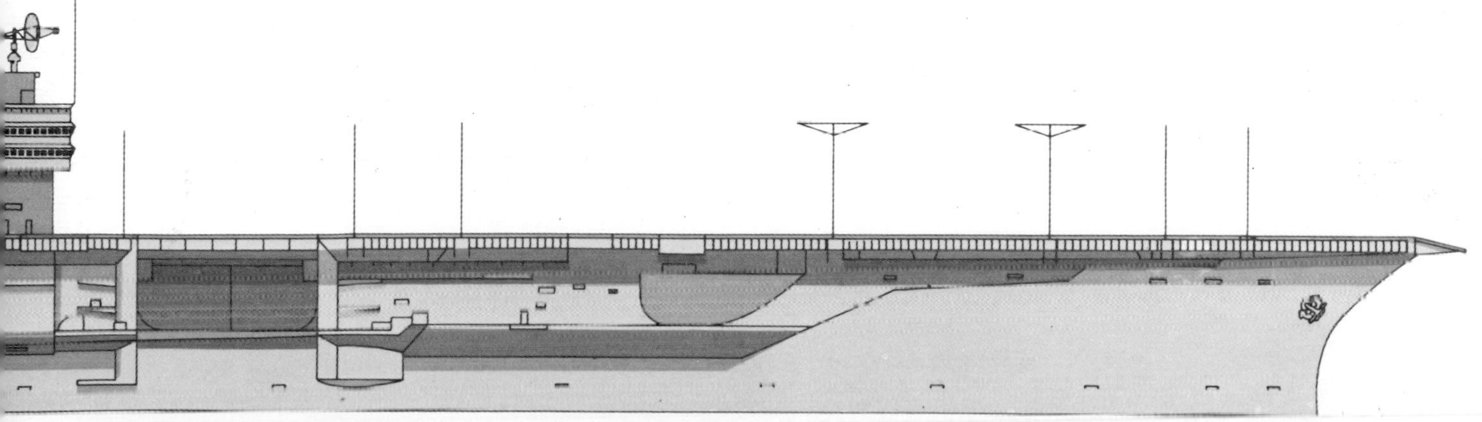

Below: Dassault Super Etendard fighter aboard the French carrier *Foch*. As with the USA, the post-war French Navy opted for a strong fleet air arm as well as a nuclear submarine fleet – while the British relied increasingly on the submarine-launched deterrent
Left: *Clemenceau* at sea. The French *Aéronavale* retains an excellent balance of anti-submarine and conventional carrier strike capability

Right: British foundation for the *Aéronavale*. *Colossus* flies the traditional outsize 'paying-off' pennant on the eve of her five-year approval period with the French Navy
Below: Helmsman's position in the French carrier *Foch*

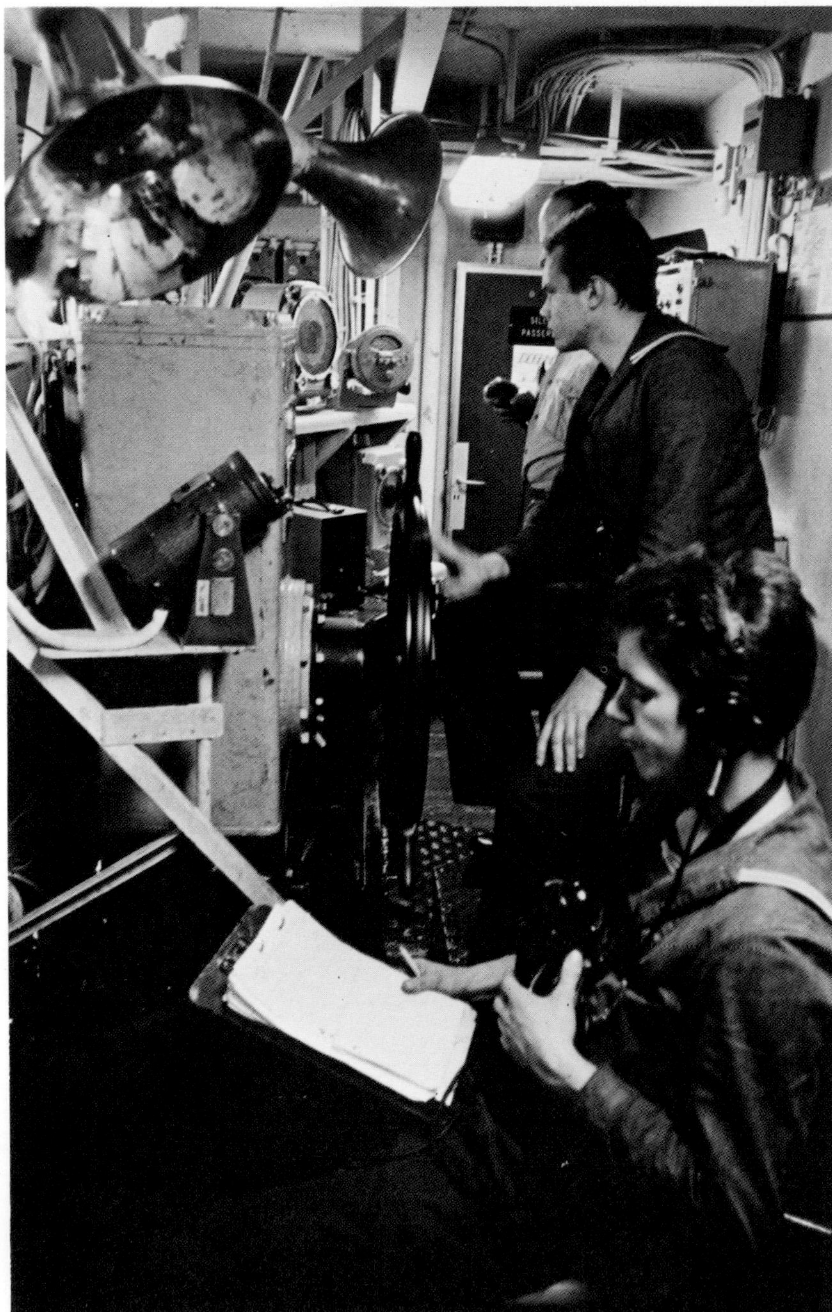

During the notorious battle of Dien Bien Phu (November 1953-May 1954) *Arromanches* and *Lafayette* strove manfully to support the troops 250 miles inland. But it was far too much of a task for two light carriers with a handful of piston-engined aircraft. In the teeth of the AA defences hemming the French in Dien Bien Phu, even the US 3rd Fleet at its wartime zenith would have been bound to suffer heavy losses for a doubtful result. The belated American sale of another 'Independence' class light carrier, *Belleau Wood* (*Bois Belleau* in the French service) came too late to help redress the balance at Dien Bien Phu.

DASSAULT SUPER ETENDARD (France)
TYPE Fighter. LOADED WEIGHT 26,445 lb. MAX. SPEED approx. Mach 1. RANGE 390 miles (*with anti-ship missile*). ARMAMENT 2 X 30 mm cannon; rockets, bombs, missiles.

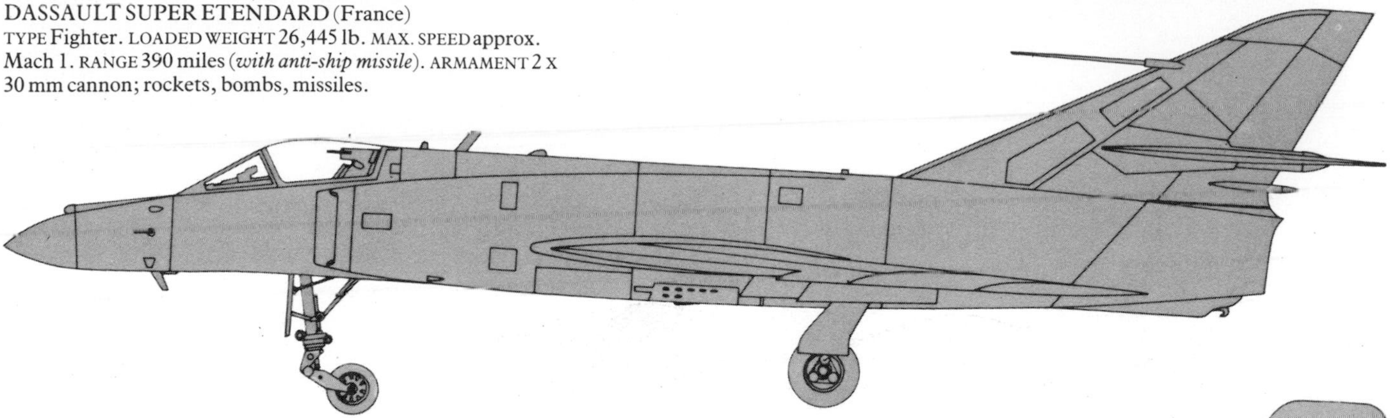

BREGUET Br 1050 ALIZÉ (France)
TYPE Anti-submarine. CREW 3. LOADED WEIGHT 18,100 lb. MAX. SPEED 254 (*knots*). RANGE 1,350 miles. ARMAMENT 2 X Matra R 530 missiles (on *Foch* and *Clemenceau*); AS.12 missiles, depth-charges OR torpedo.

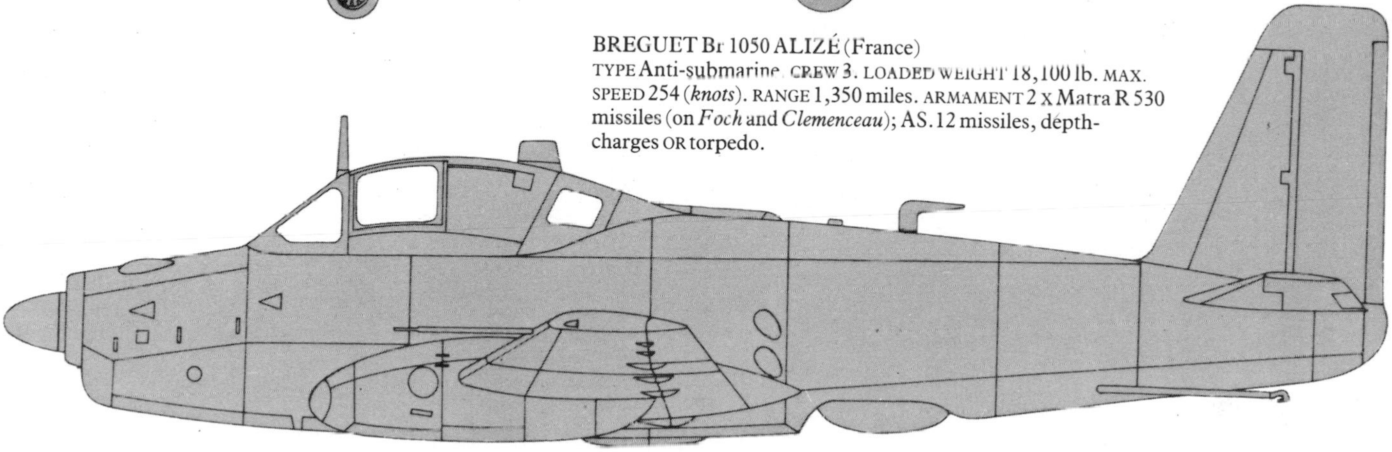

Despite the Dien Bien Phu disaster the French *Aéronavale* had gained invaluable experience, and the proper conclusions were drawn from what *had* been achieved. France's first indigenous fleet carrier, the 32,800-ton *Clemenceau*, was laid down in November 1955. She was therefore not ready when the Suez Crisis broke 12 months later, and once again *Arromanches* and *Lafayette* shouldered the load alongside the three British carriers. The French reaction to the Suez humiliation was in total contrast to the British with their orgies of self-denigration. After Suez the British sold off yet another light fleet carrier: *Hercules*, which went to India as *Vikrant* in January 1957. (The wartime fleet carriers *Illustrious* and *Indefatigable* had actually been sent to the breakers in the first week of November 1956, at the very moment of the assault on Suez.) The French, on the other hand, dourly laid down their second new fleet carrier: *Foch*, completed in July 1963.

When all associated arguments are set aside, the Suez venture had undeniably proved that 11 years into the jet and nuclear age, nothing had yet made the aircraft-carrier redundant. It had adapted readily to the new post-war technologies and transformations in naval aviation. In the form of the 'Forrestals' the carrier was preparing to assume – if only for a brief spell – the mantle of the naval strategic nuclear deterrent. But even this awesome concept was not to be the ultimate in carrier development. In the troubled aftermath of Suez planning was already in hand to add the enormous range of nuclear power-plants to the giant carrier – and create the biggest floating structures in history.

Left: Vital facility for the modern carrier – electronics workshop in *Clemenceau*

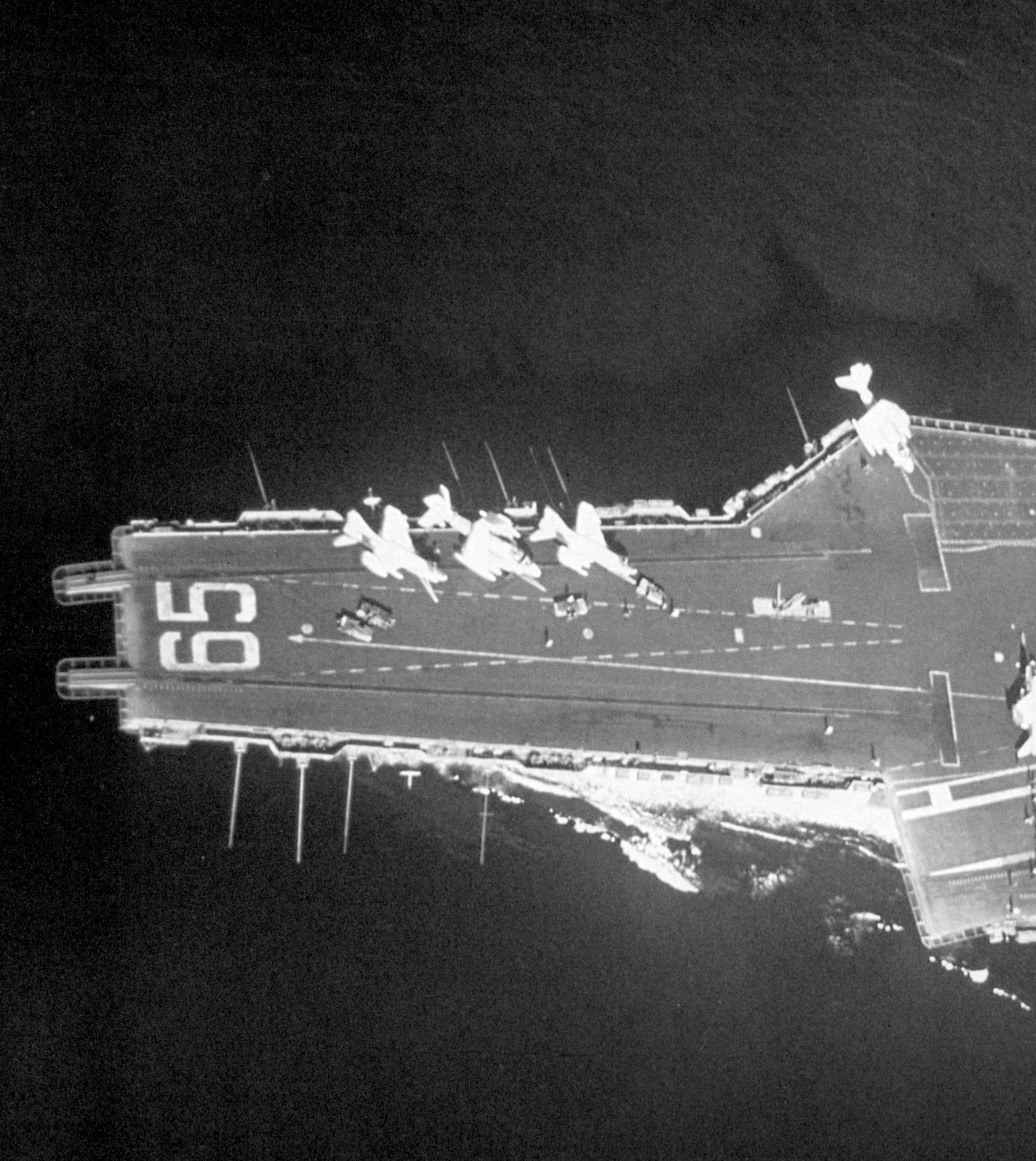
65

7. THE NUCLEAR GIANTS, 1958–1982

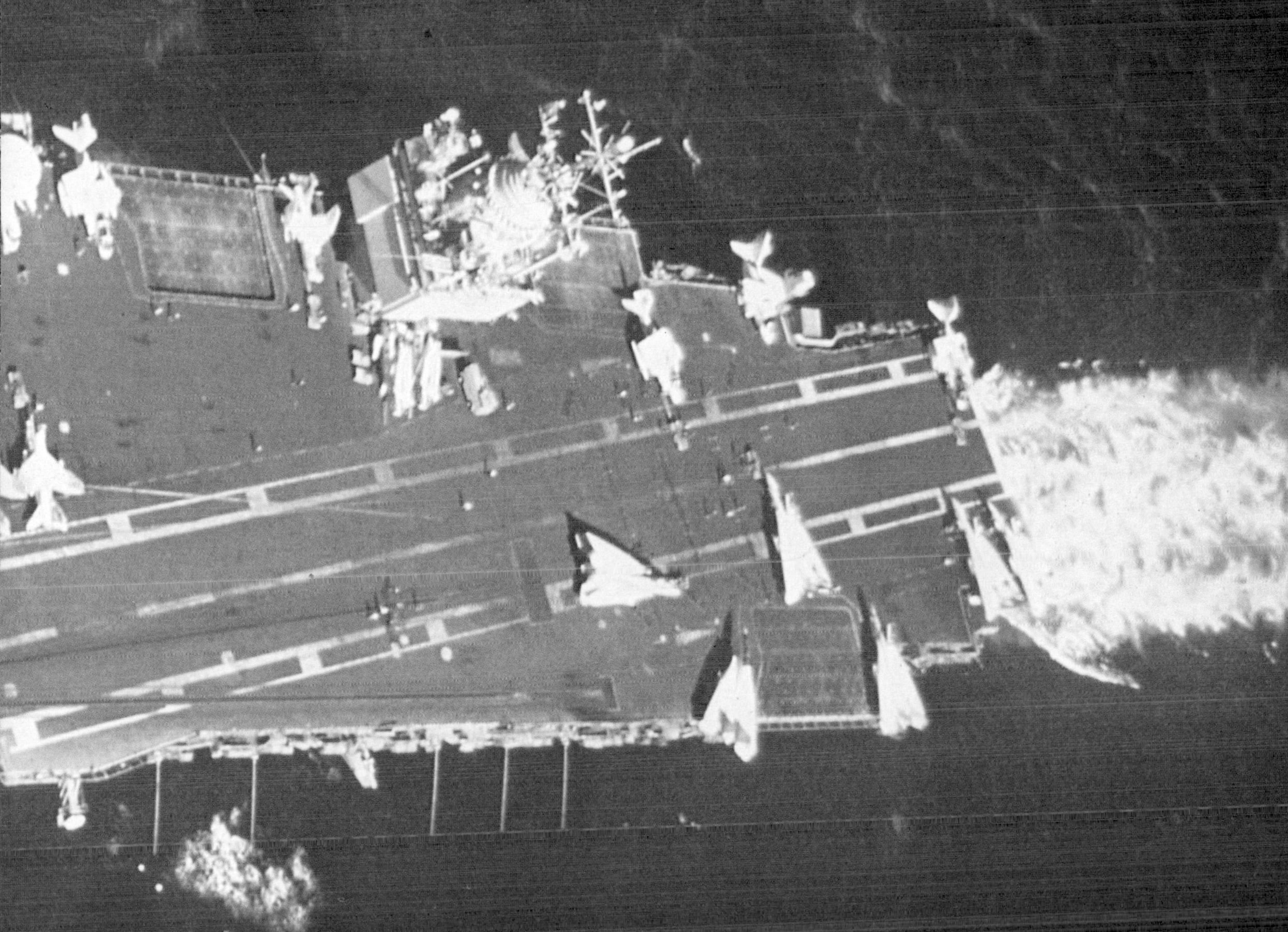

Previous pages: 'CVN-65' – *Enterprise*, the first nuclear-powered super-carrier, off southern California in 1978

THERE IS SOMETHING inimitably American about the sonorously-titled 'Nuclear-Powered Attack Aircraft-Carrier' (CVAN). They are the superlative ships, about which everything is biggest. They are the biggest ships of all time. They generate the most power. They carry the most potent strike aircraft. They are manned by the biggest crews and their food stores contain the most deep-frozen steaks! The list is endless, and it is all true – as is the fact the great American CVANs epitomise every argument which has ever been levelled at the aircraft-carrier as a big, fat, vulnerable target.

The modern submariner's verdict on the CVAN is easily reached. A CVAN is the easiest of targets for a modern attack submarine. Not so, retorts the CVAN champion; the CVAN, like any other carrier, is not designed to operate on her own, but at the heart of a concentric task group whose job it is to keep submarines at a safe distance. And even on her own a CVAN has the aircraft and weapons to detect and attack submarines. As the first captain of the CVAN USS *Enterprise* put it, in 1963: 'They say we have too many eggs in one basket; but I put it to you that this ship is no ordinary basket.'

Below: Supermarket facilities that would shame many a town ashore – ship's stores in *Dwight D. Eisenhower*.
Bottom: How crews 6,000 strong are fed – 'chow time' in *Nimitz*

Once the scientists had learned to control the heat and radiation of a nuclear pile (as well as creating giant releases of heat, blast and radiation for release as nuclear weapons) the nuclear-fired power plant was just round the corner. As far as warships are concerned, nuclear power plants consist of normal marine turbines driven by a closed-circuit steam engine, the latter being fired not by an ordinary oil-firing furnace, but by a nuclear pile. The advantages for warships had always been obvious: the ability to steam right round the world without refuelling, not once but many times. And such a prospect had physiologists and psychologists waiting in the wings, because this would be a total revolution in the essence of seafaring. Though it would undoubtedly deserve credit as one of the greatest scientific achievements of all time, all it did for the seaman was turn back the clock to the days of sail. With nuclear power, a ship's endurance would be measured not in the reserves in her fuel tanks, but in her men.

A nuclear power plant suitable for an aircraft-carrier had always been high on the US Navy's list of priorities in atomic research. Preliminary designs for nuclear-powered carriers began as early as 1950, only to be put on ice in 1953 pending results with the submarine reactor programme. By 1954 problems with the latter had been solved; USS *Nautilus*, the world's first nuclear-powered submarine, was already well on the way to completion. Work was promptly resumed on the 'Large Ship Reactor Programme', and construction of a land-based prototype power plant got under way in April 1956.

This experimental plant was an expression of the confident planning behind the American nuclear power programme in general – confidence which would be shown again to good advantage in the 1960s, with the NASA space programmes. The new plant consisted of two reactors and steam-generating equipment sufficient to drive one aircraft-carrier propellor shaft. This would represent 25 per cent of the full-size plant, which would use eight reactors, two to a shaft. 'Criticality', the moment when the nuclear 'fire' in a pile becomes self-sustaining, was achieved in the first reactor in August 1958 and in the second reactor in July 1959. The experimental shaft rig was successfully operated at full power on 15 September 1959. Until then there was no concrete proof that nuclear power was feasible for 'Forrestal' sized carriers – yet 'CVAN 65', the carrier for which the power-plant was intended, had been under construction for the past 19 months (laid down on 4 February 1958). And the name assigned to the new ship was that of the most famous American carrier of the Second World War: *Enterprise*.

'CV.6', the last American pre-war carrier to have survived (*Ranger* had been scrapped in 1947) went to the breakers in September 1958. It must be a matter of regret that the otherwise excellent American concern for historic ships – in depressing contrast to the near-total apathy of post-war Britain – failed to save the first *Enterprise* for posterity as a museum ship. If ever a ship's wartime career was unique, that of the *Enterprise* was; she had been in every major battle and campaign of the Pacific War except the Coral Sea, and she had only arrived too late for that battle by the narrowest of margins. That her name should be passed on to the first CVAN was the highest possible expression of the trust reposed in the new ship.

The second *Enterprise* naturally drew heavily on the experience gained with the four 'Forrestals' and the two improved ships which had been laid down in 1956 and 1957: *Kitty Hawk* and *Constellation*. The island was laid back towards the stern in order to permit the two starboard-side deck-edge lifts to be positioned forward, creating the widest possible aircraft 'parking area' on the forward flight-deck. The latter facility was also increased by the fact that the island did not have to accommodate smoke-stack and boiler air intakes. *Enterprise* used the 'Forrestal' catapult arrangement: two in the waist, two in the bow to permit high-speed launching by pairs when required. Somewhat startlingly, she was the first warship to be completed without any armament – the result of an effort to hold down her appalling construction-costs ($451.3 million, compared to $264.5 million for *Constellation* and $188.9 million for *Forrestal*). Space was left for the installation of surface-to-air missiles – in 1981 consisting of two 'Basic Point Defence Missile Systems' to launch the Sea Sparrow surface-to-air missile. The latter provision – or rather lack of it – was indicative of changing times. The gun was no longer the core of a carrier's defensive fire-power; in-

Nine warships from four navies. Grouped round the CVN *Enterprise* are the New Zealand frigate *Canterbury*, Canadian frigates *Gatineau*, *Kootenay* and *Restigouche*, British light cruiser *Glamorgan*, and American guided-missile cruisers *Chicago* and *Truxton* (March 1976)

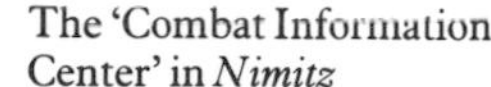

The 'Combat Information Center' in *Nimitz*

Above: *Enterprise* under way
Right: Shore/sea consultation during the Vietnam War. General Westmoreland's C-1 Trader folds its wings after landing on *Enterprise* at 'Yankee Station' for a conference between general and admiral

Above: Mission completed – EA-3B Skywarrior returns to *Enterprise* in the Gulf of Tonkin (April 1966)
Left: Modern carrier flak – a Sea Sparrow missile is launched from *John F. Kennedy*

deed, the only use for guns in carriers of this sophistication seemed to be the courtesy-role of firing salutes. *Forrestal*, laid down in 1952, had been fitted with dual purpose 5-inch guns; but she and her three sister-ships subsequently had them removed.

Quite as important as missiles in *Enterprise*'s defence was the unprecedented concentration of radars and electronic counter-measures (ECM) in the island's tower. ECM had existed from the earliest days of radio, when hostile operators would try to jam the enemy's signals. It had intensified in the Second World War with the new dimension of radar; and by the full dawn of the missile era in the late 1950s was accepted as a vital new facet of naval warfare. As radio and radar links became increasingly secure with the advance of the new technology, ECM could no longer rely on mere jamming to blank off the enemy's signals to his missile: there must be the facility for the defender's ECM to impose its own will on the enemy missile's circuits, either turning it aside or maybe blowing it up in flight by means of a violent shift in wavelength. This increasing reliance on electronic systems for ship defence is, to many diehard critics of the aircraft-carrier in the post-war era, one of the modern carrier's biggest weaknesses.

Yet one element of carrier defence patrol has always remained unchanged since the Second World War: the maxim that the carrier's main line of defence is her aircraft. Permanently orbiting above any CVAN is a radar surveillance aircraft – currently the E-2C 'Hawkeye' – whose screens scan all movement within 250 miles of the carrier. And the eternal value of CAP – combat air patrol by orbiting fighters – was shown on 19 August 1981, when Tomcats from *Nimitz* shot down two belligerent Libyan fighters.

Enterprise's first set of reactor cores lasted three years, in which time she steamed over 207,000 miles. After an overhaul and core change (with the second set of cores costing about $44 less than the first), a new set yielded about 300,000 miles of steaming.

Some 'vital statistics' for *Enterprise*, her predecessors and successor are given below:

(Comparative specifications for USS *Forrestal*, *Enterprise*, *Nimitz*)

	Forrestal	*Enterprise*	*Nimitz*
DISPLACEMENT	59,060 tons	75,700 tons	81,600 tons
LENGTH	1,086 ft	1,102 ft	1,092 ft
FLIGHT DECK WIDTH	252 ft	252 ft	252 ft
DRAUGHT	37 ft	35.8 ft	37 ft
COMPLEMENT: SHIP	2,790	3,100	3,300
COMPLEMENT: AIR WING	2,150	2,400	3,000

Nine and a half years, however, separated the ordering of *Enterprise* and the second CVAN, USS *Nimitz*. The reason for this delay was no lack of faith in the type: the CVAN was, so to speak, pushed brusquely aside to let the Polaris submarine programme through. All five of the first batch of 'George Washington' Polaris ships had been commissioned before *Enterprise* (November 1961); five more 'Ethan Allens' had followed by January 1963, to be followed in turn by the immensely costly main batch of 31 'Benjamin Franklin' and 'Lafayette' class ships. The last of these, *Will Rogers*, was not commissioned until April 1967; and it was not until that year's new construction programme that *Nimitz*, the second CVAN, was authorised. The carrier fleet had, however, received two non-nuclear additions since *Enterprise: America* (commissioned January 1965) and *John F. Kennedy* (commissioned September 1968). Both were of the 'improved Forrestal' type, sister-ships to *Kitty Hawk* and *Constellation*.

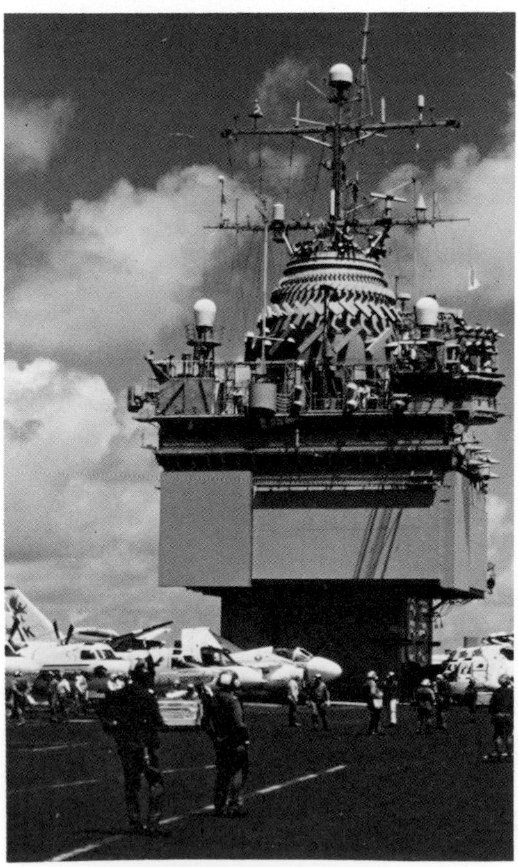

The distinctive, four-square island structure of the nuclear fleet carrier (made possible by the absence of conventional funnel uptakes) surrounded by its fixed radar arrays

GRUMMAN E-2 HAWKEYE (United States)
TYPE Airborne Early Warning. LOADED WEIGHT 51,900 lb. MAX. SPEED 325 (*knots*). RANGE 1,394 miles (*ferry*). ENDURANCE 6 hours 6 mins.

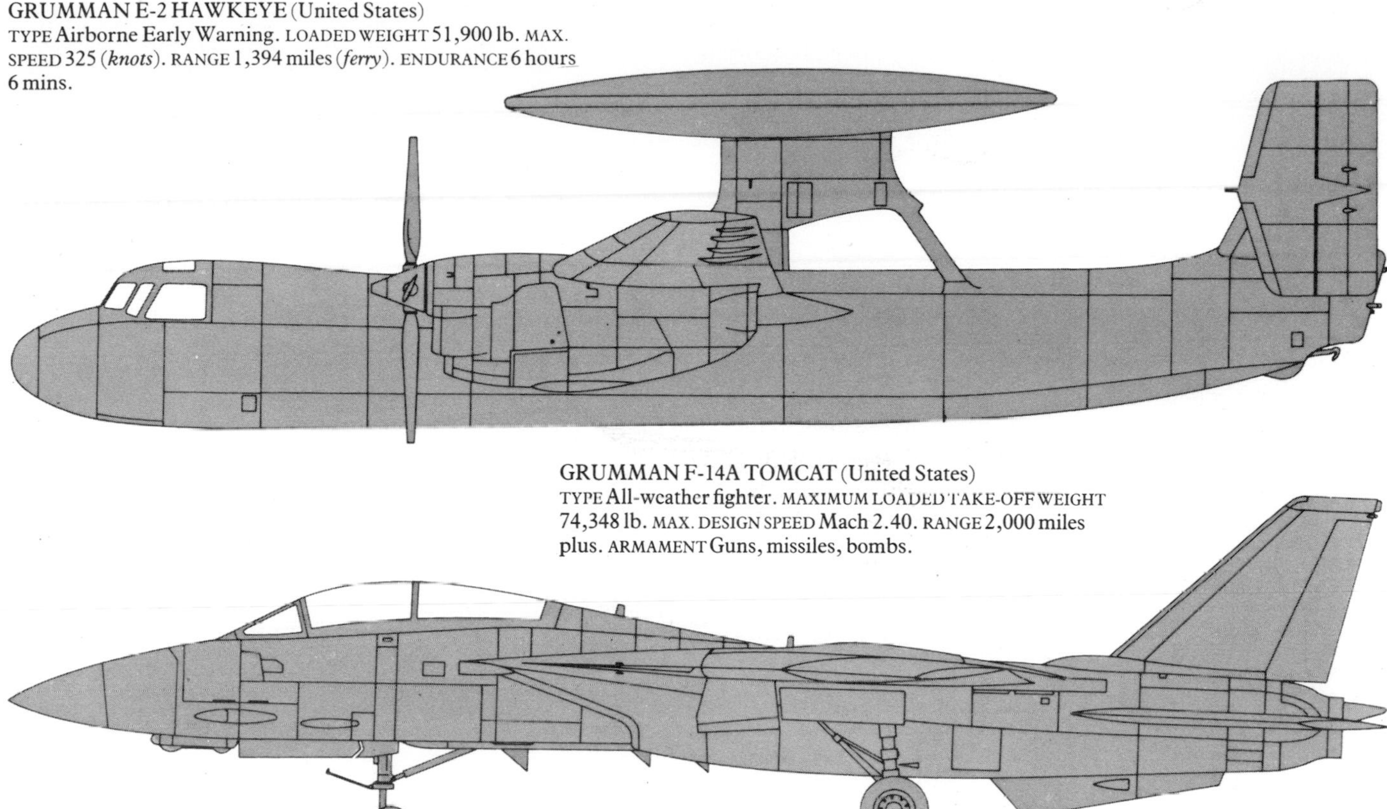

GRUMMAN F-14A TOMCAT (United States)
TYPE All-weather fighter. MAXIMUM LOADED TAKE-OFF WEIGHT 74,348 lb. MAX. DESIGN SPEED Mach 2.40. RANGE 2,000 miles plus. ARMAMENT Guns, missiles, bombs.

In this way the onus of the American nuclear deterrent passed from an attack-carrier force 15 strong to a nuclear submarine force 40 strong. But though the original motive for building the CVA fleet no longer existed, the CVAs continued to wield a formidable nuclear strike potential – the ostentatious face of nuclear deterrence, with the carrier's traditional twin advantages of mobility and high conventional striking power thrown in. But the cost was staggering. The non-nuclear *America* and *John F. Kennedy* had a combined construction cost of $525.8 million – $74 million more than *Enterprise*. Most likely *John F. Kennedy* would have remained the last CVA, and *Enterprise* the only CVAN, without the steady escalation of the Vietnam conflict into all-out war. The ensuing concentration of CVAs with the 7th Fleet in the Gulf of Tonkin, which naturally affected the deployment of the CVAs around the world, effectively assisted the case for further additions to the CVA fleet.

The performance of the CVAs during the Vietnam war re-stated all the aircraft-carrier virtues previously revealed in the Second World War and Korea. Here again was the matchless blend of manoeuvrability and hitting-power – with the accent on *selective* hitting-power. A good example of this selectivity was the achievement of the CVA-based RA-5C Vigilante. This was the photo-reconnaissance version of the A-5B Vigilante, a high-speed attack bomber which could reach Mach 2.1 (over twice the speed of sound) and carry nuclear as well as conventional bombs over a normal range of 2,000 miles. The speed, range, and multi-sensor equipment of the RA-5C Vigilante variant was exploited to complete a minute air survey of both North and South Vietnam – which in turn made possible the production of the most accurate campaign maps which it had ever been possible to achieve.

Shuttling models, flight-deck controllers plan the intricate ballet of aircraft launch and recovery aboard *Kitty Hawk* on the eve of a Canadian/US/Australian/New Zealand naval exercise ('Rimpac') in April 1975

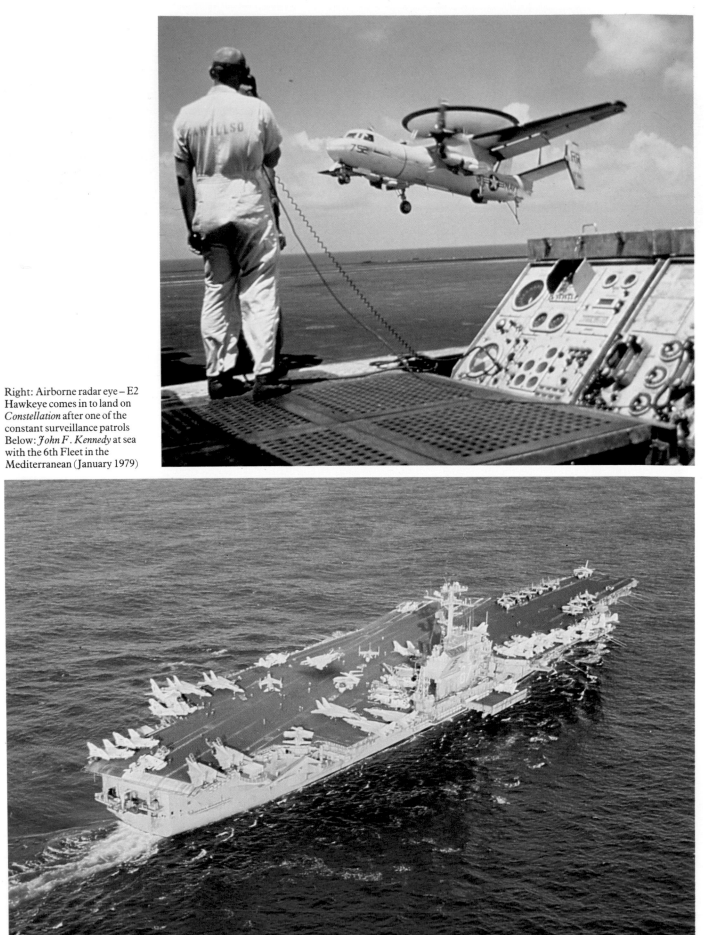

Right: Airborne radar eye – E2 Hawkeye comes in to land on *Constellation* after one of the constant surveillance patrols
Below: *John F. Kennedy* at sea with the 6th Fleet in the Mediterranean (January 1979)

Unfortunately for the United States, this was a war in which neither technological wizardry nor unlimited fire-power guaranteed victory, any more than they had for the French 20-odd years before. It must be admitted that Vietnam was not a complete combat vindication for the CVAs. Though *Enterprise* was prudently fitted with AA defences before being sent to join the 7th Fleet, the carriers were never attacked as the 3rd and 5th Fleets had been attacked by Japanese land-based aircraft in the last year of the Pacific War. Certainly one most unwelcome discovery (from the carrier fanatic's point of view) was that in a prolonged attrition campaign like Vietnam, the high cost of sophisticated modern combat aircraft made the inevitable incidental losses over enemy territory unacceptably high. Once again it was found that for short-range tactical fire support, radar-guided battleship gunfire offered similar results at a far lower cost. This was demonstrated by the battleship *New Jersey*, briefly recommissioned for bombardment trials off Vietnam at a cost barely greater than that of six downed F4 Phantom fighters. In a mere 120 days off Vietnam (1968-69) *New Jersey* fired 5,688 rounds from her 16-inch main armament. This was precisely 4,917 *more* than she had fired during her first commission, from May 1943 to the end of the Pacific War.

By the time of *New Jersey*'s arrival off Vietnam, however, the second CVAN had already been ordered and laid down. This was USS *Nimitz*, which at 91,487 tons' displacement at

Top: RA-5C Vigilante taking-off from *Enterprise* in April 1966
Above: Sustained throughout the Vietnam War – the Second World War battleship fire-support role. This is a 16-inch broadside from *New Jersey* in May 1968
Left: A-6E Intruder from *Dwight D. Eisenhower* over the Caribbean in 1979

full load deposed *Enterprise* as the world's biggest warship. The choice of a radically different power plant, with the four shafts driven by only two reactors instead of eight, understandably gave repeated teething trouble and delayed *Nimitz*'s commissioning until May 1975. Seldom if ever has the appearance of a new warship been more welcome to a nation's hard-pressed propagandists, for the internal trauma of Watergate and the ensuing resignation of President Nixon had been followed by total defeat in Vietnam. The appearance of the mightiest warship in the history of the world was, however, accompanied by a horrific final bill: $1,881 million. (The cost of *Enterprise* 14 years earlier had been $451.3 million.) The second of the class, *Dwight D. Eisenhower* (ordered 1970) was launched in October 1975 and the third, *Carl Vinson* (ordered 1974) was promptly laid down. *Eisenhower* and *Vinson* were both expected to surpass $2 billion and proposals already existed to order two more (Nos. 71 and 72). This was opposed by both Presidents Ford and Carter, optimistically blundering along

Left: Even with a loaded displacement of 78,500 tons, *America* heels distinctly as she makes a full-speed turn.
Above: Plotting ship and aircraft positions aboard *Kitty Hawk* during the exercise 'Rimpac 75'

Left: With nuclear power, a warship's operational endurance is measured in human rather than mechanical terms – hence the lavish feeding arrangements in nuclear carriers (in this case *Dwight D. Eisenhower*)

Catapult crewman signals the launch of an F-4 Phantom II from USS Constellation in the South China Sea 1972.

Above: A-7E Corsair hitched to the towing-tractor on the flight-deck of *Enterprise*. EA-6B Prowlers at left
Below: E-2A Hawkeye undergoing maintenance in the hangar of *Nimitz*

the path of 'detente' with the Soviet Union while beset with mounting financial problems at home.

A significant change had crept in to nuclear carrier classification by the time *Nimitz* entered service. In June 1975 the CVAs lost their 'A' (for attack) and were re-classified as multi-purpose – anti-submarine AND attack. This was a recognition of the enormous strides made by the Soviet submarine fleet, which had barely existed when the 'Forrestals' were laid down. Any hopes that the US Navy would retain an unchallenged lead over the Soviet Navy, either in nuclear-powered submarines or in nuclear ballistic-missile submarines, were successively dashed. By the middle 1970s, with the Soviet submarine fleet well armed with both nuclear fleet and ballistic-missile submarines, the monitoring and prompt destruction of Soviet submarines had become an essential part of the giant carrier's duties.

The six-year opposition to the fourth 'Nimitz' class carrier was to have vital effects on the global deployment of nuclear carriers in the 1980s. With *Enterprise* and four of the 'Nimitz' class, the US Navy would have been able to deploy four of the (now re-classified) CVNs simultaneously – in the Pacific, Indian and Atlantic Oceans, and with the 6th Fleet in the Mediterranean – while allowing the fifth to complete long overhauls, nuclear core changes, or whatever tasks might require prolonged periods at base. Such a deployment would have ensured that from the 1980s onward a CVN would be permanently within range of South-East Asia, the all-important oil source of the Persian Gulf, the Mediterranean Middle East, and NATO's northern flank in Norway. But with only three CVNs permanently at sea this capability was lost, and the American heavy-carrier force for the moment must continue to rely on its 'fossil-fuelled' ships to keep CVA task groups permanently at sea. Five years were to pass before the Soviet invasion of Afghanistan in November 1979 dispelled the illusion of 'detente' and reversed the decision not to build a fifth CVN. But nothing could be done to retrieve those five wasted years, or to cut down on the seven-year construction-time required for these huge and complex warships.

There can, however, be little doubt that with the 'Nimitz' class CVNs the traditional concept of the heavy fleet carrier, enjoying as it does the transformed power yields and sea-keeping endurance conferred by nuclear power, has been taken to what must be considered its final stage of development. In 1982, the 40th anniversary of Midway, *Yorktown*, *Enterprise* and *Hornet*, the victors of that classic carrier encounter, are only directly comparable to *Nimitz* and her consorts in one respect: maximum speed through the water of 30-34 knots. Comparison of other 'vital statistics' reveals the following staggering advances made during those 40 years:

	USS *Yorktown* (1942)	USS *Nimitz* (1982)
Displacement (standard light tonnage)	19,900 tons	81,600 tons
Overall length	809½ ft	1,092 ft
Max. beam	83¼ ft	252 ft
Draught	21¾ ft	37 ft
Standard horsepower (from 4-shaft turbines)	120,000	280,000
Complement (inc. air group)	2,200	6,300

In mere numbers of aircraft carried the gain over the years is zero: 90-100, according to type, in both *Yorktown* of 1942 and *Nimitz* of 1982. This is, however, an invalid comparison; it is virtually impossible to drawn up a balance-sheet between the piston-engined fighters and strike aircraft of 1942 and the air group of a CVN in the 1980s. Tactical nuclear weapons apart, the modern strike aircraft can be fitted with external 'stores', in the form of air-to-surface missile launches, which match or even surpass the destructive power of a Second World War battleship broadside. Or again, the 'average' long operating range of Second World War carrier aircraft was in the region of 300 miles. In the 1980s it would be possible for Tomcat fighters launched from 6th Fleet carriers in the central Mediterranean, given their speed of double that of sound and altitude of over 56,000 ft, to intervene in an air battle over northern Germany – over 1,100 miles from 'home'.

When all these improvements and advantages are listed and admitted, however, critics of the aircraft-carrier still have a formidable case when querying the CVN's 'survivability'. The most obvious objection, the one most frequently used by the more shameless Western politicians seeking to buy votes by making defence economies, is that 'the carrier can be wiped out by a single missile'. This presupposes that the Soviet Union has a long-range strategic nuclear missile capable of taking out a seaborne target moving at over 30 knots – and has enough of such missiles to spare to guarantee the destruction of every NATO carrier task group at sea. In view of the known advantage of NATO in numbers of long-range nuclear weapons, this seems unlikely. Air-launched medium and short-ranged missiles are another matter, but the CVN is too well equipped with aircraft, electronic counter-measures and surface-to-air missile defences for such missiles to pose an impossible threat.

Though the CVN is custom-built to exploit the latest marvels of naval aviation, its biggest peril lies not aloft but below. In the Second World War, submarines accounted for less than 50 per cent of the numbers of carriers sunk – but that was in the days when submarines could barely make 10 knots submerged. Since 1945, however, the submarine has been transformed into a nuclear-powered, streamlined menace far faster submerged than

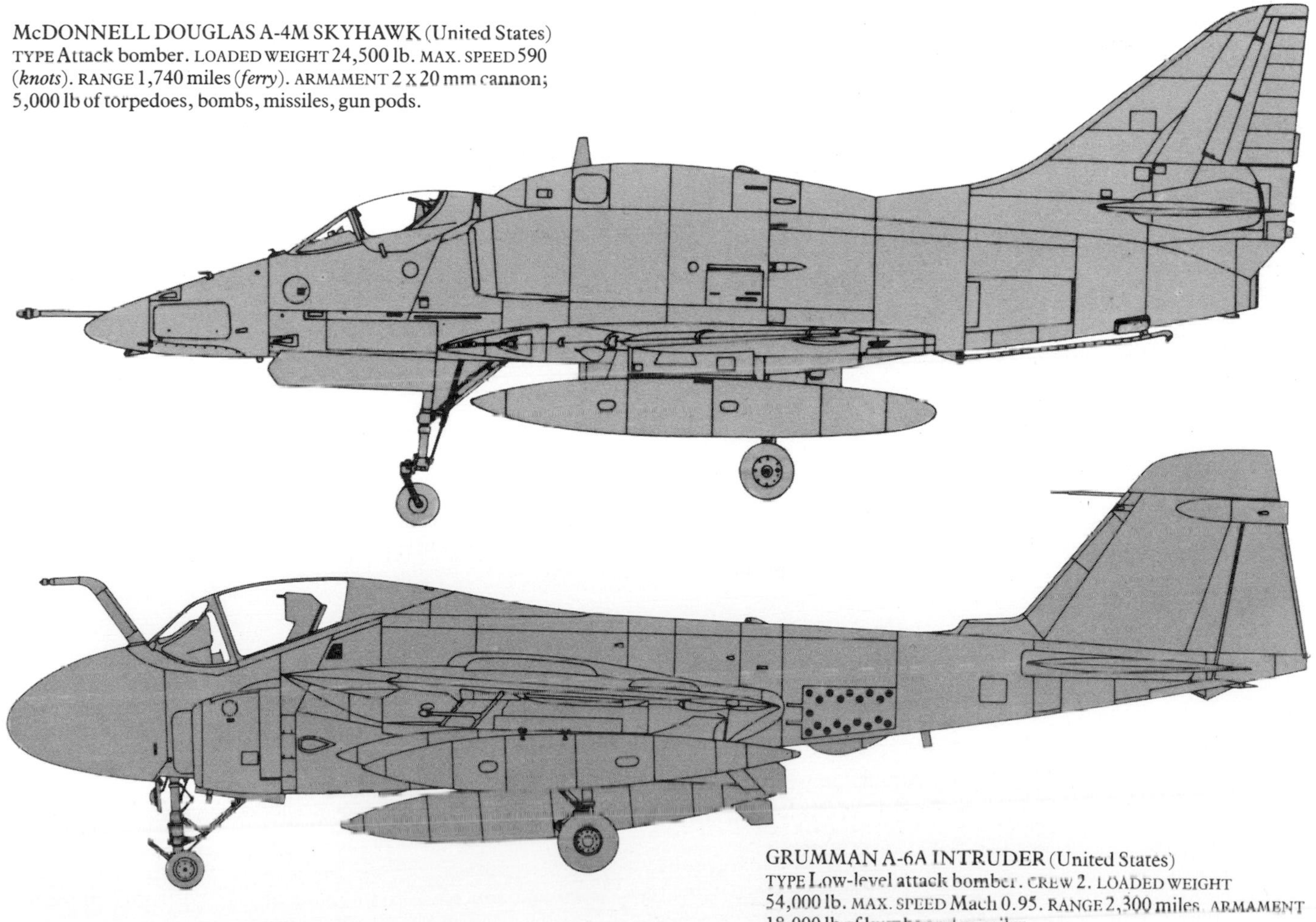

McDONNELL DOUGLAS A-4M SKYHAWK (United States)
TYPE Attack bomber. LOADED WEIGHT 24,500 lb. MAX. SPEED 590 (*knots*). RANGE 1,740 miles (*ferry*). ARMAMENT 2 x 20 mm cannon; 5,000 lb of torpedoes, bombs, missiles, gun pods.

GRUMMAN A-6A INTRUDER (United States)
TYPE Low-level attack bomber. CREW 2. LOADED WEIGHT 54,000 lb. MAX. SPEED Mach 0.95. RANGE 2,300 miles. ARMAMENT 18,000 lb of bombs and missiles.

The greatest floating structure ever created by man: *Nimitz* in the Indian Ocean (March 1980)

on the surface. The fastest Soviet attack submarines are known to have submerged speeds in excess of 30 knots, and have actually been detected making submerged speeds of 42 knots. Such speed advantages become even more worrying when one remembers that they have the bonus of superior manoeuvrability, unaffected by surface wind and weather conditions. The development of such craft has ended the years when a submarine commander was forced to lie in ambush, hoping for a lucky shot as the enemy carrier task group shot through his periscope vision. It is true that over the same period, from the début of the nuclear submarine in the middle 1950s, the detection of submerged submarines has been improved out of all measure by more sensitive devices, deployed at ever-lengthening radii by shipborne helicopters. But *detection* is one thing, *destruction* another. Anti-submarine weaponry – in the form of high-speed hunting torpedoes – has yet to reach a level when the *guaranteed destruction* of even the fastest nuclear submarines can be taken for granted.

This was the factor which led to the re-classification of the CVN's basic function in 1975, from the pure offensive to a multi-purpose role – anti-submarine as well as attack. Conceived and developed as the epitome of surface warship offensive potential, the CVN had been forced to look to its own anti-submarine defences in less than 20 years of its majestic début.

8. FATEFUL DECISIONS, 1962–1981

Previous pages: Britain's *Hermes* in 1973, in her commando-carrier role (note helicopter landing spots) before her equipment with the 'ski-jump' flight-deck to enable her to operate Sea Harriers

IN OCTOBER 1962 THE SOVIET ATTEMPT to instal medium-range missiles on Cuban soil was foiled by President Kennedy's 'quarantine' – which to all intents and purposes meant conventional surface naval blockade. The very real possibility of a nuclear war was thus averted by the intelligent use of one of the oldest conventional naval strategies in the book. The resolution of the Cuba Crisis of 1962 was therefore a triumphant vindication of the sheer *economy* of conventional sea power; and a glowing future might have been predicted for that most potent instrument of conventional sea power, the aircraft-carrier.

Despite the lesson of Cuba, however, the two ensuing decades saw the British take a step completely at variance with their American naval allies: the announcement that aircraft-carriers had lost their validity as the foremost instrument of security by sea. Less than four years after the Cuba Crisis, Harold Wilson's Labour Government announced that the British fleet carriers were to be phased out, with land-based aircraft assuming the carriers' former role. A virtual moratorium on all surface warship construction from 1964 to 1970 confirmed that Britain's Labour masters were prepared to let the Royal Navy's conventional fleet go to the wall. The new British fleet (or rather squadron) of four Polaris missile-carrying nuclear submarines was to carry the onus of Britain's defence by sea.

The fatal attraction – British nuclear ballistic-missile submarine *Renown*. Under Harold Wilson and Denis Healey in the mid-1960s, the politician's eternal weakness for the headline-grabbing option put the ownership of a Polaris submarine fleet before the maintenance of Britain's superb Fleet Air Arm

The strategic implications of this were far-ranging. Ever since the establishment of the North Atlantic Treaty Organisation in 1949, the Royal Navy had accepted responsibility for the eastern Atlantic and Norwegian Sea. The small post-war force of British fleet carriers – *Ark Royal*, *Eagle* and the modernised *Victorious* – had enabled this responsibility to be borne without jeopardising British carrier flag-showing cruises to other waters. But the phasing-out of these carriers without replacement would mean only one thing. The US Navy would have to take over the Norwegian Sea, a highly unwelcome extension of its already stretched deployment even before the exhausting and prolonged ordeal of Vietnam. Thus, in exchange for the purely *notional* contribution to NATO of 64 Polaris missiles, Britain wilfully chose to inflict the biggest *actual* tactical weakening ever suffered by the NATO deployment at sea.

When the death sentence of Britain's carrier fleet was read out in the Defence White Paper of February 1966, 22 years had passed since the last British carrier had been laid down. Over the same period the United States Navy had completed no less than seven 'Forrestals' and were already at work on the eighth: and *Enterprise*, the first nuclear-powered carrier, had been in service for the past four years. These carriers alone represented the most powerful peacetime fleet ever maintained by the USA, but they were only the tip of the iceberg. Serving behind the giant new carriers were the following veterans of the American wartime carrier fleet:

12 former escort carriers as aircraft ferries;
17 'Essex' class fleet carriers;
5 'Oriskany' class fleet carriers (improved/enlarged 'Essex' class);
3 'Midway' class fleet carriers.

In dismal contrast the British carrier fleet in 1966 consisted of:

Hermes (laid down June 1944, completed November 1959);
Ark Royal (laid down May 1943, completed February 1955);
Eagle (laid down October 1942, completed October 1951);
Centaur (laid down May 1944, completed September 1953);
Victorious (laid down May 1937, completed May 1941);
and two 'commando carriers', former sister-ships of *Centaur* but left with straight flight-decks for the airlifting of Marine commandos by helicopter:
Bulwark (laid down May 1945, completed 1954);
Albion (laid down March 1944, completed May 1954).

End of the line for Britain's last fleet carrier – *Ark Royal* leaves Devonport on her last commission in April 1978

Thus in 1966 the US Navy was still employing the services of 21 fleet carriers and ten escort carriers which had first seen service in the Pacific War. Britain had precisely one wartime carrier still in service – *Victorious* – and she was retired only two years later. With near totality, Britain had therefore rejected the most urgent lesson of the Second World War at sea: that when war breaks out a naval power has to fight with what it has. If the Royal Navy in 1940-42 had been unable to rely on the old First World War 'V and W' destroyers, it is hard to see how the Battle of the Atlantic could have been won. No sooner had the country emerged from the war, however, when all this experience went by the board. By 1950, with the run-down of the carrier fleet already proceeding apace, the Royal Navy had disposed of no less than 138 destroyers and corvettes – the all-important submarine hunters. The official British Admiralty attitude towards the wartime US Navy was that many features of the American service were spendthrift and wasteful. Yet after the war the profligacy with which British warships were sold or scrapped, while their American counterparts were thriftily laid up for future service, told its own story.

The irony was that the British had developed the carrier, had been the first to demonstrate its potential in action, and had emerged from the war with the carrier arm triumphant. The post-war stagnation had as its immediate reason the failure to develop adequate jet-age fighter and strike aircraft until the late 1950s, while at the same time British expertise had produced the angled flight-deck, steam catapult and mirror-landing sight. Uncertainty over the immediate future of the Fleet Air Arm's aircraft types naturaly affected the development of the carriers which would operate the aircraft. By the late 1950s, when the Fleet Air Arm at last had the excellent Scimitar and Sea Vixen fighters and the low-level Buccaneer strike aircraft, the decimation of the carrier fleet of 1945 was already over.

The experience of *Eagle*, *Albion* and *Bulwark* during the Suez operation, however,

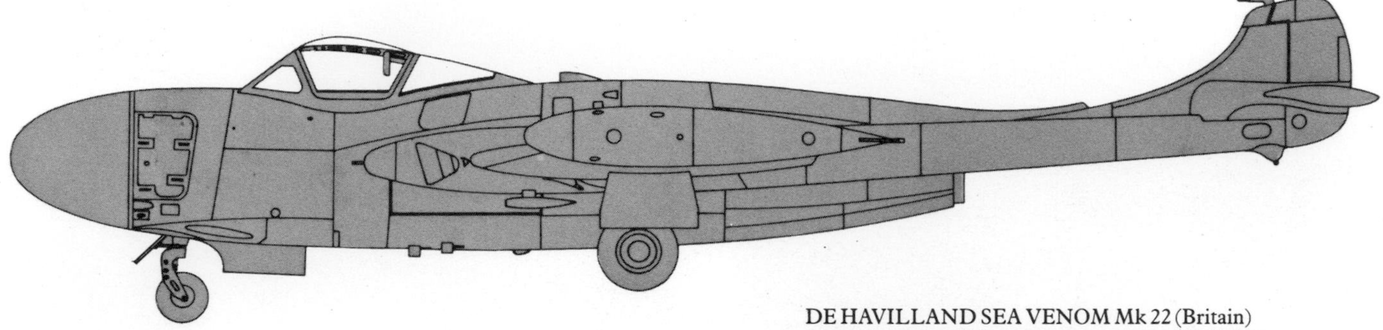

DE HAVILLAND SEA VENOM Mk 22 (Britain)
TYPE All-weather fighter. LOADED WEIGHT 15,800 lb. MAX. SPEED 575 mph. RANGE 705 miles. ARMAMENT 4 x 20 mm cannon; 8 x 60 lb rocket projectiles.

did lead to definite planning for Britain's first post-war carrier. Borrowing American nomenclature, the new ship became known as 'CVA01'; but this certainly did not imply a British imitation of the 'Forrestal' class, or indeed anything like it. 'CVA01' would have begun where the cancelled 'Gibraltar' class carriers of 1946 left off. With a displacement of 45,000 tons, 'CVA01' implied a British version of the 'Midway' class carriers – at least 15 years behind the American lead. The hastiness with which the 'Gibraltar' class carriers had been cancelled in 1945 now stood revealed. 'CVA01' was still nothing more than a name as the 1960s opened. The demise of the new carrier, when it came, was easy to accomplish.

Throughout the 1950s, with the United States and Soviet Union drifting ever faster towards nuclear-powered super-carriers and intercontinental ballistic missiles, Britain's so-called 'independent nuclear deterrent' had become increasingly threadbare. The Royal Air Force, campaigning with ever-greater mendacity to keep the ascendancy over the Navy established after 1945, argued that the life of Britain's ageing 'V-bomber' fleet would be safely extended with the purchase of the American 'stand-off' bomb, Skybolt. In a humiliating sequence of events, destined to be repeated 20 years later with uncanny accuracy, the fate of the 'independent British deterrent' was settled by a shift in American weapons policy. This was the American cancellation of Skybolt in 1962, by which time the first Polaris test-firings had been made and the system proven. The result was the Macmillan/Kennedy Nassau meeting of December 1962, which agreed on a five-submarine Polaris fleet for Britain.

At no stage during the negotiations was the British Admiralty bluntly told that the 'pound of flesh' for Polaris would be the cancellation of CVA01. Moreover, fears that the cost of the whole project – estimated at £60 million for four ships without missiles – would prove exorbitant, were firmly discounted. (The final bill was £156.29 million.) The future of CVA01 was still a real issue when Harold Wilson brought the Labour Party back to

Victorious in 1961, equipped with angled flight-deck, in the Indian Ocean

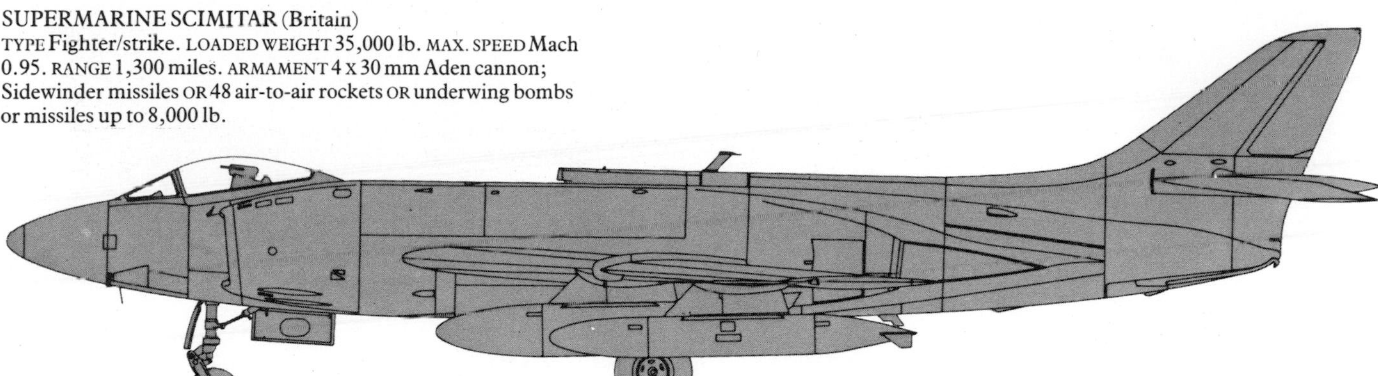

SUPERMARINE SCIMITAR (Britain)
TYPE Fighter/strike. LOADED WEIGHT 35,000 lb. MAX. SPEED Mach 0.95. RANGE 1,300 miles. ARMAMENT 4 x 30 mm Aden cannon; Sidewinder missiles OR 48 air-to-air rockets OR underwing bombs or missiles up to 8,000 lb.

HAWKER SIDDELEY BUCCANEER S.Mk 2 (Britain)
TYPE All-weather low-level strike. CREW 2. LOADED WEIGHT 56,000 lb. MAX. SPEED Transonic (*low-altitude*). RANGE 1,150 miles. ARMAMENT Nuclear weapons (in bomb bay); underwing missiles, bombs or rocket packs.

power in October 1964. With only a narrow Parliamentary majority, Wilson made brilliant use of the defence issue to enlist electoral support for his party and won a solid majority in a second election 14 months after the first. Ever since the Nassau agreement, Wilson had made it appear that Labour in power would scrap Polaris. This guaranteed him the support of the anti-Polaris nuclear disarmers. Once in power, however, he realised that the Polaris programme was the biggest British naval shipbuilding programme since the war; that Barrow and Birkenhead, where the Polaris submarines were to be built, naturally approved the programme for the jobs it created; and that the jobs in question had been created by the derided Conservatives. If, therefore, Wilson wanted to slash his majority to nothing merely by doing away with jobs provided by the opposition, scrapping Polaris would be the way to do it.

The compromise finally approved by Wilson and his Defence Minister Denis Healey was to confirm that the Polaris programme would be retained, but with four submarines instead of five; and institute an exhaustive 'defence review' to ensure that the British people got the most cost-effective Navy that money could buy. There was much staunch but vague governmental assurance that the Wilson Government would not blindly copy American practice – just enough to win general approval without bringing the champions of CVA01 out into the open, demanding embarrassing answers. Meanwhile Healey, already only too well aware of the soaring costs of the Polaris programme, had decided on his pound of flesh: not merely the cancellation of CVA01, but the decision not to replace *any* of the British carriers still in service. The Fleet Air Arm was to be allowed to wither and die, the governmental line being that land-based RAF bombers could cover every stretch of ocean formerly covered by Fleet Air Arm carriers. This monstrous lie was, of course, the penultimate round in the 'Battle of the Blues' – the Navy/Air Force struggle which had continued ever since the birth of the independent Royal Air Force in 1918. That decision had merely doomed British naval aviation to slow obsolescence for 19 years. The Wilson/Healey Defence White Paper of 1966 sentenced the Fleet Air Arm to death. Healey even went so far as to hint that possession of a carrier Navy was an outdated relic of imperialism, leading to moral outrages such as Suez. 'Experience and study have shown', announced the 1966 White Paper with breathtaking impudence, 'that only one type of operation exists for which carriers and carrier-borne aircraft would be indispensable: that is the landing, or withdrawal, of troops.'

Other gems worth quoting from the Healey Defence Statement of February 1966 show how easily political arrogance and ignorance could forget all the lessons of recent history.

'Strike capacity against enemy ships will be provided by surface-to-surface missile.' This effectively condemned Britain's surface fleet to fighting without the principal advantage of the aircraft-carrier: the ability to destroy your enemy before he can destroy you. Moreover, it serenely neglected the fact that without carrier attack capacity to destroy at long range, it would be quite possible for British warships to be destroyed without striking a blow, merely by longer-ranged enemy surface-to-surface missiles (SSMs). And then there was the claim that *'Close anti-submarine protection of the naval force will be given by helicopters operating from ships other than carriers.'* The point here was not so much the wilful surrender of an outer defended zone formerly patrolled by carrier helicopters; the statement was an invitation to disaster in the age of the nuclear attack submarine with speeds of over 30 knots.

The biggest absurdity of Denis Healey's death-sentence on the carrier arm was the fact that it unscrupulously used the old anti-carrier chestnut: 'one missile' could destroy the carrier at sea. And yet the nub of the proposal was the transference of British naval aviation from ship to shore: from mobile bases virtually impossible to target accurately, to shore airfields which could be minutely pinpointed by Soviet ICBMs. Even if the nuclear menace of ICBM bombardment were left out of the equation, airfields ashore were no substitute for carriers afloat. For every historical instance of a triumph over warships by land-based aircraft, it is possible to counter with an instance of a land air base being suppressed by carrier aircraft. And the 1966 decision to scrap the Fleet Air Arm was entirely dependent on the acquisition by the RAF of an aircraft which was neither fully proven nor in British hands: the American 'swing-wing' F.111.

Within two years it was obvious that the Healey Defence proposals of February 1966 already lay in comical ruins. The F.111 deal had fallen through; the dwindling British carrier force continued to demonstrate, with

The airborne marvel which spelled resurrection for the British Fleet Air Arm: Sea Harriers landing on *Invincible* in 1980, after the new carrier's appallingly delayed completion

LT CDR T J H GEDGE

Bulwark, Britain's 'Rusty B', flying-off helicopters in her final incarnation as a commando-carrier

perfect efficiency, that it had never been better equipped. But the decision to phase out the Fleet Air Arm was not reversed – either under Wilson or his successors. From 1968 the extraordinary versatility of a new potential fighter and strike aircraft, the V/STOL or 'jump-jet' vertical take-off Harrier, opened new vistas. With a force of sea Harriers armed with the latest air-to-surface missiles, and able to take-off and land-on *vertically*, all that would be needed was hangar space and launch platforms aboard the bigger surface ships. Obviously the cruiser format would be best; it happened that by the late 1960s the Navy was due for its first heavy surface warship to be laid down since the war. The new cruiser, then, would operate the Sea Harrier; it would also be best if it carried anti-submarine helicopters as well. This combined facility added up to a light aircraft-carrier, particularly when it was suggested to fit her with a flight-deck for maximum economy of operations. It would have been unthinkable for the Wilson Government to have gone back on its decision to scrap the carriers; and so the deceitful phrase 'through-deck cruiser' was coined, slyly avoiding the emotive terms 'flight-deck' and 'carrier'.

The appearance on the scene of the Harrier and the 'through-deck cruiser', which took shape in the 1970s as the admirable 'Invincible' class light carrier, was the latest extension of the strong British thread running through the aircraft-carrier's story. It was crowned with the introduction of the vertically-curved or 'ski-jump' flight-deck, brought in to counter the downward sag of heavily-loaded aircraft as they leave the carrier at launch. The ski-jump flight-deck proved ideal for the Harrier, the fuel expenditure of which is naturally high in vertical flight. With a modest ski-jump deck extension inclined at no more than 6·5°, a Sea Harrier needs so much less thrust on take-off that it can carry 1,500 lb more in weapons.

Given the fact that the ageing fleet carriers were due for withdrawal by the late 1970s, some urgency in bringing in the new 'Invincibles' might have been expected. Instead the 'Invincibles' took shape at a snail's pace. HMS *Invincible*, the first of the class, was laid down in July 1973 but not launched until May 1977 – and not *commissioned* until June 1980. Displacing 16,000 tons standard and 19,810 at full load, she is designed to carry ten Sea King helicopters and five Sea Harriers – and has been designed with space to carry the next generation of both species of aircraft. The 'Invincibles' therefore represent a completely new concept of light carrier, able to serve as a task group command ship, operate one of the

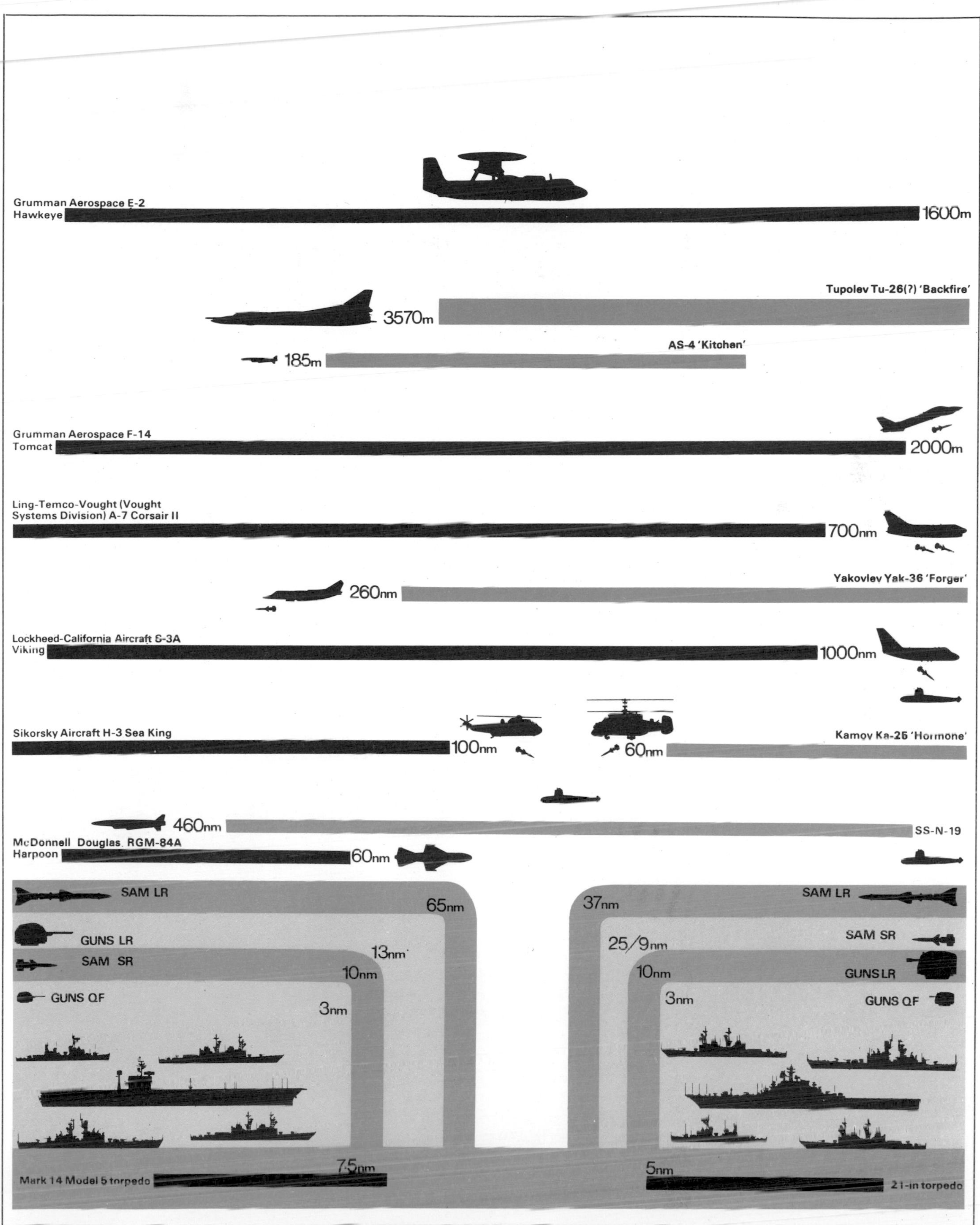
Grumman Aerospace E-2 Hawkeye
1600m
Tupolev Tu-26(?) 'Backfire'
3570m
AS-4 'Kitchen'
185m
Grumman Aerospace F-14 Tomcat
2000m
Ling-Temco-Vought (Vought Systems Division) A-7 Corsair II
700nm
Yakovlev Yak-36 'Forger'
260nm
Lockheed-California Aircraft S-3A Viking
1000nm
Sikorsky Aircraft H-3 Sea King
100nm
Kamov Ka-25 'Hormone'
60nm
460nm
SS-N-19
McDonnell Douglas RGM-84A Harpoon
60nm
SAM LR
65nm
GUNS LR
13nm
SAM SR
10nm
GUNS QF
3nm
SAM LR
37nm
SAM SR
25/9nm
GUNS LR
10nm
GUNS QF
3nm
Mark 14 Model 5 torpedo
7.5nm
5nm
21-in torpedo

Above: *Hermes*, fitted for the Sea Harrier era with 'ski-jump' flight-deck, in company with the destroyer *Broadsword* (November 1981)
Right: Triumphant return of the light carrier format – *Invincible* in commission at last (March 1981). Her puny Sea Dart missile launcher can be seen just aft of the open forecastle

most versatile strike/reconnaissance aircraft in the history of aviation, while operating a potent anti-submarine helicopter force. The type deeply impressed the US Navy when first tested in Atlantic manoeuvres. With three 'Invincibles' ordered, the Royal Navy seemed set fair to reopen the old carrier debate: was one big carrier better than several small ones?

Instead disaster struck at the embryo British light carrier fleet from a totally unexpected direction. In 1966 CVA01 had been slain by ministerial decree, a sacrificial offering to counter the devouring costs of the new Polaris programme. Fifteen years later, with the first 'Invincible' already in service, the second launched and the third building, the politicians did it again. This time the culprits were not of the Labour Party but the members of Margaret Thatcher's Conservative Cabinet, determined to replace Polaris with the new American Trident missile. For the second time in two decades, *notional* striking-power was set higher in the scale of priorities than *actual* security by sea. Despite passionate denials that he was sacrificing the surface Fleet on the altar of Trident, Defence Minister John Nott announced the sale of *Invincible* in March 1982 – *before* the official decision to order Trident had been made. Though *Hermes* was reprieved from the scrapyard until 1983, last of the old light fleet carriers, the Royal Navy was to be left with only one 'Invincible' by the middle 1980s.

Given the excellence of the class – which, unlike CVA01 in 1966, *was already in existence* – the Nott Defence Statement of 1981 and its aftermath would have been reprehensible enough. What was positively unbelievable was the fact that the decision had been made *after* the appearance of a totally unexpected phenomenon: the construction of a new fleet of aircraft-carriers for the already-formidable Soviet Navy.

9. RESURRECTION: THE SOVIET MENACE, 1966–1982

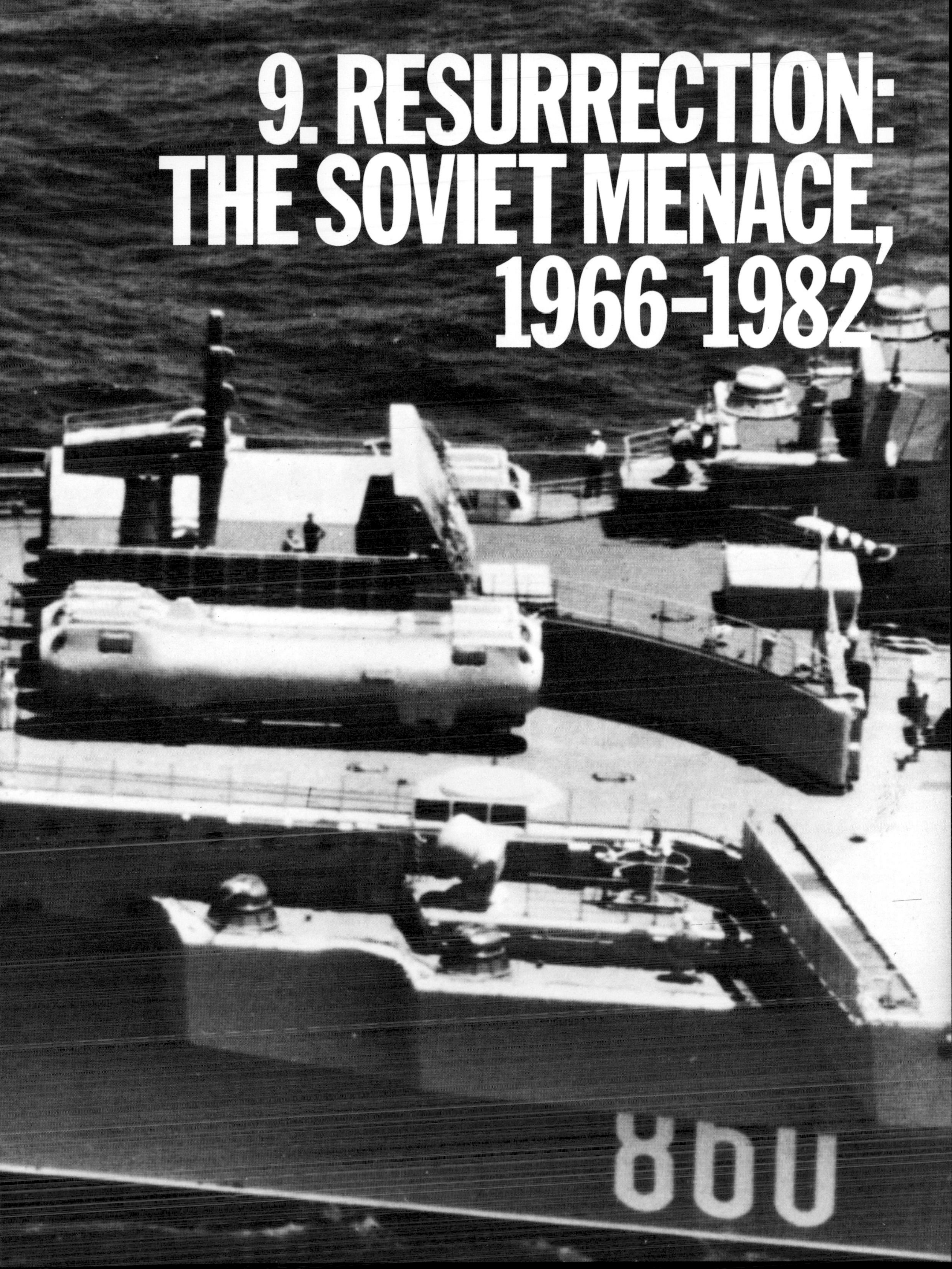

Previous pages: *Kiev*'s massive surface-to-surface fire-power (her portside SS-N-12 twin launchers). Each of the superb new Soviet carriers has the surface-to-surface fire-power of a Second World War battleship

THE BRITISH DECISION TO ABOLISH the Royal Navy's carrier arm, and American limitations (if not outright reductions) on the size of the US Navy's carrier force, have been rendered totally untenable by the rise of a Soviet fleet air arm. If the aircraft-carrier's brief combat life has one lesson to teach, it is that a fleet without carriers has little or no chance against a fleet with carriers. Unfortunately for NATO, British and American politicians are almost totally ignorant of recent naval history. The same obviously does not apply in the Soviet Union, where the Brezhnev regime has built a formidable naval striking force to the recommendations of a highly gifted naval theorist: Fleet Admiral Sergei Gorshkov.

Gorshkov is unique. He has been Commander-in-Chief of the Soviet Navy, *without a break*, since 1956. No less significantly, he also holds the post of Deputy Minister of Defence. He has argued his political colleagues (not masters, because Gorshkov's naval and Party career have always advanced hand in hand) out of the Stalinist obsession with reliance on a strong submarine fleet. He has evolved a naval strategy tailored to the uneasy balance of nuclear deterrence and tactical confrontation; and has given his country the tools to make rapid Soviet victories at sea an almost inevitable feature of any Third World War.

Gorshkov's first concern was to provide the Soviet Navy with a surface fleet strong enough to beat Western anti-submarine surface forces on the hunt for Soviet submarines – above all Soviet missile-carrying submarines. At the same time he accepted that the biggest natural menace to the Soviet surface fleet was the unbeatable preponderance of Western naval aviation. He therefore stipulated that all additions to the fleet must be armed to the teeth for instant victory in any clash with Western surface forces. At the same time they must be given no less potent anti-air defences to beat off Western carrier aircraft. This separation of the surface-to-surface and surface-to-air defence capacities should, but has not, given Western naval planners the gravest concern. For example, the Soviet 'Kara' class guided-missile destroyer has a surface-to-surface armament of eight SS-N-14 missiles and a *separate* surface-to-air system, also consisting of eight launchers. She also has four 76 mm guns and four 30 mm Gatlings. But the British 'Sheffield' class (which, like the 'Karas', entered service in the 1970s) only has one twin Sea Dart launcher, which has to double as surface-to-surface *and* surface-to-air armament.

Nor does the Soviet Navy rely on volume of

'Kara' class cruiser, which like every other major unit of the modern Soviet fleet – carriers included – packs an ominous surface-to-surface punch . . .

. . . unlike NATO equivalents such as Britain's Type 42 *Newcastle (right)*

Above: *Kiev* in the North Atlantic, shadowed by the British frigate *Danae*, in August 1976

fire alone: it has selected the hitherto decisive advantage of superior range. The later SS-N-12 missile has an estimated range of 250 nautical miles – against the British Sea Dart's 25, the French Matra's 112, the French Exocet's 26 and the American Harpoon's 50. It is true that the Soviet missile requires mid-course guidance – but the long-range aircraft of the Soviet fleet air arm are there to provide it. This ability to wipe out the opposition at ranges safely outside Western missile range was to be retained in the first Soviet carriers.

Never too proud to imitate good ideas, Gorshkov approved the construction of two helicopter-carriers, *Moskva* and *Leningrad*. These were laid down well before the British decision to abolish the Fleet Air Arm, being launched in 1965 and 1966 respectively. But their enormous after flight-decks were the first indication that the Soviet Navy was feeling its way towards the development of fleet carriers.

Such was indeed the case. The Soviets had anticipated the West in producing a V/STOL aircraft: the Yakovlev 'Freehand', first demonstrated in 1967. In 1970 the first Soviet carrier was laid down: the 32,000-ton *Kiev*. Like her contemporary, the British *Invincible*, *Kiev* was not announced as a carrier; her official designation (as with *Moskva* and *Leningrad*) is *protivo lodochny kreyser*, or 'anti-submarine cruiser'. For all that, she has the surface-to-surface fire power of a battleship: eight SS-N-12s in four twin mountings. She also has eight surface-to-air SA-N-3s and 4s, a twin launcher (SUW-N-1) for anti-submarine missiles, plus eight 76 mm guns and eight 30

Soviet carrier Kiev in the Mediterranean, July 1976
Opposite: Helicopter-carrier *Leningrad* on her majestic passage through the English Channel in August 1981. Thanks to politically-imposed economies Royal Naval attendance, to escort the intruder through British home waters, was conspicuous by its absence
Left: Yakovlev Yak-36 'Forger' hovering over *Kiev* in August 1976. Unlike the British Harrier, the Yak-36 lacks the supreme advantages of vectored-thrust propulsion

Kiev heads out into the Mediterranean on her maiden cruise in July 1976

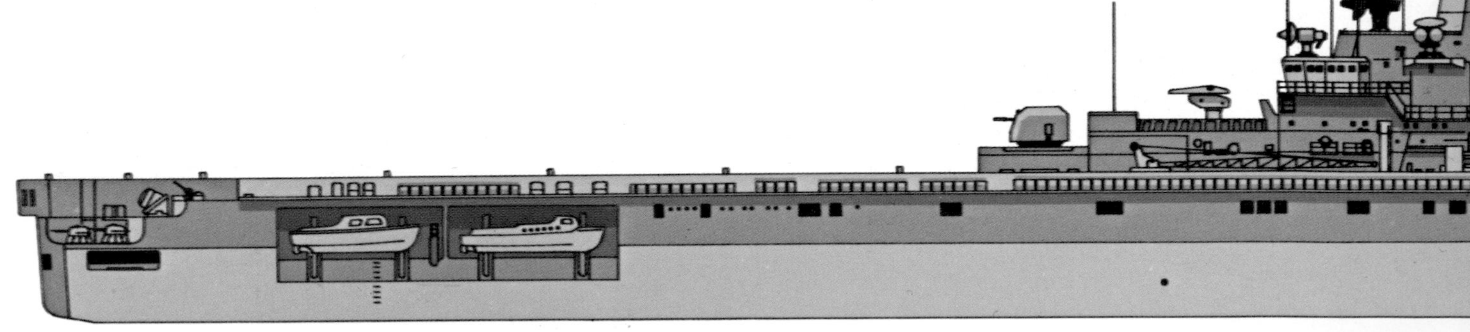

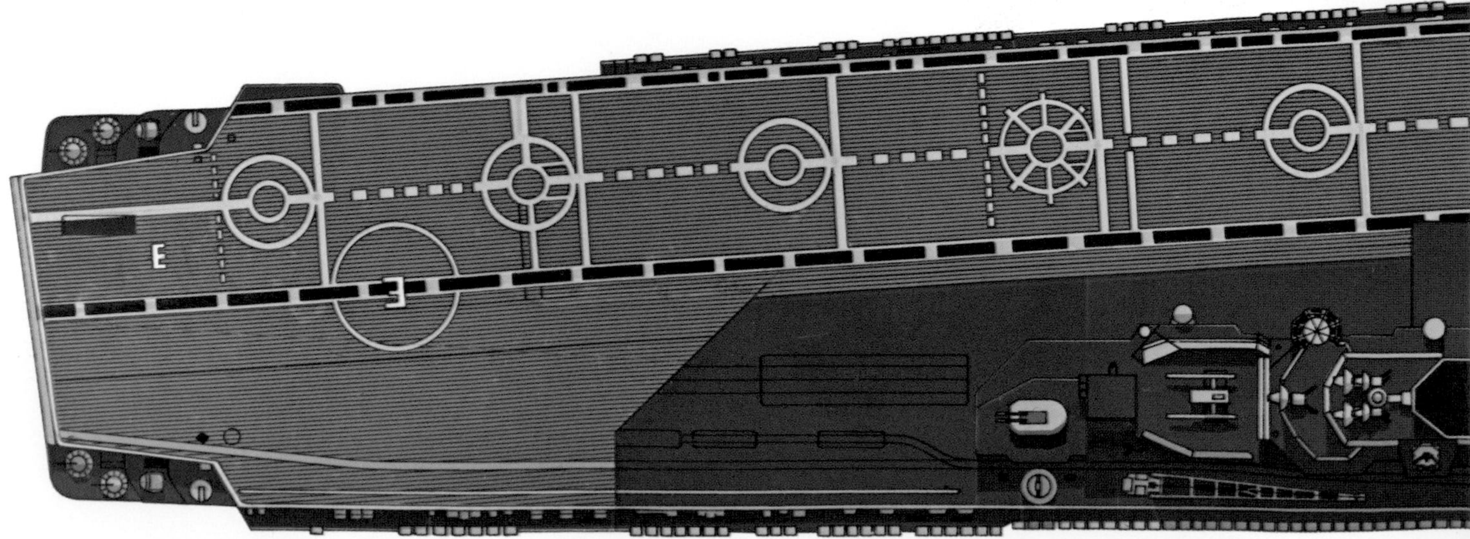

mm Gatling mounts. Britain's *Invincible*, however, has only one twin Sea Dart launcher – *and she was completed four years after* Kiev *sailed on her first operational cruise*. Two sister-ships, *Minsk* and *Novorossiisk*, have been completed to the time of writing.

As none of these advantages, apart from the lavish anti-aircraft defences, could prevail against the strike potential of the American CVAs, the only conclusion seems to be that Gorshkov's carrier fleet has been custom-built for easy victory over NATO forces lacking carrier support. This could give the Soviet Baltic Fleet a quick breakout into the North Sea at the expense of the West German, Danish and Norwegian navies.

It could also, most ominously for Britain, give the Soviet Northern Fleet (based on Murmansk) a clear run down to the North Atlantic sea-lane, NATO's lifeline to Europe, after the liquidation of the Royal Navy. All this could happen without a single strategic nuclear missile, in which so much defence trust is confidently invested, being fired.

How many 'Kievs' the Russians will build remains to be seen – as with the reported construction of the first Soviet nuclear-powered fleet carrier. Hopefully the appearance of the latter warship will reverse the Western blind faith in strategic nuclear missiles, and cause the British to look again to their carrier defence.

KIEV (Soviet Union)
DISPLACEMENT 32,000 tons. DIMENSIONS 898⅔ ft x 157⅓ ft x 27⅓ ft. MACHINERY 4-shaft steam turbines: 180,000 SHP. SPEED 32 knots. ARMAMENT (*Surface-to surface*) 4 twin SS-N-12 missile launchers; (*surface-to-air*) 2 twin SA-N-3, 2 twin SA-N-4 missile launchers; 4 x 76 mm guns; 8 x 30 mm Gatling gun mounts; 10 x 21-inch torpedo tubes; 2 x 12-barrelled anti-submarine launchers. AIRCRAFT (*estimated*) 35 x 12/13 Yak-36 VTOL 'Forger' helicopters; 22 Kamov Ka-25 'Hormone' helicopters. COMPLEMENT 2,500.

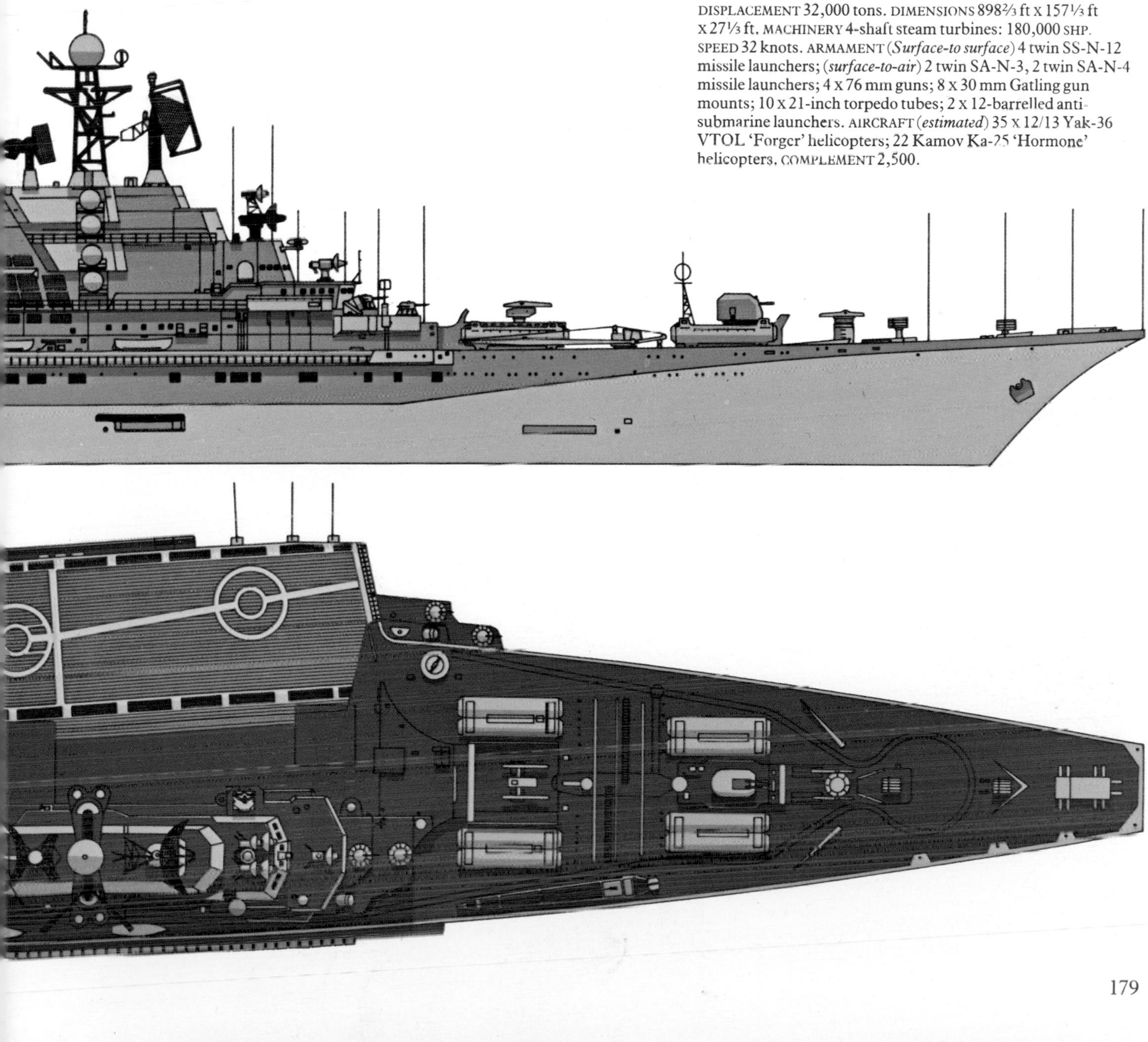

10. BALANCE SHEET, 1982: DINOSAUR OR PHOENIX?

USS Carl Vinson (CVN-70) on sea trials in the Atlantic Ocean in 1982.

IN THE EARLY 1980s the debate goes on, with the same arguments being raised in attack or defence of the aircraft-carrier as have been heard since the type first came into being, but one fact is clear. Whatever the truth of the carrier's viability in a future war – which only a future war can reveal – reports of the carrier's demise have been greatly exaggerated.

Beyond doubt it is the United States which have mastered the art of getting the most prolonged service out of aircraft-carriers. *Coral Sea* and *Midway*, the last carriers completed in the Second World War, are scheduled for phasing-out by 1985. The 'Forrestals', however, will not follow until the late 1990s. A staggered schedule of reconstructions will phase out the 'Forrestals' year by year until *Constellation*'s departure in 2010. *Enterprise* will go the following year, then *America* (2012) and *John F. Kennedy* (2014). *Nimitz* will follow in 2020, but no deadline has yet been put forward for the withdrawal from service of *Eisenhower* and *Vinson*.

This will add to the aircraft-carrier's laurels, making the type the longest-serving class of warship in modern naval history. Indeed, the only warships ever to exceed the carrier's longevity have been ships-of-the-line from the age of sail, such as *Sovereign of the Seas* (1637-1696). Pride of place, of course, is held by NATO's oldest warship still in commission: HMS *Victory*, completed in 1778!

Below: The catapult officer aboard USS Coral Sea prepares to launch a KA-6D Intruder tanker.
Right: USS Enterprise (CVN-35) underway in the late 1970s.
Inset: USS John F Kennedy about to launch two A-7B Corsair II strike aircraft.

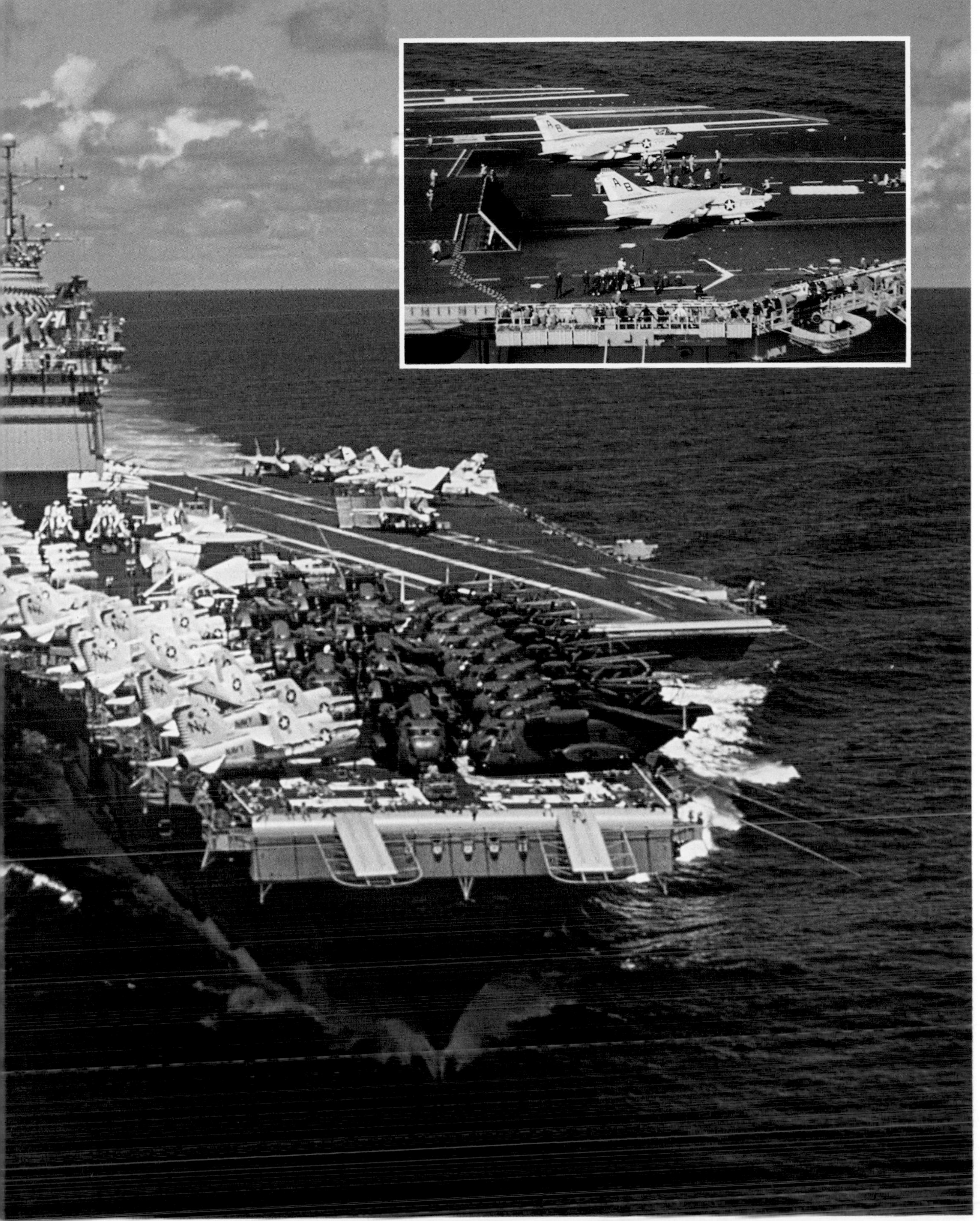

Right: Crewmen aboard the USS Nimitz (CVN-68) handling hoses during sea trials cruise off the Virginia coast in 1975.

Below: USS Nimitz during her first NATO exercise in the Atlantic Ocean in 1975.

Left: AN S-3A Viking of Air Anti-Submarine Squadron VS-37 aboard the USS Constellation in the western Pacific in 1978.

Right: HMS Invincible leaves Portsmouth naval base during deployment of the Falkland's Task Force in April 1982. Her VSTOL Harriers were to prove to be an extremely potent weapon system.

Inset: Harriers and a Sea King aboard HMS Invincible at the time of the Falkland's conflict.

Those who criticise the high-risk aspect of carrier operations were grimly vindicated in June 1981 by an appalling accident aboard *Nimitz*. The culprit was a Grumman EA-6B Prowler, whose role is described in the jargon of the current era as 'ECM/Elint' – electronic counter-measures and electronic intelligence-gatherer. Approaching to land, the Prowler came in too high and well off the centreline. It missed the arrester-cables and ended a costly glissade along the flight-deck by crashing into six fuelled Tomcats. The fuel and the Tomcats' weapons erupted and in the ensuing blaze 14 men died, with 48 more seriously injured. The Prowler was totally wrecked, along with two of the Tomcats; which meant that the mere financial cost of one bad landing topped $111.6 million.

This represents the costly debit of maintaining a carrier fleet. The credit side of the ledger is represented by another modern incident, also involving *Nimitz* in 1981 (19 August). When the Libyan dictator Colonel Gaddafi arbitrarily decided to extend his country's territorial waters, *Nimitz* entered the area to proclaim the freedom of the seas. Two of Gaddafi's fighter pilots, apparently possessed by a death wish, attacked and were shot down by *Nimitz*'s Tomcats. The lesson was plain: there is little point in laying claim to water which cannot be controlled by your ships.

The most intriguing question-mark hangs over the Anglo-Soviet naval confrontation which, since the Thatcher Government's measures of 1981-82, has left the tactical initiative firmly with the Soviet Northern Fleet. The Soviet Navy has already demonstrated its ability to operate carrier task groups on both sides of the world simultaneously – *Kiev* in the Atlantic, *Minsk* in the Indian Ocean. The feckless British, having divested themselves of all viable conventional defence to pay for a new generation of fancy ballistic missiles, may yet see their last warships with enough fuel to put to sea wiped out in a conventional sea war. If this were to happen, the core of the victorious Soviet task force would be the weapon Britain did so much to invent and perfect – the aircraft-carrier.

Finally, a few words on the wholly unexpected fillip given to the aircraft-carrier story by the Falklands Conflict of April-June 1982. Humiliated by the Argentine *coup de main* against the Falkland Islands (2 April 1982), the British Government reacted with what can only be described as a strategic rush of blood to the head. The only two operational British carriers, *Hermes* and *Invincible* – the latter already sold to Australia as part of the surface

Above: HMS Hermes sails out of Portsmouth as part of the Falkland's Task Force. Aboard were Royal Marine Commando forces and an enlarged complement of Harriers. However, her inability to operate Airborne Early Warning aircraft proved costly to the Royal Navy.

fleet reductions of the past 18 months – were rushed off to the South Atlantic as the core of an amphibious 'Task Force'.

Judged by every lesson of carrier history, this was an act of utter folly. Operating at an awesome 8,000 miles from their home base, with a frantically-improvised 'fleet train' including converted civilian tankers, bulk carriers and luxury liners, the two carriers between them could put up no more than 20 Sea Harriers. This tiny air group had to handle all reconnaissance, combat air patrol, interceptor, bombing and tactical strike missions – all in the teeth of superior Argentine land-based air power at odds of over three to one. Admittedly, on paper the Argentine fleet was heavily outmatched by the Task Force, with only one elderly carrier: *Veinticinco de Mayo* (ex-*Karel Doorman*, ex-'Colossus' class *Venerable*). But given the assurance of land-based air cover, the odds against the Argentine fleet were far less than the odds against the US Pacific Fleet on the eve of Midway 40 years before. The despatch of the British Task Force, moreover, was rushed ahead as though the Soviet Navy did not exist. It effectively denuded the United Kingdom of any viable air/sea defence, and promised a grievous long-term weakening of NATO forces. And yet the Falklands campaign of April-June 1982 revealed how misleading paper strengths and theoretical disadvantages can be.

As soon as they arrived within striking range, the British carriers should have been the supreme Argentine objectives, to be destroyed or incapacitated at whatever cost.

With *Hermes* and *Invincible* sunk or rendered incapable of operating aircraft, the British would have been unable to land on East Falkland (22 May), or 'leap-frog' the follow-up consignment of RAF Harriers ashore to operate at close range against the Argentine garrison troops. A succession of massed land- and carrier-based air strikes could easily have swamped the Sea Harriers and eliminated the British carriers. Instead, the Argentine persistence with 'penny-packet' air attacks on the Task Force, though inflicting grievous losses on the skimpy screen of frigates and destroyers, allowed *Hermes* and *Invincible* to fulfil their vital role of covering the troop landings.

The Falklands Conflict revealed the utter folly of the run-down of the British Fleet Air Arm over the previous two decades; but the most telling reaction came from the United States, not Britain. On 14 May, a week before the British landings on East Falkland, the US Senate approved a massive $178,000 million defence budget – to include the cost of two new CVNs. In Britain, the Thatcher Government contented itself with furtively postponing the imminent Defence Statement with its burden of further fleet reductions. There was fulsome governmental praise for the magnificent achievements of the Task Force – against odds which need never have been so high but for sustained and wilful political delinquency. Once again the unique versatility of the aircraft-carrier, enhanced as never before by the superb all round qualities of the Sea Harrier, had been demonstrated to the world.

INDEX

Numbers in italics refer to illustrations

006